OLGA IN KENYA

Repressing the Irrepressible

By
Elizabeth Watkins

Pen Press Publishers Ltd

First published in Great Britain by
Pen Press Publishers Ltd
39-41, North Road
Islington
London N7 9DP

ISBN 1-905203-74-8

Printed and bound in the UK

A catalogue record of this book is available from
the British Library

Cover Illustration by Steve Foote

This book is dedicated to Olga's twenty six great grandchildren

The Montgomery Family:
Roberto and Paulo Salvucci,
Sally and Fiona Montgomery,
Poppy and Jade Montgomery,
And in loving memory of Amber.

The Hughes Family:
James, Sarah and Robert Hughes,
Michael, Sally, and Charles Hoare,
Anne, Julia and Andrew Francombe.

The Knowles Family:
Rachel & Rebecca,
Emma, Clarissa, and Zuleika,
Anna and Eleanor,
George, Olivia and Tom,

AUTHOR'S FOREWORD

Owing to a multitude of interruptions, this book has been much too long in gestation. Initially I had hoped to write about both my parents together, but this was not possible. Olga always bolted with the book, while my father Oscar had made quite a different, and very important, contribution to Kenya's development.

Olga was a person who committed every fleeting moment, every passing idea, and every discussion to paper. She kept every cheque stub, every note on the back of an envelope, every bill, school or medical report, scattered between her three homes in Austria, Kenya, and England. When we were clearing the homes after her death, I went through the different lots, discarded many and stored the rest where I could. I was myself following a peripatetic husband through his career and did not manage to bring all the papers together until after our retirement.

It has been difficult to choose the activities and quotes that show her as both the family and the wider world knew her. It is notoriously difficult for a daughter to write about her mother; the relationship is so close it is difficult to distance oneself. This was slightly easier for me than for many daughters, for I left home soon after my eighteenth birthday to join up, and by the time I was ready to return home, she was dead and there was therefore no home to which I could go.

Most people lose their wish to put the world to rights at around the age of thirty. Olga never lost hers. For example, when she visited me in Oxford just after the war, she found that certain old ladies had to do their own shopping and then carry their packages home. She wanted me to start a shopping service for them and persuade fellow undergraduates to adopt one or two old ladies and do their chores for them twice a week. Had she been in my place, she would certainly have had a flourishing organization going in no time, and she was disappointed in me when I point-blank refused. However, I did explain that I was already helping my own landlady bring back not just the rations, but also the coal. At the same time, she was continuously upbraiding me, telling me that I had filled my university days too full and was working beyond my strength. Yet it was her own kind heart that constantly led her to exhaustion and overwork.

Many people have helped me write this book and I would like to thank them, especially my husband who has not only put up with my constant pre-occupation and an even untidier house than usual, but has chauffeured me to various places of research and accompanied me through numerous archives.

I am also grateful to the various libraries, the Central Registry at Kew, the Newspaper Library, and the ever-friendly Rhodes House librarians. Joan Considine and Nicholas Knowles have each read the manuscript at least twice, and my sister Ronny has given me the Wispers papers, photographs, and more stories than I have been able to use. Christopher Kump, the present owner of Schloss Matzen, has given me family papers and photographs that were abandoned there when the Schloss was sold to his grandfather. I am grateful to them all. The shortcomings of the book are mine, the opinions mostly Olga's.

* * *

Ancestry

The Grohmann Family

Johann Grohmann self made merchant banker and owner of Dams Coffee shop in Vienna. He married Marianne Franzoni in 1810. In 1838 he bought the recently dissolved monastery, Schloss Wolfgang, on Wolfgangsee near Salzburg, There were two children, Lora and Adolf.

Adolf Grohmann 1822 - 1876 married Fanny Reade in Wales in 1848. When Adolf became ill, Fanny and her five children were made wards of Court. Fanny defied her guardians and sold her personal possessions to buy ruined castle, Schloss Matzen inTyrol.

.

Her eldest son, Willie Adolf Baillie Grohmann, 1851-1922, anglicized his name to Baillie-Grohman in 1872 and married Florence Nickalls in 1886. - They had two children, Tom 1888 - 1979 and Olga 1889 – 1947. Tom joined the Royal Navy and became an Admiral.

Olga married first Douglas Thompson, with whom she set up a farm, Khitari estate, at Koru in Kenya. He was killed in 1915. There were no children. In 1917 she married Oscar Watkins, and by him had three daughters.

Olga Penelope, known as Pella, married Oliver Montgomery.Grace Veronica, known as Ronny, married Patrick Hughes. Elizabeth June known as Tiny Wee and then June, married Oliver Knowles.

The Nickalls family

Tom Nickalls was the eldest surviving child of failed pioneers in Chicago in the 1830's. He was brought back to England by Quaker relatives in 1847 and found a job as an office boy on the London Stock Exchange, where he progressed to make a fortune and by 1860 was financing his parents and four much younger siblings. He married Emily Quihampton, a farmer's daughter from Essex, by whom he had 13 children, 11 of whom survived into maturity.

Florence (Flo), the eldest child, was born in 1861. Others mentioned in this book are the Oxford oarsmen, Guy and Vee Nickalls; Olga's favourite aunts, Grace and Maud Nickalls; and Flo's favourite sister, Nina Simpson. Flo married Willie Baillie-Grohman in 1886 and pioneered with him in British Columbia. She had two children, Tom and Olga.

*   *   *

CONTENTS

Olga Baillie-Grohman and Douglas Thompson's wedding at
St. Margaret's Westminster January 14 1914

Chapter One

A HURRIED ARRIVAL

Olga Baillie-Grohman was born in the early hours of April 21 1889, within a few hours of two other characters who proved notable throughout her life: Adolf Hitler and Charlie Chaplin. She was born with one foot in Kent like Chaplin and the other in Austria like Hitler. Although she achieved neither the same fame nor the same notoriety as these two giants on the world stage, she shared many of the same characteristics, the same unstoppable energy, the same sense of pathos and drama, and the ability to bring the two together. As early as 1934 she saw the evil Hitler would bring about.

She pioneered women farming in Kenya, and in particular she pioneered excellent conditions for her workers. She was the first woman on Nairobi's Municipal Council, the first to stand for Kenya's Legislative Council, and the second to be elected. She had three daughters, of which I am the youngest, and for the fifteen years of her second marriage was the wife of Kenya's senior Commissioner, a job with many responsibilities which in itself kept most women fully employed. She was known for her kindness and hospitality, two virtues which constantly interfered with her longing to write. She published one book and dozens of articles in a very wide range of magazines.

Her birth took place quickly before the doctor, who lived an hour's ride away, could arrive. She was to remain in a hurry for the rest of her life. At the time of her birth, her mother, Flo, was staying at a farmhouse called Bellevue, near Hythe in Kent, which belonged to Flo's father, Tom Nickalls. The Nickalls family did not live there, but Tom used it as a stud farm for hunters and racehorses. It was also a useful place to send his twelve children for seaside holidays or convalescence. His eldest daughter, whose husband came from Austria but lived in British Columbia, was permitted to use it for the arrival of his second grandchild. The house still stands on the edge of Lympne Airport.

Flo's mother, Emily Nickalls, came down to the farm from the family home, Patteson Court, at Nutfield near Redhill in Surrey. Flo had brought with her an English nanny from Canada who had been looking after one year old Tom, known as Young Tom to distinguish him from his grandfather, Old Tom. Olga was named

Olga because, as a small girl, Flo had read a book about a little girl of that name. The storybook Olga had run away from the family with whom she had been placed after her mother died. She was befriended by another girl of the same age who hid her in her room and managed to feed her for several weeks before she was discovered and re-united with her father. Flo was so struck by this book that she determined to call any daughter she had Olga. If these were the qualities that Flo most admired, she certainly managed to inculcate them into her daughter. Olga had the courage and impatience required to run away, the charm to befriend a stranger into helping her, the ability to plan an original way to remain hidden, and the instinct to combine all three to carve her own very original path through life.

Olga had pioneering blood in her veins. Not only was her father pioneering in Kootenay in Canada, but Tom Nickalls' father had also pioneered and was a self-made man. He was descended from a long line of Quaker flour millers and shopkeepers from Folkestone and Dover. In 1836, when he was five years old, he had accompanied his parents, Patteson and Arabella, to New England where he was to work in his uncle's brewery. Patteson, however, found his Quaker conscience did not allow him to work in a brewery, a decision which Arabella found reasonable, although she could not think why he had waited until they had crossed the ocean to make it. Instead he moved to Chicago, which at the time had only 5,000 inhabitants, and built a flour mill on the Chicago River. This growing settlement needed a lot of grain, but the siting of his mill on the Chicago River showed equal lack of foresight. The river froze in winter and therefore prevented the movement of flour and grain for five months of the year. It was cheaper to export the corn before it was milled rather than store the milled flour through the winter months. The livery stables, which followed the flour mill, were no more successful. The Chicago River was on the North side of the small settlement, whereas potential customers for the livery stables were mostly new migrants who, on arrival, lived on the rapidly expanding South side. Eventually, the family could no longer afford to move, which prompted Patteson to write with great charm to his maiden sisters in England suggesting that they invest their minuscule capital in his ventures. Fortunately, Arabella wrote with even greater fervour begging them not to do so.

In 1846, at the age of fifteen, 'Old' Tom wrote a thank you letter for a Christmas present to the same aunts in England. He wrote: "Mother says I am a great big lumbering lout of a boy." He then described how he and other boys stoned wolves to death to earn a dime for each wolf-tail they brought in. He also described how that same year he had been the only person in the cabin when his mother Arabella was delivered of another son and commented: "As if we have not enough mouths to feed already!" The aunts acted quickly, and that same year the lout found himself back in England with his father's Quaker cousins. They found him a position as an office boy with a broker on the Stock Exchange, dressed him in a sober black suit and starched white collared shirt, and endeavoured to iron out of him the loutishness, particularly the Yankee accent. Tom travelled to work in the city and back to Redhill each day with a Quaker uncle. In old age he had only to travel on that same route to recall learning his tables, the rules of English grammar, and the scraps of correctly pronounced poetry that were taught him on the journeys.

What impressed him even more than the importance given to such things as cleanliness, learning and pronunciation was the railway on which he travelled, as he recalled the frozen river in Chicago and the problems of the livery stables. By the 1840s, railways were being built in America, financed by the London Stock Exchange. Tom's childhood may have robbed him of an education, but it had given him an early understanding of the importance of improved land transport across the great open spaces of the New World. He advanced rapidly in his job and, when he was ready to set up on his own, his concentration on American railway stock, and his practical knowledge of the problems involved, earned him a fortune. By the 1850s he was financing his parents who had returned penniless to England. By 1860 he had married Emily Quihampton from Totham in Essex and had bought a small house in Croydon where his eldest daughters, Flo, and Nina, were born. Emily bore him 14 children, and by 1870, after several moves, he had installed his young brood in a large Victorian villa, Patteson Court, at Nutfield near Redhill, the same house to which he had been brought 25 years earlier. He bought the house to oblige the uncle who had given him a start, but Emily greeted the purchase with tears, saying her family had already outgrown it. He promised her she could enlarge the villa as much as she liked and agreed that she could build new stables and a dairy.

Emily's father had been a farmer who was famous for the splendid Punch Shire horses he bred. Her mother had died young and Emily had been obliged to step into the role of farmer's wife at a very early age, bringing up her younger siblings and running the dairy. Now the stables and dairy she had planned became showpieces, attracting visitors from afar. On one occasion, the crown prince of France, the son of the Emperor Louis Napoleon, rode up to the gates intent on seeing her livestock. Flo, then a little girl of ten, was playing in the garden and refused to open the gate for him, saying her father had told her not to admit strangers.

In 1880, Old Tom bought the farm Belle Vue at Lympne in Kent, a place where he always said he would retire. However, with twelve children, there was never a suitable time for the family to move to a smaller house. Although they lived at Patteson Court for just thirty years, it became as rooted in family memory as firmly as any hereditary country seat. The perambulator, which had stood in the hall since they arrived, was moved to a stable loft in 1885, only to be fetched back three years later for grandchildren.

In August 1885, when Flo was 24, Old Tom looked around his crowded breakfast table and said: "Now who would like to come to America with me?"

"Yes please," said Flo, "Me too!" said Nina, who was inseparable from Flo. "Include me," said Norman, who was waiting to join his regiment in the New Year. "I suppose I have to go back to college!" said Guy, who was making a name for himself as an oarsman at Oxford, and the eight younger siblings, all in serious education, sighed at what they were missing. "Not me," said Emily from the other end of the table, "I shall be seasick all the way!" "Oh no, I am not travelling without you!" said Tom. Emily did not argue. She went and was seasick both ways.

Flo was not seasick, and she kept a detailed diary of the trip. She spent the allowance her father gave her for clothes to enrol secretly at the Slade School of Art. Studying art was considered most unladylike, almost as bad as studying medicine because it demanded a close knowledge of how the human body was put together. Old Tom was furious when he found out, even more so when he discovered that Flo had been travelling second class to London, often on the same train on which he himself travelled first class. Emily had encouraged her eldest daughter, and helped her to make her own clothes to save money for her studies. Flo did not follow the fashions of the day, nor use the new paper patterns much advertised in women's magazines. She designed her outfits from the great pictures she studied. They were plain-tailored and plain-coloured, even when the fashion was for flowers and frills on every garment. Emily hand stitched them faithfully, following Flo's designs. By 1885, Flo had completed her course at the Slade and was wondering what to do next

The entire journey was an ideal adventure. Flo recorded how her father changed the minute he stepped off the ship at New York, walking and talking like a Yankee. He wore his hat at a different angle, and none of them could understand a word he said. On the return journey from New York to Liverpool, Flo and Nina stood at the ship's rail guessing the nationality of embarking passengers.

"Look at that man," said Flo. "He looks just as if he had stepped straight out of an Austrian farmer's house!" The man wore a green hat with a gemsbart that made him look even taller than his six foot two. His coat was of grey loden and his breeches were made of leather. He wore battered mountain boots over heavy woollen socks and carried a battered rucksack over one shoulder.

"Only an Englishman would dress so eccentrically," said Nina.

"No, I bet you half a crown he is Austrian," said Flo.

Both girls listened carefully as he came aboard and exchanged greetings with the ship's officers. He spoke perfect English with a slight brogue. Was he Irish? Surely not! At close quarters they could see he was dark, weather-beaten, and very handsome. The girls told their brother Norman to find out more about him and Norman duly scraped up an acquaintance with him in the smoking room. He reported back that both his sisters were right: W.A. Baillie-Grohman was half-Irish, half-Austrian, and although he had grown up in Austria, he had been educated in England. He had been in America for about ten years and was a well-known sportsman. He had written several books and had a wonderful fund of Wild West stories, as well as an even better collection of photographs. He held the record for shooting both the biggest wapiti in North America and the best chamois head in Austria. Everyone on board watched with amusement when two predatory widows started competing for his disdainful attentions. Flo told me that she fell in love with him while he was giving a talk on his work in the Kootenay Valley, but she spoke to him only to thank him for the talk and to comment on the photographs he handed round. It is likely that Emily's seasickness may have helped, because it allowed Flo to take early-morning, unchaperoned walks around the deck before the widows appeared. Willie also liked to exercise early in the morning, and Nina tactfully developed early morning headaches which prevented her from joining them.

The ship docked in Liverpool a few days before Christmas. Tom Nickalls had reserved a first class compartment on the boat train for his family. In those days railway carriages did not have corridors, and as Norman was sitting by the window, he saw W.A. deliver a clinging widow to another carriage. As he looked down the train searchingly, Norman opened the carriage door and invited him to join them. In the course of conversation, the Nickalls family discovered that he had nowhere to spend Christmas since his mother lived in Austria, so Emily invited him to Patteson Court. W.A. proposed to Flo on New Year's Eve 1885. Flo was quite taken aback, and said she would like to meet his mother, Fanny, before she made up her mind.

Old Tom did not approve, as his own impoverished childhood had taught him to distrust pioneering projects. He came to the conclusion that, to be pouring thousands of pounds into digging canals in a valley shortly to be by-passed by the completion of the trans-Canadian railway, W.A. must be as financially inept as his own father had been. Once again, Emily supported her eldest daughter. A few years earlier, Emily had put a seal on their newly gained wealth by presenting her two elder daughters at court, escorting them through a season of debutante parties and dances. Tom was Master of the Surrey Hunt, and there were frequent hunt-breakfasts and balls at Patteson Court. There had always been plenty of eligible young men around, attracted by Tom's hunting and horse racing activities as well as by his wealth. Flo had shown no interest in any of them. Now that she had fallen in love with a man ten years older than she was she felt she should be allowed to marry him. Old Tom could never stand out against Emily for long. Willie invited Flo and Nina to visit his mother, Fanny, who was wintering in Dalmatia with her eldest daughter.

Even Emily was taken aback when W.A.'s mother insisted on meeting Flo's parents immediately. Fanny moved to Florence to be nearer them, and Flo and Nina stayed with her while Willie was sent to escort her parents from Surrey. Fanny wanted them to learn the family's secret before the engagement was announced. That secret was that W.A.'s father had suffered from manic depression, had attempted suicide, and had spent the last fifteen years of his life in an asylum. On hearing this, Old Tom wanted to call the engagement off. The two mothers, Emily and Fanny, decided that the young couple, who had known each other for just two months, should wait for one year. Willie was furious, fearing that Flo would change her mind under pressure from her father, but she agreed it was a reasonable request. They were married early in 1886, with Flo refusing the society wedding her father wanted to give her. He was generous in the amount of money he settled on her, but was careful to arrange the settlement so that it could not disappear down Kootenay canals.

By now the Pacific Canadian Railroad was completed, and they were able to travel direct to Victoria, where they found a house to rent. Flo loved the beautiful scenery of sea and snow-covered mountains, the feeling of space, and the friendliness of the people from all walks of life. She loved the ponies that flourished there and rode all over the island. However, she did not accompany Willie to Golden that year because there was a baby on the way, and Harold Tom was born in February 1888. After the birth, Flo was very ill with puerperal fever and only discovered later that the doctor was known for this disease, with five of his seven most recent patients having died. When she recovered, although she had a wonderful nurse, she found she could not feed young Tom because she had lost all her milk with the high fever. During the summer, she left the baby with her nurse, Jane, in Victoria and travelled with Willie to his work camp at Canal Flats, which was a five-day journey. When her Chinese cook left at short notice because he had lost a lot of money gambling and was afraid of retribution for his unpaid debts, Flo undertook the work herself, feeding large meals three times a day, often to as many as ten people.

The camp was a long day's ride from Golden, which was the nearest railway station, and visitors could be seen from a distance. One day, when Flo went out to the woodpile, she noticed three riders approaching.

"I have just seen someone who looks exactly like my father!" she said to Willie. He took his binocular outside.

"It is your father, plus Nina and Vivian," he remarked. Old Tom had heard of her illness, and wanted to make sure she was being properly looked after. When he saw the work that was being undertaken, he agreed to put some money into the scheme, but insisted that Flo must come back to England for the next baby which was obviously on the way.

So it was that Olga's birth took place in Kent, a county where the Nickalls had been rooted since the fifteenth century. Genealogically, they are an easy family to trace because for generation after generation they appear in court records. They became Quakers early on and refused to pay the King's shilling, refused to fight his wars, insisted on helping poor migrants from other parishes even when the poor law forbade it, and obeyed the law only when it coincided with their own strict consciences. Olga inherited the same strict conscience and the same reluctance to abide by laws and regulations that she considered stupid.

As soon as they could travel, Willie returned to Kootenay and Flo set out to Austria to introduce the two children to their paternal grandmother and eight Austrian cousins. It was not until Olga was six months old that it was considered safe to travel back to Canada. By the time Olga had children of her own, she could travel with them when they were only a few weeks old.

Three years later, Willie's pioneering dream was over. By digging the canal, he had hoped to drain the Kootenay valley of its annual floods and thus open up a vast area of new agricultural land. To achieve this work he had employed Chinese labour. After Willie left his project, three succeeding firms endeavoured to complete the work he had started. All three failed. It was eventually achieved amid soaring food prices half a century later during World War Two, long after Willie was dead. This time, the project was completed with the help of mechanical diggers.

In 1893, soon after Olga's fourth birthday, the bankrupted family returned to live with Willie's mother in the Austrian Tyrol. Instead of returning across Canada, they crossed from Victoria to Seattle and took the train across the United States. When they reached Minneapolis, Olga and Tom developed chickenpox and were not permitted to stay on the train. No hotel would take them in either, and they had to be admitted to an isolation ward of a local hospital. Flo and Nanny were also admitted as they had been in close contact with them, and every time they went out, they had to go through a complicated fumigation procedure. Willie had to kick his heels holed up in the cheapest hotel he could find, and he was so short of cash that he sold his treasured firearms to pay the bills.

Fanny was particularly worried by their delayed arrival in Austria, and was perhaps the oddest card in Olga's family pack. She was Anglo-Irish and, during the Irish famine when she was 15 years old, her impoverished widowed mother had been evicted from her home. Fanny had been farmed out as companion to a rich cousin whom she accompanied on a grand tour of Europe. She developed into a stunning beauty and did her job well, surrounding her plain thirty-something widowed cousin with admiring young men wherever they went. She was only sixteen when she was persuaded, against her better judgement, into marriage with a wealthy young Austrian, Adolf Grohmann. Adolf was the son of a merchant banker, Reinholt Grohmann, who had made his fortune in coffee. Adolf did not possess Reinhold's ability and turned out to be a manic-depressive, a condition which was not recognized as long as his parents were alive to draw his anger. However, when they died, his anger turned against Fanny and their five children. He became more and more aggressive with the children as well as Fanny and, in 1861, she was compelled to have him certified.

At the age of 30, Fanny and her five surviving children became wards of court and fell prey to inefficient guardians, who let her fortune slip away while they limited her every action. Worst of all, they sold the family estate for a song and refused to let Fanny buy a home in the country. Fanny hated town life and hated being moved from one set of rented rooms to another. She hated having to consult elderly, pompous, stick-in-the-muds over every detail of domestic life. She was obliged to consult them before she selected a governess for her daughters or a school for her sons or even a rented villa for their summer holidays. In 1871, she eventually defied them, sold what valuables she had, and bought herself a ruined castle in the Tyrol. She restored the old castle slowly, room by room, assisted by her second husband who came from a family of artists. By 1884, she was living out her life as a matriarch, accommodating each of her four children in their own set of rooms within the castle. The fifth child, Dolfy, another manic-depressive, had been sent on a sea voyage for his health and later married into a German family of coffee planters in Mexico. Coffee was to remain a recurrent theme for our family.

In Fanny's castle, Schloss Matzen, Willie was allocated his own spacious flat and turned the sacristy of the Castle's chapel into a study where he concentrated on his writing. He had published two books as a very young man and now, as well as contributing to sporting journals, he published a number of other books. Tom and Olga grew into mischievous, headstrong, and very handsome children. Soon after arrival, the four-year old Olga had a tiff with Nanny and ran away. Five-year old Tom tried to dissuade her, but when he failed, he decided he should go too to look after her. The two infants were picked up eight hours later, hungry and tearful, hidden in the ruins of another castle two miles away.

Tom and Olga Baillie-Grohman

Soon after, old Tom Nickalls went shooting in Norway and, seeing skis for the first time, decided these were just what dear Flo needed in her snowed-up Austrian schloss, and despatched a bundle of skis to her. Skis were unknown in Tyrol and, when they arrived at the Austrian customs, the customs men sent for Willie and indignantly demanded the reason he was importing firewood into Austria. Was there not enough wood there already? Willie and Flo never really took to them, but young Tom and Olga did. They thought skis were wonderful as they gave you such freedom of movement in winter.

Old Tom continued to treat Flo generously, but never took to Willie. When he and Emily visited them in Matzen, Old Tom told Flo how disappointed he was. He was concerned that Flo, with her beauty, talents, and fortune, had buried herself in the country with a man who could not even give her a home of her own. Olga always remembered Flo's reply: "Life is what you make it, you can make something worthwhile of any situation!" Thirty years later, Flo was the first woman, and the first foreigner, to be awarded the Gold Medal of the new Republic of Austria. It was in recognition of her and Willie's work in setting up childcare centres to save children from the famine which followed World War One.

At the age of nine, Olga was sent to a Quaker school in England, despite Willie's protests that girls did not need such an education. Fanny, who had insisted on a good education for Willie's three sisters, agreed with Flo. Both women stood firm in their view that a girl must be educated, and Willie was no match for them. Before Olga left, she spent days pretending her large family of dolls were suffering from a serious illness. They all 'died' and a funeral cortege was organized to bury them in the garden, with Young Tom draped in a white tablecloth officiating as the priest. Olga then retired to bed and cried herself to sleep. At the age of ninety, Young Tom's eyes still filled with tears when he told this story. Only Miss Cocoa survived, a splendid black doll wearing a red coat and hat trimmed with real white fur. I spent years digging in the garden looking for the dolls that Olga had buried, but never found them. Fifty years later, Miss Cocoa left Matzen for Kenya, treasured by Olga's eldest granddaughter.

"Why didn't you bury her too?" young Tom had asked all those years ago.

"She's different! She's strong!" replied Olga.

Olga did not like her school, where she was always hungry. The school said she was disruptive, untidy, and always in mischief. "Just what they said of me!" said Granny Fanny, recalling with pride the day she broke the lavatory window for a bet. Three years later, again despite her father's protests, Olga was sent to the Godolphin School in Salisbury. Just before she left home, she replaced the space bar on her father's typewriter with the letter 'y', and roared with laughter at Flo's description of his rage when an important letter started "DearySiry".

When she was twelve, Theodore Roosevelt came to visit Willie. The two men had met in America and Willie had described the shooting reserves of the Austrian Empire as the only way to prevent extinction of game, an extinction to which both he and Roosevelt had extensively contributed by their passion for shooting. When Roosevelt telegraphed that he was arriving, Willie had to cancel an outing he had promised the children. At the end of the day, when Willie walked him down to the station, Roosevelt put his hand in his pocket and with some surprise found a hot baked potato, then another and another. The other pocket was equally stuffed with squashy hot potatoes. Willie was suitably embarrassed and said, "So sorry, Roosevelt, my son, I'm afraid. Boys will be boys…." But Roosevelt would have none of it. "Not your son, Grohman, but your daughter!"

Olga adored her new school, laughed at what she considered the silly regulations, and started a house magazine in which she made fun of everyone, including her housemistress. Miss Edwards became a life long friend and admirer, and years later wrote to Olga that of all the girls who had been through her hands, she had been the most outstanding. But at the time, she wrote in Olga's report: "Olga has been here four years. She has never yet done anything ladylike, nor has she done anything ungentlemanly!"

From the age of nine, Olga was expected to travel from Innsbruck to London and back again alone. She would be seen across London to Victoria station by one or other of her many aunts. Young Tom told me that she rarely arrived with her luggage, which usually had to be telegraphed for from Calais or Dover, but she always had a pile of vulgar papers in French, German and English. He felt so embarrassed that he would take the papers and burn them before anyone else saw them. Yes, he admitted, he did read them first.

I asked Tom why he had joined the Royal Navy, not the most obvious career for a man of mixed Austrian and Irish blood who was heir to an ancient castle in the Tyrol. "My father often took me on shooting expeditions when he was acting as a guide to Prussian magnates. At night we slept in simple lodges, and I overheard them talking politics, running down the English, telling father what they were going to do to them. Father had been born in Austria of an Austrian father, but he had been so angry at the way his mother was treated as a ward of court that he decided to become British on his 21st birthday, and this he could do because his mother had been born in Ireland. It amazed me how gently Father turned away their anger – he was known for his peppery temper. It was only later that I realized how urgently he needed the money these gentlemen brought. When I came home from one such expedition, I told my mother: 'When I'm grown up, I'm going to have my own battle-ship, an English one!' and when she asked me why, I said: 'So I can shoot those Prussians before

Olga, Flo, Willie and Tom

they reach England! As a Lieutenant in the first war and an admiral in the second, that is just what I have done.'"

When Olga left school, her mother decided to "bring her out". Willie's writing had proved sufficiently successful to pay for a flat in Artillery Mansions just behind the Army and Navy Stores, and it was from this base that Olga was presented at Court and then attended a season of dances and parties. The following year she spent the season in Vienna, attending another round of balls and parties. Although she was widely remembered as a beautiful girl full of fun and vitality, she told me she hated every minute of both seasons, and when I asked her why, she explained:

"It was all such a waste of time, of life." Then her voice grew indignant. "I felt I was on a marriage market, and nobody bid for me!" This may have been partly true. Despite her beauty, she was very tall, totally unmusical, a clumsy dancer, far too quick with witty repartee, and frighteningly able. The thought of living a submissive, frivolous life in Edwardian suburbia, in the capital city of either the British Empire or of the Austrian one, was anathema to her. Her school friend, Eileen Hayes, the daughter of an Oxford don, was going to Oxford and Olga wanted to go too. Mrs Hayes suggested that both girls could become home students and that Olga could live with the Hayes during her years at Oxford.

"No blue stockings for me – that is too much, and far too expensive!" shouted Willie, and this time he won the argument. Olga did not go to university. Yet when the family was at home in the Alps, she was allowed exceptional freedom. She spent nearly four years at home, and long days in both summer and winter were spent on excursions into the mountains, often quite alone and for days at a time. She had many adventures: she dislocated her shoulder and wrenched an ankle while skiing in winter; found her path home along a steep mountain side blocked by a land slip; and had to retrace her footsteps some fifteen miles up one valley and down the other side in summer. When she needed help she would go to the nearest farmhouse. On her excursions, Die Matzener Olga became a familiar figure. She was always made welcome, for she was genuinely interested in the farmers and their problems and had a great gift for amusing sick children.

The Austrian peasant farmers had been freed from tithes to land-lord and church in 1848, and now, two generations later, were self sufficient yeoman farmers, jealous of their independence and well adjusted to survive the vagaries of a harsh climate. Each family lived almost entirely on what they produced. They wove their own linen, made their own breeches from the hides of their animals, built their own houses, grew their own corn and baked their own bread, buying in only such 'Colonial wares' as sugar and coffee. It was a way of life Olga greatly admired. Later it became her dream to create this kind of life for African farmers in Kenya.

Leaving school in no way diminished Olga's sense of mischief. Because of the cold winters it was difficult to install water sanitation in the old castle, and old-fashioned lavatories over a pit that was cleaned out once a year were still in use. Water was poured down these from a jug, and one day Olga noticed a beautiful copper jug in the maid's lavatory. Her father was an avid collector of antiques, and villagers who had fallen on hard times would bring in oddments for him to buy. She polished the jug carefully, then went to the lowest courtyard, rang the bell, waved away the servant who was going to answer it, and stood there apparently talking to someone. She took the jug to her father's study.

"There is a woman selling this jug, and she wants thirty kroner for it," said Olga.

Willie examined the jug intently. "It is a good one, offer her fifteen!" Olga went off down the spiral staircase and came back to say the imaginary woman would take twenty-five.

"Too much," said Willie, "try her with twenty!"

"Twenty-two fifty!" said Olga on her third journey upstairs. "I'll pay the last two fifty if I can put the jug in my rooms!"

Willie wanted to get on with his writing. "All right!" he said. On her way back to her rooms she passed her grandmother, who looked at the gleaming jug and said: "Where did you find that, Olga, it is one from Schloss Wolfgangsee!" (the home which Fanny had been forced to sell forty years earlier.) Olga confessed at once.

"Father has just paid me 20 kroner for it, and I can have it for my rooms." This became one of the old lady's favourite stories

"That is the only time I have known anyone get the better of Willie – that girl will go a long way!"

When Olga was staying with cousins in Vienna and was invited to a grand ball, a clumsy young man asked how to apologise in English when he bumped into anyone. "Hey ho, bumps a daisy!" said Olga and giggled irrepressibly when she saw eyebrows being raised as the young man bumped his way round the room with a cheery. "Hey ho, bumps a daisy!" On another social occasion, everyone had to perform a party piece, recite a poem, sing a song or play some music. When Olga's turn came, she stood up and said: "I'm going to show you how the average English girl sings!" And tone deaf and tuneless as she was, she sang a popular song and brought the house down with laughter. When the ever musical Viennese hostess said: "My dear, you must be very good to give such a clever impersonation of tuneless singing, now show us what you can really do!" she politely declined. Luckily it was considered bad manners for the same person to perform twice.

Back at Matzen, Fanny, who had so loved the mountains as a girl, was not so sure that she approved of Olga going on day-long skiing expeditions alone. Flo had made Olga a new ski-skirt of heavy wool. The trouble with skirts was that they swept up the snow, which first melted and then froze again, making the skirt as stiff as a board and a hindrance to quick movements. On one outing Olga became so frustrated that she took out a pen-knife and cut off six inches, leaving the skirt well above her ankles. A few falls later, the skirt was still bothersome, and out came the penknife and off came another few inches. She arrived back with a skirt only just below her knees.

"I can't ski in stupid skirts, I can't! I can't!" wept Olga when her mother reproved her. There was no way she was going to be allowed out in trousers.

When Granny Fanny died in 1908, the castle was left to Willie and his three sisters, each of whom had a flat in it. Willie bought his sisters' shares and proceeded to make improvements to the castle, giving his son and daughter their own flat each. Olga had the sunny south wing, and spent much time planning how to improve the rooms exactly to her liking. The coachman was a good carpenter, and panelled one room for her with packing cases found in the attics. She found a set of tile moulds, and carried them one by one on her bicycle to the potter five miles across the river, who cast them for her. Olga carried the even heavier tiles back one by one to the castle where the coachman set the stove in her sitting room. They were beautiful tiles, early eighteenth century representations of the twelve apostles and of the prophets.

Her rooms were exceptional, neither over decorated and fussy as was the Edwardian trend, nor following the gothic and renaissance styles of the rest of the castle. Instead, they reflected the simplicity of the Austrian farmhouse. There was a table in one corner surrounded by a bench, a green tiled stove with another bench in another corner, built-in seats set at tables under each window, and a single cupboard matching the panelling. Her bedroom was whitewashed – no expensive brocaded wall paper here – and furnished with an inlaid bed and two wonderful chests of drawers, which her grandmother had left her. The floors were polished parquet, the rugs few and well worn. These simple rooms remained Olga's ideal throughout her life, and parts were copied again and again each time she built a house, an occupation she loved.

Schloss Matzen

With her rooms comfortably organized, Olga started writing. To her father's dismay, the Baillie-Grohman name appeared in publications he scorned as vulgar such as Titbits, Woman's Weekly, and Home Chat. When he complained, she promptly sent an article to Country Life, a paper to which he was a contributor. They published it. He was proud of his daughter, yet dismayed that she should be so able to compete in a very masculine world.

Young Tom was now in the Navy. The deep companionship of their early childhood had disappeared. He envied her the comfort in which she lived, her own comfortable rooms, good food, and a personal maid, while he struggled to make a career for himself in the Navy. Olga was envious of his freedom, the interesting training he was provided with, his demanding job, and the prodigal son's welcome when he came home. Like many young women, she loved her home yet felt imprisoned by it, and found it tedious to help with the flowers and attend an endless succession of elderly guests. Young Tom agreed with his father that it was high time Olga got married.

By 1909 skiing was becoming popular in Austria, and English skiers were frequent visitors. Skiing on her own above Innsbruck, Olga stopped to assist another skier so entangled in her skirts and boards that she could not get up. Olga disentangled her and helped her to her feet. She was an English girl, Dolly Thompson, about her own age. The two girls shared their packed lunches and later made their way down together to the Tiroler Hof Hotel in Innsbruck where the Thompson family was staying. It adjoined the station and Olga had arranged to meet her own parents there so she could travel back to Matzen with them. The two families were introduced, and over hot chocolate the Grohmans invited the Thompsons to lunch the following week. Dolly's brother, Douglas, came along too. Douglas was a regular officer in the King's Own Dragoon Guards and was on his way back to join his regiment, then serving in India, after his first English leave. For him it was love at first sight. He was so enchanted by Olga, that he wanted to postpone his departure to court her, marry her and take her back with him. His father, a retired colonel from the same regiment, would not hear of this. Douglas was only 22 years old, and depended on his father for an allowance, so father's views prevailed. In four years time, when he next returned to Europe, he would be twenty-six, and that was time enough for a man to marry.

Olga never forgot the hurt puppy-dog look on his face when she agreed with this dictum, and told him that she would make no promises but that she would write to him regularly and would make a decision during those four years. She was not nearly as smitten as Douglas seemed to be, recording in her diary that she found him: "Young, blasé, likes to be thought clever, and dull." Olga's tolerance for dull people was very low, which was another reason that such a beautiful girl had not yet met her match. Men found her keen intellect, fertile imagination, and forthright repartee threatening. Here was no clinging vine, but a young sapling that threatened to grow into a mighty oak.

Although the prospect of life in an Indian cantonment did not sound exciting, it would undoubtedly be better than English or Austrian suburbia, and she took the first steps to prepare herself by training as a nurse. To do this she once again had to fight her father's prejudices – nursing was not considered a suitable profession for a lady. When Olga told him that she wanted to train at a famous London hospital, he shouted: "Do you think I want my daughter looking after the sweepings from the street in some London hospital? You will have to wash, and do other things, to men!"

Olga's voice was as strong as his as she yelled back: "Just look at what happened to your Aunt Betsy – she buried five children in India. Do you want your grandchildren buried there too?" Flo said nothing, but when they were next in London she enrolled Olga at the Great Ormond Street Hospital for Sick Children and arranged for her to live with Aunt Nina while she did her training. Once again, Willie found himself outmanoeuvred.

Nursing sick children was hard, demanding work. Olga found that she could handle children well but she never learned to dress a major wound without retching, She also found she was peculiarly susceptible to blood poisoning, and after two years had endured so many infections that the doctors said she must give up nursing. During these two years Douglas had been regaled with every heart rending incident from the children's hospital, and Olga had received surprisingly lively accounts of life on the cantonment. They were not love letters, and did not touch on matters of emotion or longing, but were a bulletin of daily events in their lives. So Olga heard about the mosquitoes which bit his ankles while he was out shooting, the subsequent attack of malaria, and finally the news that Douglas was to be invalided back to England on long sick leave with possible discharge from the Army. Olga was deeply disappointed, thinking that it meant accepting the restrictions of suburbia for the rest of her life, or waiting for another man. She had come to like Douglas more through his letters than in real life, and his next letters were best of all. He had decided to break the journey at Mombasa and travel up country for some big game shooting in British East Africa, as the future colony of Kenya was then called. He travelled as far as Uganda, which in those days meant taking the train to the railhead in Kisumu and crossing Lake Victoria Nyanza on a steamer. This new railway, cheerfully dubbed the Lunatic line, was heavily in debt. The then governor of British East Africa, Sir Charles Eliot, was determined to encourage white settlers to produce enough crops to make both the railway, and the protectorate, pay. Land which was seemingly unoccupied was being allocated to white settlers in blocks of 2,000 acres. On his way back through Kisumu, Douglas, with Olga's encouragement, put his name down for an allocation of land. It proved too expensive for him so he bought jointly with three other men, each man taking 500 acres. Choosing business partners from unknown people singled out by their lack of funds was not the wisest way to start a business, but at the time it seemed the only solution. Douglas remained in Kenya for the rest of 1912 and most of 1913, camping on his land with his three partners. The surveying skills acquired in the army were useful and enabled him to earn money. He arranged for a mortgage; planted some thirty acres with coffee, and mapped out his future farm, encouraged in all his activities by Olga's delighted letters. He could not be such a stick in the mud after all, she told herself, and she would certainly marry him now and be mistress of his farm.

Olga knew exactly why she wanted to emigrate. She was too brimming over with life to want to be tied down to the Edwardian social calendar, too intelligent to want to trivialise time away. She had no interest in the occupations of most upper middle class women – fussing over fashion, the social round of the seasons, Ascot, and Henley, theatre and opera, balls and receptions, bridge and tennis. These were the frills of life and she had no time for frills. What did you do if you felt like this in Edwardian England? You migrated – temporarily to govern the empire, or permanently to settle it. She had yet to come to terms with the inconsistency of her hopes and longings. Although she decried suburbia, she loved the noisy, jolly Nickalls family, the endless family gatherings for parties and celebrations. She was bridesmaid to her aunts, godmother to their children. She loved visiting the Henley Regatta, where her Nickalls uncles, Guy and Vee, were making such great names for themselves. This was not trivial socializing, this was family. Yet this way of life was determined by the suburban values of newly rich middle classes, on the one hand aping the habits of the aristocracy, on the other preaching the virtues of hard work and integrity.

Douglas took his discharge from the army in 1912 and they announced their engagement. Both sets of parents expressed delight at the match. "Olga has so much vitality and drive, I am sure she is just the girl to wake Douglas up and make a man of him!" Olga overheard Mrs Thomson remark to her parents. Willie usually left social chitchat to Flo, but he had replied vehemently: "Olga needs a good steady boy like Douglas! I just hope he is firm with her, and does not allow her to go off on her madcap jaunts!"

"Madcap jaunts?" Mrs Thompson sounded distressed.

"Oh, he means Olga's long walks," Flo quickly interspersed. "She's inclined to go off into the mountains for several days at a time, just like her father does! Usually when her grandmother was expecting guests whom she considered dull!"

Olga described Douglas in a letter to her Aunt Clare: "He is half pure Scottish and half Irish, and I never thought what a good mixture that could be! He is nice looking, about two inches taller than self (she was 5ft 11 inches), dark, and aged twenty five. I think that is a faithful description. His father and mine were both born on April 1, and that is the day we became engaged!"

Olga decided to train herself in skills a pioneer would need. In the 1910s, it was as difficult as it was unusual for a girl who was expected to employ servants all her life to learn about such practical matters, but Olga had set about it in her usual direct manner. She returned to Bellevue farm where she was born, and although Old Tom was now dead and Bellevue belonged to someone else, the farm manager who had once taught her to ride was delighted to teach her anything that would be useful. On the land where Lympne aerodrome now stands, the ploughman taught her to lead the great Shire horse out of the stable, to harness him to the plough, and to plough a straight furrow. She found keeping the furrow straight the most difficult thing she had ever tried to do. The dairyman taught her how to milk, and his wife showed her how to manage both dairy and poultry, making her handle the animals and inspect them closely for signs of disease. Back in London, she went to the London residence of a rich estate owner, a shooting acquaintance of her father's, and persuaded the cook to give her lessons, to make bread, and cakes, to show her how meat and fish were salted and how all kinds of food sent down from the estate could be preserved.

For the first time in her life, her father approved her activities. He considered Olga had been ridiculously pampered all her life and was pleased to see her take an interest in domesticity. His hoyden daughter would become a good wife yet. Flo showed her pleasure by taking her on extensive, and expensive, shopping expeditions. Her own pioneering days in British Columbia told her just what a pioneer needed. At Harrods they spent £500 on a prefabricated bungalow recommended for the tropics, and other famous shops provided everything to go in it. The bed came from Maples, the linen from Harrods, the tin trunks from the Army & Navy stores, and Olga's stout leather boots were hand-made in Austria. Her trousseau was plain – pioneer women did not dress up – and consisted mainly of serge skirts, linen shirts, lawn camisoles, white pleated night-dresses, and frilly white drawers (knickers), each item hand-sewn by the dozen.

In January 1914, Olga and Douglas were married at St Margaret's Church Westminster, with eight bridesmaids selected from Olga's forty-odd first cousins, and with his sister Dolly in charge. Both sets of parents sealed their approval with an allowance of £250 a year for five years, by which time the farm should be developed sufficiently to support them.

It was 33 years later when I, her youngest daughter, became engaged that Olga told me that her own honeymoon had been a wonderful voyage of discovery. Most girls of her generation were married with little knowledge of what were then called the facts of life. Flo had told Olga just what to expect and warned her that she might find it disappointing and painful. In turn, Olga told me of the wonders of sex, how she had never imagined that it could be so physically satisfying, and how a man could be so gentle, so willing to please, so sensitive. And later, as I read articles and papers by her, I realized that it was at this point that she had fallen in love with Douglas and forgotten about his dullness. Nobody could be dull with Olga around. Only three weeks later he sailed for Kenya, taking the bungalow with him, and leaving her a bulldog puppy as a parting gift. We know exactly what happened to Bully, she kept a diary for him as well as for herself.

The House at Koru – 1914.

Chapter Two

THE COUNTRY OF THE UNEXPECTED

This chapter is taken from Olga's unpublished manuscript: The Adventures of Olivia & a Woman Coffee Farmer in Kenya.

In her early writing, Olga constantly referred to her first journey to Africa, but to us children it was rarely mentioned. The reason behind this was because the voyage was concerned with Douglas; he was referred to in hushed tones and questions about him were not welcome. The voyage was ruined by what today would be called sexual harassment, and her experience of dealing with it would have been useful to us all, yet it was one of the few subjects not discussed. A young and pretty woman travelling alone was prey to every bored man on board, and there was no way of escape.

Conditions on board ship were very different from those on today's cruise ships. Cabins, even first class ones, were small and cramped and Olga shared hers with two strangers. There was one small washbasin in each cabin, a tiny wardrobe, and just space for three wardrobe trunks. Laundry was difficult and, as the climate changed from a northern winter to that of the Red Sea, and because passengers were expected to dress for dinner every night and to play deck games by day, they needed an ample wardrobe. Most baggage had to be kept in the baggage room, to which there was access only two or three times a week. First class cabins usually had portholes, but were unwholesomely hot for much of the voyage. The cabin was no place to sit quietly and read or write; once they reached the Red Sea, Olga decided it was no place to sleep either and would creep out on deck at night to sleep in a hidden corner on a wooden chair.

The real problem for young women travelling alone was that there was nowhere to escape an aggressive male. If she happened to be both pretty and yet disinterested in a board ship romance, she had to plan avoidance techniques with care. Upper middle class girls of that generation were so protected in their upbringing that they had no idea how to deal with sexual harassment, a term unknown in those days. Olga was noticed boarding at Genoa by a predatory Prussian en route for German East Africa (GEA) as the present day Tanzania was then known. He was an experienced traveller and tipped the head steward in the dining room to ensure he was seated next to her. Olga had insufficient experience to approach the same steward a day or two later to request to be seated away from him. The Prussian only spoke heavily accented English and, because she was bilingual in German, they conversed in that language. However, to her acute embarrassment, everyone assumed they were travelling together.

As it was her first journey and she knew no one, he made her life a misery. He intruded on her conversations with others and, if she attended the almost nightly dancing on deck, he insisted on dancing every dance with her. In the end she did find a solution. She adored children, who were not allowed on to the main passenger deck but had a space on the lower, second-class level. Olga found that she was extremely popular organising games, giving the nannies time off to do the laundry. She took some of the children to visit Bully in his cage on the aft hold, where she gave him a walk round the deck and put him through his tricks. Next, she took her typewriter to the second class dining room and tried to do some writing. However, she was constantly interrupted by stewards bringing her cups of Bovril and stories of life at sea, of cramped quarters, poor pay and food, the harshness of the discipline, and the perpetual fear of unemployment before the days of the welfare state. Olga always had a sympathetic ear for the underdog, and ten years and eight journeys later published articles about how conditions for seamen were worsening rather than improving.

The pattern of this voyage was the forerunner of her later ones. She must have made the journey at least twenty times, a number of which I shared with her. She always had quality time for children, her own and other people's, time for those who worked for her, time for herself and her work, very little time for what she regarded as social frivolities, and none at all for board ship romances. She was never to enjoy the voyages, the sense of relaxation they brought as one travelled suspended between two worlds and out of touch with both of them. The many entertainments provided for passengers were, in her eyes, a waste of time. Even as a young woman she was very serious and almost puritanical in her self-discipline, an attitude well disguised by a tremendous sense of fun and mischief.

In April 1914, when she arrived at Mombasa, the deep-water harbour of Kilindini was not yet finished and passengers were ferried ashore on lighters. As usual, a group of government officials stood watching them alight, looking out for newly arrived officers and old friends returning, hoping to glean 'home' news and gossip. One of these, an administrator called Oscar Watkins, stood watching fascinated as Olga stood up in the lighter, with Bully in a rucksack on her back. She ignored helping hands held out to her, and leaped from the lighter on to the quayside in one jump into the arms of a young man even taller and thinner than herself, and wearing a yet larger hat. He recognized the man as Douglas Thompson. Oscar had been in the office at Kisumu when Douglas came in to take up a land claim. He had spoken to him on several occasions, and thought him a dull fish, but he must have had something in him to attract a girl like that one. He decided that he must treat himself to lunch at the Mombasa Club to catch another glimpse of the Thompsons. Everyone waiting for the boat train lunched at the club.

Sure enough, they came in just after him, with Olga clasping Bully even though dogs were not allowed into the dining room. They chose a table near his, and he watched as Bully was put through his repertoire of tricks. Olga placed a morsel of food on his nose and said: "Trust!" Bully drooled with anticipation, and sat until she said: "Good Dog!" He immediately tossed the food into the air and caught it in one slobbery bite. He sat up and begged, offered his paw to be shaken, and repeated various other routines until the command of "Die for your country!" At this he rolled onto his back and waved his four fat paws in the air. Finally, the words "Good Dog" were accompanied by the last morsel of meat from Olga's plate. She never did like meat.

Bully was now three months old, devoted to Olga and possessive of her. The train had no corridor and the coupé they occupied had two bunks and they were allowed to take him into their railway carriage, Bully insisted on sitting on the seat, trying to insinuate his body between them. Soon after dusk, the train stopped and the passengers clambered down for dinner, an elaborate five course meal of mediocre cooking, served in a long hut near the station. When passengers returned to their compartments, they found their bunks had been made up. But when Olga tried to go to bed on the lower bunk, Bully would not allow Douglas near her. Laughingly they moved to the top bunk, and found it wider and, at the frequent stops, more private. Bully lay spread-eagled on the bunk below them, snoring loudly.

* * * * * * *

At Nairobi station, Douglas and Olga were met by the Stanley Hotel ox-cart with eight oxen in span and taken to the little wooden hotel which stood in Sixth Avenue, a road planned so wide that sixteen span of oxen could turn in it. At the moment the rains had broken and it was difficult for any wheeled vehicle to move, let alone turn, in the thick clinging mud. Douglas had reserved two riding mules at the hotel so they could go shopping. Olga's mount was a small one suitable for a lady, so despite her bulky skirt, when she sat astride it her long legs reached to the ground on either side. The mule had to be forced to start with a sharp crack of the whip, and plunged forwards suddenly straight into a drainage ditch which was so full of red mud that it could not climb out again. Neither could Olga move, she was up to her thighs in mud. Both of them had to be dug out. Bully, high on her back in his rucksack, was warm and dry. Douglas went shopping alone.

Next day, they both went down to Nairobi station to check the stores they had ordered. Olga was accustomed to seeing the shopping of huge Edwardian families but she had never seen shopping on quite this scale, sacks of flour, sugar, rice and maize, two-pound tins of butter and jam each by the dozen, condensed milk by the crate, biscuits by the five pound tin, paraffin oil by cases of four four-gallon tins, lamp glasses by the dozen, blue and yellow laundry soap by the dozen bars. Finally, Olga could not believe that the two of them needed such supplies and questioned Douglas. He told her they were still living in a camp with the other three partners, and it would be a while before they could move into the bungalow.

It was July before Olga wrote to her favourite aunt. She was richly endowed with aunts, with a total of nine real aunts and a number more by marriage. Any child with so many is bound to have favourites, and Olga's was Grace Nickalls. Aunt Grace lived with her sister Maud in a Georgian house built in the grounds of a ruined abbey at Boxley in Kent, where Grace managed the domestic affairs and Maud turned the ruins of the Abbey into a magical water garden. She also grew a plentiful supply of fruit and vegetables in the monks' old walled kitchen garden. The sisters needed these supplies as they had become the types of persons indispensable to any large family. The Aunts had long been dispensing hospitality and tender loving care to generations of nieces, nephews, and their families. Sitting in her Harrods bungalow in Kenya, Olga conjured up the witty, kindly woman who had so understood her frustration with her father when he forbade her wish to go to University. Her letters to Aunt Grace were illustrated by funny drawings, never mind that Olga could not draw, (at least, not pictures).

"We have had so many adventures since we started from Nairobi that I do not know where to begin. In the first place we went straight into grass huts, because the neighbours could not have us. The huts are large and roomy and built in different shapes. There is quite a colony of them here now. One hut is a large dining room, with a door used as a dining room table and another on two whisky barrels as a sideboard. We have a good deal of furniture in use already, for the things brought from the station could not be brought up here packed. I had not been warned of this, and when Douglas's agent came to meet us at the station with forty Africans, and sixteen oxen with ridiculously inadequate harness, and a small water cart, I was not well enough up in the ways of the country to know what to expect.

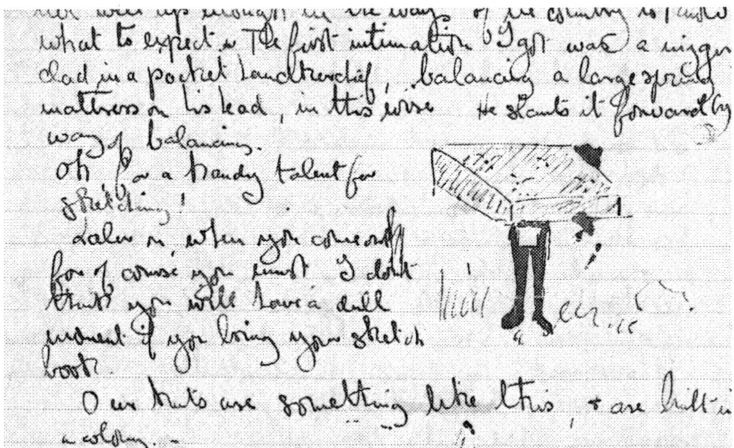

"We went on ahead; it is a five mile walk from the station and it was very muddy. The first intimation was the arrival of an African clad in a pocket handkerchief balancing a large spring mattress on his head. The next thing was two armchairs with two pairs of legs to each. These were rather comic, for they did not walk in step so frequently fell over each other.

"There was nowhere to put the mattresses as the floors are full of insects. However, eventually the bed-stead arrived and we were able to put it up. Maples sent the wrong fittings for the bed, so it cannot be used properly and it is too small for the mattress.

"It has taken some time to settle down, to get provisions into lock-up places which are handy, and so on. Now we are quite comfortable but this is pre-eminently the country of the unexpected. The whole life is hand to mouth. Provisions are difficult to obtain regularly. The store cheerfully runs out of oil, flour, and jam at the same time, leaving the district in semi-darkness, breadless, and tealess.

"The house-hold servants, field boys and cattlemen sign on by the month, yet one is never surprised to wake up in the morning to find that the household has decamped in the night, or that the cattle have not been let out because the herdsmen have flitted.

"At other times the trains are knocked off. The time-table gives us one a day in each direction, and even when they run provisions of any kind may arrive distinctly high. It takes a letter a week to arrive in Nairobi, and telegrams are often not delivered. Nothing, absolutely nothing, can be counted on for certain."

Aunt Grace was spared many details recorded by 'Olivia'; the kitchen that was a mud hut set some twenty yards from the house, with a smoky wood burning stove, no running water, and little light. The cook, a strapping teenager straight from mission school, was naked except for football boots and blue garters. He stood at the inefficient wood-burning stove clutching a harp in one hand and a wooden spoon in the other. When asked why he wore the boots and garters, he replied because if he took them off they might be stolen, and he did not like to put his harp down for the same reason.

Both Douglas and Olga had worked extremely hard. Douglas had finished surveying his land and that of his neighbours and had surveyed the new roads they would need to put in when the dry season started. He had planted out a coffee nursery with seedlings for another fifteen acres, while wheat and maize had been planted in their prepared plot. He had made a start on breeding up hardy African stock with imported bulls – his cows had to travel 150 miles by rail to Nakuru for this service, and he viewed his burgeoning farm with pleasure. What pleased him most was the way Olga had taken to farming in Africa, and how fast any work proceeded once she put her unstoppable energy behind it. She had organized a small poultry farm, using the small local chickens and when he escorted his cows to Nakuru he had always to bring back half-breed Rhode Island Red cocks to improve her chickens. She had also set up a dairy and now made her own butter and cream, and sold them to the neighbours.

On the domestic side she had made even more progress. The bungalow had been finished inside to look like a replica of her sitting room in Austria. The walls were panelled with their packing cases, planed and stained an ancient brown; a corner table had a bench built round it. Her collection of pewter plates from Austria gleamed on the shelves of a Welsh dresser from Bellevue, the house where she was born. Near the door stood old Tom Nickalls's desk, so deep in papers that her typewriter was quite buried. Douglas was a tidy person who liked everything to be neat and in its place, yet he loved to watch Olga delving into the deluge on her desk and producing just what was wanted; darning wool, secateurs, Bully's worm pills, safety pins, or her current notebook and pencil. And he realized that since Olga had arrived, there were always workers seeking work, yet overall so great was the shortage of labour in that district that most settlers were urging the government to force Africans out to work. Two years earlier, in 1912, the government had set up a commission, which had found there was indeed a shortage of workers. There were insufficient young males available in the country to fulfil the requirements of the new settler farms, and those who did go out to work would choose the farmer who offered the best conditions. The government had no intention of using compulsion to force Africans to work for settlers. Neither Olga nor Douglas had heard of this report, research for which had been carried out two years before she arrived by a man called Watkins, the same one who had watched her at Mombasa. Olga just thought it was her duty to provide as good conditions as she could for labour, at least as good as the Austrian farmer provided for his hired men.

Most of their workers came from the lower plains round Lake Victoria, but up in the highlands it was much colder at night. Olga insisted that their huts should be properly built and weather proofed. She encouraged married men to bring their families. She insisted that water was piped from the stream to a convenient fetching point near the workers' huts, and she used her nursing skills to treat the children for their various complaints. Every child had to parade at the house every day to be given milk, and while they were drinking it she would walk down the line, picking out any ailing ones. She now wanted to set up a school for them. She had been on the farm just three months.

Despite the hard work, it had been for both of them a garden of Eden, full of adventure and excitement yet almost totally isolated from the outside world. They both wanted a child and the impatient Olga waited each month with baited breath. Douglas decided they needed a break. August bank holiday was celebrated in Nairobi by horse-races on the Muthaiga race course, and there would be plenty of entertainments put on for the up-country settlers who gathered in Nairobi. There would be amateur plays and concerts, dances, parties and picnics. The farm needed more stores and building materials, the bank manager must be placated for an extended overdraft, while Olga was keen to get some clothes more suited to farming in the tropics than the long drill skirts and starchy white blouses of her trousseau, all now stained by the reddened river water in which they were laundered by pounding them with stones.

* * * * * * *

It was only when they arrived in Nairobi that they realized the extent to which they had opted out of the world. For months they had met no one but half a dozen fellow farmers; the local newspaper published in Mombasa took a week to reach Koru. English papers came in batches, taking five or six weeks to arrive. It took time to read them and the light from flickering oil lamps did not make reading easy. Now in Nairobi the talk was of the Austrian arch-duke shot dead in Sarajevo and the likelihood of war. The bar in the New Stanley buzzed with rumours and excited anticipation as to whether the war, if it came, would be fought in East Africa. That evening as they sat by candlelight over their stodgy evening meal and made lists of all the things they must do the next day, they did not know that tomorrow was the day that their world would change for ever.

* * * * * * *

The following day they set out early on foot, walking up Sixth Avenue towards the post office. They would start at the far end and work backwards. All the way up Sixth Avenue posters screamed at them: "Germany Invades Belgium", "England declares war on Germany." When confronted with problems, Olga always talked them through and now she went through all uncles and cousins, those who would join up immediately, those who were already soldiers or sailors, and those who were too old or too young. At least eight men on the Nickalls side would probably join up; her own brother was an officer in the Royal Navy. The same number of men on the Austrian side would also join up and the thought of these two families warring against each other was too terrible to contemplate. And what of her parents now, British subjects resident in Austria, would they be able to survive the war? Were they already in a prison camp? Was there any way to communicate with them?

Douglas let her talk – he liked to think problems through, and by the time they reached the post office, he had made up his mind. It was a difficult decision, taken with much heart searching, for what would happen to Olga, "my darling baby" as he called her. What if she was even now pregnant? But he was a soldier by choice, trained for war, happy to defend the great empire into which he had been born. The decision was speeded by a big notice on the far side of the road saying: "Recruitment Office for the King's African Rifles." He turned to her and told her to go into the post office and buy up fifty rupees worth of stamps. It was an absurd amount, and Olga protested loudly but he insisted. There was a long queue and Olga noticed, between long conversations with others in the queue, that every one seemed to be buying up stamps. Local post offices often ran out of them and with no telephones and an unreliable telegraph service, letters were the only means of communication,

When she came out of the post office, Douglas was not to be seen, and she walked to the level crossing to watch the down-train from up country pass. Passengers were leaning out of the windows looking to see who was in town that day but she did not see anyone she knew; she knew so few people in this strange land.

Suddenly Douglas was behind her, talking into her ear, a new note of urgency in his voice. She was to go to the bank and take out all their money, and then go down to Elliots, the grocers, and order all the groceries they needed for a year. Olga remonstrated that they did not need any more stores. He spun her round so that she was facing him, keeping his hands on her shoulders, looking into her eyes.

"Baby, there is a war on. I shall be happier if you have ample supplies and money on the farm. Now be a good girl and don't argue."

"But of course we shall have enough money and stores. What is all this about?" Then over his shoulder she caught sight of the recruitment poster. "Douglas, you haven't joined up?"

"My country needs me, Baby. I must do my bit!" People really did speak like that in those days. The enormity of the situation reached her. She tried to bury her head on his shoulder but her terrai hat got in the way.

"I need you too, Douglas. What about the farm, and" – a large sob caught her unawares – "my parents?"

"We have all got to be very brave, Baby, that is what war is about. You can save us both a lot of time and money by looking after the farm while I am away. Now off you go to the bank and you do the shops near the station. I am going down Bazaar road for tools and nails and spares. Remember, a year's supply of everything you can lay hands on." "Except my new outfit!" thought Olga, but for once was wise enough to keep her thoughts to herself. Down in Government Road she tucked the bundle of rupee notes into her belt and walked back to Whitakers and then on to Elliots. Six sacks of wheat flour, twelve of maize, four cases of paraffin, each of sixteen gallons, twenty four bars each of blue and yellow soap, six extra hurricane lanterns, spare glasses and wicks for all the lamps, a case of tea, another of tinned ham, four sacks of sugar and one of salt. Fortunately a ship-load of luxuries had arrived recently and Olga ordered them all: tinned peaches, sardines, gentlemen's relish, bacon, marmalade, Worcester sauce, tomato ketchup. She paid cash and arranged immediate delivery to the station.

Back in the hotel to do their packing, Olga's mind filled with dread. She did not like two of Douglas's partners, one of whom ogled her even with Douglas around. Would he try it with Douglas away?

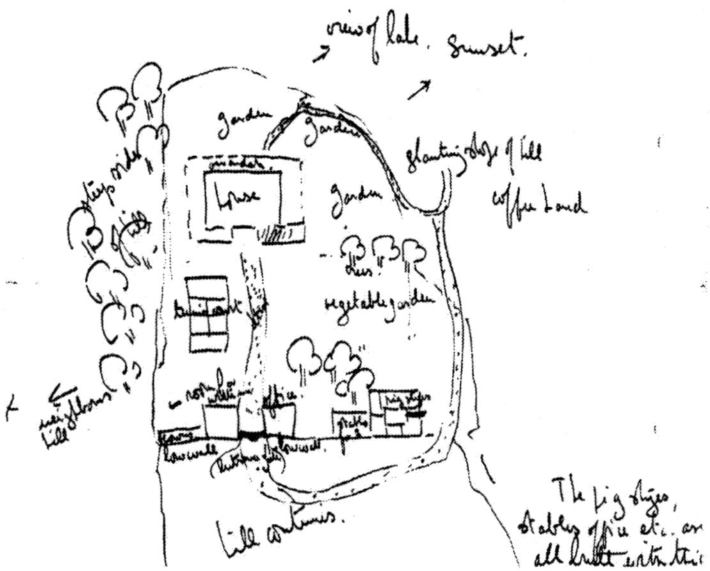

The original plan for Khitari.

The bungalow from Harrods had been erected but the doors did not fit. She could not get cook to wear any clothes at all. She still did not speak the language. Two cows were in calf, and although she could milk, she had never seen a calf born. Another fifteen acres of coffee were to be planted before the short rains. How could she do all this without Douglas? Douglas came into the room and threw down his topi.

"Baby, I've got seven whole days before I need report for duty! And even then I am only going to Kisumu!" He did not add that he had sent a telegram to rejoin his own regiment, which was now in England. He hoped the reply would reach him before he took up a commission in the KAR. Olga went to him for comfort, and this time her head fitted neatly into his shoulder.

"I'm so frightened, Douglas," she whispered.

"So am I, Baby," he stroked her hair. "I'm frightened down in the pit of my stomach. But it is not fear which makes us into cowards, it is how we face it."

"You mean, I really have to look after the farm while you go off?" Olga always jumped several stages in any reasoning process.

"I'll close down all I can, and we shall postpone any extensions." There was so much to talk about, but next morning when they arrived at Koru in the chill air before dawn, Douglas was shivering too much to talk. It was the first return of the dread malaria since the bad attack five years before. It took a long time to find the cart men sound asleep in different huts, round up the oxen, load the cart and stack the remainder tidily in the goods shed. They set out walking behind the cart, hand in hand but in silence. Douglas did not say anything because it was as much as he could do to keep going and Olga sensed the worsening of the attack in the hand which held hers, now hot, now cold, now trying in vain to control the shaking rigor which overtook it. After a while she gently persuaded him to ride in the ox cart, resting uncomfortably on the heap of sacks. As one side of her mind worried over the fever, the other kept rejoicing: "He won't be able to join up! He won't be able to leave the farm!"

Despite her nursing training, Olga had never seen an adult delirious before. It was hard when Douglas did not know who she was and kept calling for the bearer he had had in India. He remained delirious for two whole days, Olga constantly at his side, sponging him down, feeding him sips of barley water, crushing the quinine tablets into sweet tea and spooning the bitter mixture into him. In those two days she took charge, sending the cart off to the station each morning and supervising the careful stowage of the stores when it returned, giving orders, making decisions. On the third day he was able to sit on the verandah, and supervise the carpenter she had found to plane down the doors,

To her relief, the partners' camp was now empty. Douglas's three partners, Scott, MacFarley, and Smith were each in their own houses while visiting prospectors and agents had moved on. As they sat looking out over their land, home-made lemon barley water in their hands, their headman, Ansa, came up to the verandah. He was a magnificent young warrior from the Luo tribe, his dark shiny skin wonderfully set off by a necklace of hippo teeth. His only other clothing was a tiny toga of colobus monkey fur slung over his left shoulder. Olga did not know that hippo teeth and colobus monkey fur were symbols of authority and that in his tribe he was a junior elder, a man of standing and responsibility. He stood on one leg, leaning on his spear, and started talking in a very excited manner, so excited that Douglas had difficulty in understanding him.

"I am not happy with his news," Douglas said eventually. "There is trouble brewing in the district. I am going over to MacFarley!"

"But Douglas, you are much too weak to walk four miles."

It always seemed to Olga absurd that each man had built his house on the furthermost corner of the land from the others, so that each could be of the least possible use to his neighbour.

"It is only a mile and a half each way," Douglas always put down Olga's exaggerations. "You come with me and carry me back, Baby!"

MacFarley knew all about the trouble: "It's the Nandi. The KAR regiments stationed there were sent down to the Tanganyika border within hours of war being declared, while you were in Nairobi. The Nandi warriors at once threatened to raid the Luo – the two tribes have been enemies for generations. Your headman is Luo and so thinks he is going to be killed now the KAR have gone. He may well be right."

They walked home thoughtfully, hand in hand again, climbing the steep hill to their own house slowly. Douglas was wondering to himself if it was safe to leave Olga alone on the farm. As they passed the old camp, two strangers came out, white men newly arrived to take up more distant allocations. They had heard about the camp on Douglas's land and asked if they could stay there. Douglas welcomed them and immediately asked them to supper that night.

"Damn!" said Olga when they were alone. "There goes another of our precious evenings together!"

"I am glad to have friendly men around while we are away. Be brave, Baby, don't cry!" He put his arms round her. "Do you know something, when I leave for Kisumu, I am going to take you with me. It should be easy to find lodgings for you with some official's wife, and then I can visit you when I am free!"

"What about the farm?" asked Olga.

"Don't you see, that is where the visitors come in. They look after the farm; my wife looks after me. Now don't argue, Baby!"

The visitors certainly proved their worth that night. A house left empty might well be looted. Once the servants had gone to bed the four Europeans spent the evening burying Douglas's and Olga's possessions, some of them unopened wedding presents. The two strangers dug holes in the garden. Olga bundled everything up in newspaper and sacking – there was the canteen of silver, the silver tea service and lamp, the heavy silver hairbrushes from her dressing table, the sewing machine and type-writer, spare ammunition, riding saddles, new linen, the blanket box. Douglas labelled and numbered each package, then carried it out to the diggers, returning to mark its burial place on his map.

The next evening was the last but one. Olga was in the kitchen with her naked cook, trying to concoct a supper which Douglas would enjoy, when he called her over to the house and spread a letter scribbled on a page torn out of a note book in front of her:

"A runner has just brought this from Kisumu. We have all to report in at once, the men to join up, the women and children for safety. I have to sign this and send it on!" He signed the letter, folded it back into the envelope, and returned it to the runner. Olga heard him explain how to get to MacFarley's.

"Well, we have to leave anyway to morrow night," said Olga as Cook carried supper in.

"This means we leave tonight and catch tomorrow's train." As she well knew, the train from Nairobi arrived at dawn and paused only a few minutes before continuing to Kisumu, only three stops down the line.

"We'll leave at 4 a.m. as that should give us plenty of time!" said Douglas firmly. "And Olga, pack lightly. I shall only take two men down to act as porters. Not more than one suitcase each!"

When Olga woke at four, it was because Bully was restless. She went out to the kitchen to see if Cook was up, and when she found the kitchen empty she called to him over the kitchen wall. His room was next door and the partition did not go up to the eaves. There was no reply. She took her lamp and walked round to his door. It was open, and the room empty. The other house servants' huts were also deserted. There was no one about, no one to carry their luggage, no one to leave in charge of the livestock. MacFarley had been right. The Luo were so sure that the Nandi would murder them that they had walked away from the farm.

Fortunately there were the two new arrivals who had dined with them the previous night and who had brought with them servants from a different area. Olga and Douglas quickly transferred their most essential belongings into light hand-bags, Olga using an ancient rucksack she had brought from Austria. Armed with a hurricane lamp, they went down to the night paddock, let out the cattle, and drove them up the road and into the camp. The fenced paddocks where each partner had kept his cattle when he first arrived were empty now, and in the glow of early dawn they drove their cattle in. Douglas took his dog to the strangers' huts and roused them. Olga insisted that Bully must accompany them.

With the dog at heel and a rucksack at her back she started on the way down to the station, saying she would wait for him at the tiny shop-cum-post office a mile down the road. She had to knock up the Scotsman who owned it. He was weak with fever, but he telephoned for her – it connected only with Koru Station and post office. He asked the stationmaster to hold the train for them.

"No matter," replied the Indian stationmaster happily, "Train seven hours late!"

There was time for breakfast. Olga's appetite never failed her. She now turned her attention to the food shelves in the shop. The only provisions which could be eaten without preparation were tins of peaches and of sardines. She and Douglas sat on the wooden steps sharing a tin of each. Olga crammed some spares into her over full rucksack and they set out for the long walk to the station. By the time they arrived, the mid morning heat had set in and both were parched with thirst. The shop in Koru was bereft of soft drinks, and nowhere could they find drinking water. The station-master was horrified to see Olga.

"Have you not heard of the Nandi rising?" he intoned in his sing-song voice, as he turned on the tap of the water tank used to fuel the train to give Bully a drink. "All women and children left on train for Nairobi last night – very bad, very bad you here. No memsahib should be here!" he said again and again.

There was no waiting room and they had to wait either in the open air or in the goods shed. The shed exuded a strange smell compounded of dust, hot tin roof, and sacks of maize. Yet it was cooler in there than in the shadeless, dusty yard. They did not dare eat anything, the sweetness of the peaches and the salt of the sardines would only aggravate their thirst. There was nothing to do. It was very frustrating – they could have used the time so much better at home. The day stretched endlessly before them. They played noughts and crosses in the dust on the floor, and improvised a draughts board, using pebbles and maize kernels as counters.

The afternoon passed slowly into evening. Douglas stopped sweating and started shivering. They dared not leave the shed in case they missed the train. The stationmaster told them that it only stopped if someone stood on the rails waving a lamp, and his lamp had failed. Douglas lit theirs and gave it to him. At last they heard the busy puffing little train. There was a first class compartment with Douglas's name on it, with a bed made up, and a filter of drinking water. They each managed a tin of sardines and shared one of peaches. Two hours later, when they woke up in the top bunk, they were in Kisumu. Douglas drew the blind and they went to sleep again.

*   *   *

Chapter Three

DOUGLAS GOES TO WAR

The facts and many of the phrases are taken from Olga's ms: Olivia's Adventures.

Olga records that on her first visit to Kisumu she must have been seeing the world through rose coloured spectacles, declaring she was totally unprepared for the beauty of the place. Her brief glimpse of Mombasa had revealed the decaying buildings and narrow crooked streets of an ancient seaport, while Nairobi was a muddy sprawl of corrugated iron sheds, unkempt and grubby, incongruously set out along wide straight roads. In Kisumu the sun sparkled on the bright blue water of the lake, the red roads ran smooth and straight between the neatly white-washed little bungalows with their green painted roofs. There were flowering shrubs and trees everywhere, jacaranda, flame trees, oleander, frangipani, alamanda, bougainvillaea. It was more like some exotic garden suburb than an African outpost.

It was not long before she learned that this order could be attributed to one man, John Ainsworth, who had been Provincial Commissioner for six years. Before he came the place had been a fever-ridden swamp, so depressing that two government officers had committed suicide there. Now it was a flourishing port, the main link between the two East African Protectorates, later known as Kenya and Uganda. It was also an important link to other towns around the lake, including Mwanza and Bukoba, both in German East Africa, (now Tanzania). Olga was soon to learn that the landscape was not the only thing which obeyed Ainsworth's command.

After their enforced fast the day before, they were both ravenous with the hunger of youth, and dwelt on the joys of breakfast as they crossed the road to the hotel. Hotel? Could such a name be given to the long, low, ramshackle building which housed passing strangers. The central building was an ordinary wood and iron bungalow on legs like all the others, its entire floor space occupied by the dining room and bar. On either side stretched a line of similar wood and iron rooms, also up on legs, with a verandah which doubled as a passage-way in front. These open passages overlooked a small strip of garden, then a hedge and the main road.

Despite the early hour, the dining room and its verandah were already crowded by men in a variety of improvised uniforms and buzzing with excitement. Olga was the only woman. A number of men knew Douglas and came over to greet him. The Thompsons learned that Kisii, an Administrative outpost about forty miles south of Kisumu and only 15 from the boundary with German East, was being attacked by German soldiers. To Olga's anxious questions they replied that all women and children had indeed been evacuated from Kisumu the day before, but that a few women with qualifications had been allowed to stay, including the hotel proprietor's wife who was bustling about the dining room supervising the serving of breakfast. Nurses were urgently needed. The wounded were beginning to come back from the front, as the frontier with German East Africa lay only some fifty miles to the South and frequent skirmishes took place.

From their table on the verandah Olga saw a man get out of a rickshaw with a Gladstone bag. She left the table hurriedly.

"Are you the doctor? Can you find me a job? I'm trained. Great Ormond Street..."

"Here and now, come with me." Olga cast a longing glance back at her half-finished breakfast and followed. He paused in a little lobby to explain:

"This is not a sick child, but a man, a very tough man, a white hunter, Major Gray. He was wounded last week, in a skirmish near Kisii, and was brought in delirious last night. Apparently after being wounded, he walked twenty miles to Kendu Bay with neither food nor water. An Indian shop-keeper gave him a ginger beer and helped him on to the boat to Kisumu. Then he passed out. Nobody knew who he was. He was carried in here last night and the hotel keeper recognized him. We had to amputate his arm at once and he has not yet come round. If he does, and it is touch and go, he will not know where he is nor what has happened. You must stay with him all the time, and tell him. I need the medical orderly who was with him last night for our African wounded. We have no hospital to which to send him. Can you cope with a haemorrhage? Good. I'll call again at lunch time. The proprietor will get me if you need me. You can give him a little water, nothing else."

Her patient did not stir until three o'clock that afternoon. When he came round his mind was clear. Olga could even see in his eyes an appreciation of her beauty. She told him as gently as she could what had happened to him, leaning slightly against the bed as she did so.

"Don't touch there," he pleaded, "it's very painful." Olga looked down, and realized that her hand rested where his arm would have been, had it not been amputated. He faded again into unconsciousness. His room was near the hotel bar, crowded with men newly in uniform. The noise was deafening. Every now and then she summoned courage to penetrate the bar and beg for quiet for the man she believed to be dying, but the noise grew louder and as the evening drew on her appearance there was greeted with leers and jeers.

At last Douglas came in wearing the uniform of the KAR with two pips on his shoulder. He had had a telegram to say that his regiment in England definitely did not want him. "The recruitment office here seemed delighted to have ex-regulars and have promised me a third pip before Christmas! More pay for the farm!" He was to join the reinforcements at Kisii. He looked wistfully at Olga as he held her in his arms to say good night and made his way with the reluctant Bully to his lonely room at the other end of the verandah. Olga had to stay with her patient.

"Tired?" asked the doctor, as he walked in at dawn.

"Not a bit," Olga lied. To admit to tiredness was a sign of weakness.

"Splendid. Your patient will turn the corner today, one way or the other. Stay on the job and I will find someone to relieve you tonight."

But he did not. Olga stayed with him all day and all the next night too. When Douglas came by the Major had eaten well and was now asleep, but Olga would not leave him. His balance was still badly disturbed, and he might easily fall out of bed and start haemorrhaging. Douglas placed a little table in the doorway of the room, and there they ate their dinner, Olga sitting inside the room, Douglas in the passage. It was not exactly private but as they held hands and looked at each other in the soft lamp-light they became oblivious to the chilly evening air, to people squeezing by, even to the mosquitoes. For each, in that charmed circle, only the other existed. Yet once again, the night had to be spent apart. Olga rolled her coat into a pillow and slept on the floor.

The following afternoon Douglas went off to join his draft. Major Gray continued to recover. He was moved to a quieter room, the one next door to Olga's, and a fortnight later she was receiving regular letters from Douglas in Kisii and finding ways to teach the Major to dress himself with his left hand. And since her patient could now be left for short periods, Bully enjoyed two walks a day and shared Olga's bed.

A few days later she packed the Major's bag ready for Mrs Gray to collect him. A tiny, trim figure of a woman turned up, impeccably dressed. Olga noted with dismay how fashionable her clothes were, how tiny her hands and feet, "Just another decorative woman!" she thought scornfully, "Too preoccupied with her appearance to visit her own husband when he was so ill!"

The Grays planned to leave on the night train so Mrs Gray invited Olga and the doctor to dine with them that evening. During the meal she explained that she had not heard for some time that her husband had been wounded. He had heard about the war while he was hunting in Uganda, earning money while she looked after their 2000 acre farm single-handed. He had hidden the ivory he had shot and had walked for three days with one bearer to carry his spare fire-arms, to reach Entebbe on the lake. While crossing to Kisumu he had heard about the fighting at Kisii, so had continued on the same boat to Kendu Bay, only twenty miles from Kisii. He had walked by night, reached a British camp where he breakfasted and had gone into action with them. As he had not enlisted, no one knew who he was or where he was from.

The first news she had was from John Ainsworth, followed by Olga's letter dictated by the Major himself. She had gathered from this letter that he would soon be ready to come home and had postponed visiting until she could fetch him. They were breeding up livestock which meant constant dipping and dosing of the higher grade animals, and could not risk leaving them to untrained men. The success of the farm was even more important to them now that her husband had lost his arm and could no longer earn as a white hunter or shoot a bit of ivory when times were hard. The doctor told her that Olga had saved the Major's life. Mrs Gray questioned her on the development of Khitari. She was touched to find, after they left, that the Grays had paid her hotel bill. Some months later a beautiful half-bred bull calf arrived on the train; a gift to Olga to help her improve her own herd.

Olga had made her first Kenya friends and, perhaps even more important, had gained sufficient confidence to risk making an enemy. If Mrs Gray could run a huge estate single-handed, Olga too could make herself useful, and 'do her bit'. She might be allowed to nurse the wounded African soldiers she had seen lying on stretchers on the ground near the railway station. Or she might go back and run her farm like Mrs Gray had been doing – she felt she too could take on a farm in Kenya.

The following morning, with Bully at her heels, she strode out to beard the famous Mr Ainsworth in his office, nearly a mile away at the top of the hill. Olga knew all about successful, managing, elderly men. They were tall, good looking, had delightful manners, and were charming to pretty young women. She breezed cheerfully into his office.

"Good morning, Mr Ainsworth. I am Olga Thompson and I'm looking for something to do."

Ainsworth did not get up; he did not look up; he did not hide the fact that she was an unwelcome interruption. "Well, don't do it here, I'm busy!"

For once Olga was dumbfounded; here was someone as direct as herself. She remained silent. He put his papers down but kept his eyes on them.

"Well, what can you do?" he asked.

"Nothing much. Some nursing. Fluent German."

"Oh, you are the girl who nursed Gray?" He looked at her for the first time. "The doctor told me you did a good job. Do you enjoy nursing?"

"I would rather run our farm, but I suppose none of us can do what we like in war time. Nursing is useful. I would like to nurse Africans. I saw the wounded being unloaded in the port."

"No," he said firmly, and looked at her thoughtfully. This woman, a new comer to the country, had recognized that the Africans deserved good nursing, and was prepared to undertake it herself.

"You said you spoke German. Can you read the Gothic script?"

"Yes, of course." All German was written in Gothic script in those days. Olga had had an enormous box of the letters of the alphabet to play with as a small girl.

"College, I suppose?" said Ainsworth, taking up a piece of paper and starting to write. Olga heard the sneer in his voice. College women were not popular.

"No, I wanted to go but my father would not let me!" Olga was defiant, resisting his put down. Ainsworth was too busy writing to notice.

"Take this note down to the bungalow next door but one to the post office. I think you can help."

It was just another little wood and iron bungalow standing up on tree trunk legs, steps leading to a verandah on which sat a man in a deck-chair, with three large sacks before him, a dictionary and a pile of letters on the table beside him. He hardly glanced up at Olga's approach, and only when he had read her note did he speak to her.

"Can you read letters handwritten in Gothic script?" he asked.

"Usually, yes. My home was in Austria." She saw his frown. In future she would be more careful about mentioning Austria. "My parents are British, so British that at the moment they are prisoners of war. My husband has joined up and gone to Kisii."

"It was at Kisii that we caught these mail bags a few days ago. There are certain things we are looking for. Were they expecting war or was it as sudden to them as it was to us? Are they going back to Europe to join up or are units being formed to fight locally? How many units are there in any one area? Any mention of soldiers or training is important. Are they using African tribesmen to stir up trouble among our tribes?" He scribbled each question on the back of Ainsworth's note as he mentioned it, placed the list on the table, and gestured Olga to the other deck chair and a sack of letters.

It was a revelation to Olga, to sit there reading other people's letters; the revelation of how others lived. One man was writing passionate love letters to three different girls; another, a business man, was writing to his wife saying how successful he was in his new life, and to his partners in Europe that he was failing and must have more money. A third man was writing long affectionate letters to an old aunt and pornographic ones, complete with pictures of African women in indecent poses, to his men friends. By the end of the fifth day she had finished. She had amassed five pages of notes, had lodgings in a railway official's house, and a badly poisoned foot from a jigger, the fleas that burrow into one's flesh and lay their eggs in little sacks. Bully had learned how to empty the sugar basin when Olga was absorbed in her letters, and repeated this performance at her lodgings. It was not a habit which endeared him to her hostess.

This time it was Ainsworth who sent for her. The Postmaster had reported that they had finished the letters.

"You did those letters very quickly, Mrs Thompson."

"It took five days!" To Olga, five days of sitting reading letters had seemed an eternity.

"The Postmaster said it would take a month!"

"I expect he is a college man." She was pleased to see that he flushed as he crossed to his safe and took a file from it.

"Did you see a signature like this?" He paged through to find a scrap of paper.

"Yes, at least half a dozen letters."

"Was he expecting war? Do you remember?"

"Yes, but he was surprised that it came so soon. It's all in here." She put her typed sheets of notes on the desk.

"You've typed them?" he asked in astonishment.

"Yes, the hotel manager let me use his office type-writer!"

"Captain Meinertzhagen, who is in charge of Military Intelligence, is visiting soon and wants to meet you. Meanwhile, I have another job for you. Do you speak the language as well as you read it?"

"Better, but with a Tyrolean accent."

"A regional accent is an excellent disguise. Three wounded Germans have been brought in. We have turned a government bungalow into a hospital. One of them is unlikely to live through the night. I want you to question them."

"No! I won't badger dying men!" Olga was vehement.

"Your husband is at the front. If we have information, many casualties can be avoided."

"You are asking me to do something terrible."

"War is terrible. Missing vital information will make it even more terrible for our men. I am not giving you an order, you are not being paid!"

"That would not make any difference. Pestering the dying is not a job I would do for money."

"If you were in the Army, you would obey orders, however unwelcome. Anyway, think it over." He nodded and Olga knew she was dismissed. She did not go.

"Supposing I do this job, may I go back to our farm afterwards?"

"I will have to review the situation at the time. I don't see why not, but you must get that foot better. With soldiers coming back from the front, we cannot spare the doctor to visit you!"

Olga went back to her landlady for lunch. It was true, her foot was very painful, she was limping badly and the throbbing went all the way up the leg to the groin. The doctors at the Great Ormond Street hospital had warned her to be careful if she got blood poisoning again. Olga's host was a tall sallow man, and most people would have called him a senior mechanic, but he called himself a railway engineer, a position which filled his wife with social importance. They both peopled the world with those above us, whom we should call on and fawn on, and those below us, who should be ignored. Olga as a settler belonged to the latter category. He doubted whether it had been wise to allow her into his house, and he had only done so because her husband was an officer at the front. His wife was always grumbling about that pesky bulldog and the way Olga scattered newspapers all over her room.

The post was never delivered to houses in East Africa, but was sorted into individual boxes at the post office from which the recipient must fetch it. The engineer brought it home with him and on this day he handed her a letter from Douglas. She opened it at once, aware that he was watching every movement critically. She read it quickly for news and then turned to him:

"A friend of my husband's, Lieut. Bradley, is coming on the train tonight and will take things down to him. Douglas has sent me a shopping list," she waved the letter at him, "and I will have to buy everything this afternoon. Do you think you could send me down to the shops in that little hand-cart your messenger uses?"

"You? Ride in that cart? With a nigger pushing you? Mrs Thompson, have you no sense of propriety?" She realized her free and easy ways must have been niggling him for a long time. Now his wife joined in.

"Now you have joined *us* I really do think that you should be more careful about the way you behave, dear," she spoke in her most refined voice. As Olga limped painfully down to the town, she tried to think what *us* she had joined, what false pride had prevented them letting her use the hand-cart. Then she realized her own arrogance, assuming that she was the equal of anyone. As a settler she was nothing to them, but now because Douglas had joined up she had become an officer's wife, a status of importance. It was a moment of insight; in future she would make friends with everyone.

When she had finished her shopping, she took it to the station. Once free of it, she limped towards the lake and chose a shady tree to sit under while writing to Douglas. When the letter was finished she sat on, thinking of her problems.

For the first time in her life she had to make her own decisions. Somehow she had to placate the old rock of Gibraltar, as she had nicknamed Ainsworth, so that she could go back and run the farm for Douglas. She had had enough of living in unwelcoming digs. She did not like the idea of spying.

Another problem was her clothes. She was dressed in the long serge skirts and tight linen shirts with boned collars of her trousseau. The skirts were so heavy they dragged her down and swept up burrs and blackjacks; the shirts rubbed her chest and neck unbearably, causing patches of prickly heat. If she was going to work in the tropics as hard as she had done these last few weeks, as hard as she would have to do alone on the farm, she would have to dress differently. She started sketching on her writing pad. The only garment which had given her freedom and comfort was the gym-tunic she had worn at school. She tried to draw one, and decided she would wear it over britches coming to below the knee, which would tuck into men's knee-stockings. Olga was not good at drawing but she limped painfully back into town and took her sketches to the Indian tailor who had made Douglas's uniform. He wore a long white shirt in fine muslin, draped over baggy trousers made from two layers of the same material.

"What a sensible outfit!" thought Olga, as the tailor turned her sketch upside down and said:

"I see, wear shirty outside trousers, like us." Days later, when Olga went to fetch the clothes, she found he had not understood but had made her a long man's bush shirt instead of a tunic and long baggy shorts instead of britches. She was to wear clothes like this for the rest of her life, gradually lengthening the shorts into full length trousers. When in 1940 someone asked her why she wore the same uniform as service women, she replied:

"I designed these clothes in 1914, so the women's services have copied mine!"

Olga found her foot too sore to walk back, and when she had finished watching the sun set over the lake she went to the station waiting-room to wait for the train. The bench which she and Bully shared was very hard, and it proved a very long wait. It was nearly two when the train arrived. Bradley came straight towards her as she stood on the platform and took charge of the boxes and letters. She waved him goodbye as he crossed to where the boat waited to take him to Homa bay, and then went back to the hard bench in the waiting room.

At dawn the tailor arrived with a hand-cart to collect his supplies, Olga asked him to find her a rickshaw; there were none, so he offered to send her home in his hand-cart. The pusher of the cart was a huge African, who thought this task a great joke and sang in a loud voice to make sure no one missed the sight of him pushing the beautiful young woman up hill. He was probably singing a praise song, the sort of song which would touch his passenger's pocket rather than her heart and prompt a handsome tip. It served only to publicize her return home in the early hours of the morning, apparently legless. Where had she been all night? Her host and hostess were on their verandah to greet her. No doubt she would have another telling off for letting the side down, for not behaving like one of us. She scribbled a note to the Indian tailor asking him to send the delivery cart up for her later that evening.

* * * * * * *

The tailor's cart did not arrive until dusk. Olga directed the messenger to push her over to the improvised hospital. The nurse on duty was expecting her, and showed her into the living room of the bungalow, now the ward for three wounded German soldiers. Olga paused by the first bed, and said "Gruss Gott" the Tyrolean greeting, informal and friendly. The young man showed a flicker of understanding, clutching at his sheet, and she touched his right hand. He gripped hers desperately, opened his eyes to look at her wonderingly, said "Who are you? You come from Tyrol?" closed his eyes, and lost consciousness. Half an hour later he died. The other man in the same room lay weeping quietly at what was happening to his friend. The third man, on the verandah, had seen Olga arrive and called out to know who was there. Presently the dead man was moved out and the live one moved in from the verandah. Olga spent all the night in that ward, talking to the two men who did not want to sleep because their friend had died.

"You are a Bavarian," she said to one.

"Yes, and you come from Tyrol!" he grinned. It was like a Yorkshireman meeting a Lancastrian. He had joined the army to see the world, and had ended up an officer with a unit at Mwanza, headquarters of Tanganyika's Northern Province. She did not have to ask questions to obtain the facts, but because she was there, and understood, torrents of lonely words poured out. One of the nurses came in and dressed Olga's foot for her, soaking it in hot water, painting it with a blue disinfectant, and bandaging it professionally. She gave her a deck chair to rest in and brought a stool for her foot. The night seemed to pass quickly, as each soldier vied with the other in telling his story, attracting her attention. Each ended with how he had been captured and wounded, how wrong German tactics had been, then each started again, and all three talked of Germany and skiing and walking in the mountains. After a while they all dozed, and when dawn came her foot was easier and she decided to limp back to her lodging. She did not get very far.

Outside the hospital a young white policeman was waiting for her. Very embarrassed, he told her she was under arrest. It was well known that she came from Austria, and now she had spent the night consorting with Germans. He had instructions to take her into custody, to go to a prisoner of war camp. For the time being he was taking her to the hotel, where she would be guarded in her room.

"You must take me to Mr Ainsworth," Olga insisted, knowing she must say no more.

"You will go before the magistrate tomorrow, Monday. Today is Sunday!" he replied.

The hotel was comfortable, the food generous, and the only discomfort was the African policeman placed firmly outside her door – he slept across the door step at night – so she could not go to the lavatory without disturbing him. Mrs Samuels had packed up her things and sent them over, so that they arrived a few minutes after Olga. There was no doubt who had reported her.

The junior magistrate was on duty on Monday morning, and was as puzzled as the policeman as what to do with her. She would have to be sent to Nairobi, but who could be spared to guard her? Certainly not one of the white policemen, and it was unthinkable to send a black one with her. John Ainsworth was due back the next day. The magistrate sent Olga back to the hotel to await his arrival.

Ainsworth travelled back from Nairobi with Captain Meinertzhagen, head of British Intelligence. When he heard what had happened to Olga he came down at once in his own rickshaw to fetch her and took her to his home. She remained closeted with the two men for the whole morning, while Mrs Ainsworth fussed over her foot, bringing in frequent hot fomentations. Olga had spent the days in the hotel typing up her conversations with the prisoners. Meinertzhagen handed her a pay cheque for the work she had done on the letters and said he would be in touch with her later.

"I wonder what that means?" she pondered, as she sat alone in her hotel room. "Tomorrow evening we shall arrive home!" she announced to Bully. "Home with all those lovely things to chase on our evening walks."

* * * * * * *

It was strange going back to the farm alone, trekking up the long hill in the dark with nothing but her hurricane lamp, her rucksack on her back and Bully nervous and trembling at her feet. It was a moonlight night, full of noises and grunts of animals, strange rustlings which made her jump and Bully whimper. The house was cold and silent without Douglas, her bed unbearably empty, and despite a muddy Bully seizing the opportunity to snuggle up to her, she cried herself to sleep.

In the morning she found 63 men and ten boys were waiting for work, all their old work force plus some extra. They must have heard she was returning before she knew herself. Weeds were growing thickly in the young coffee and the seedling nursery was in urgent need of attention. The maize and wheat needed weeding. Both cows had calved and were flourishing, while two other heifers appeared to be in calf. As she walked round her boundaries from one neglected corner of the farm to another she remembered the tidiness, the order of Kisumu, and felt deeply ashamed. It was up to her to meld this slice of raw Africa, this conglomerate of humanity, into an orderly, productive whole. If that old rock of Gibraltar, John Ainsworth, could do it for the whole of Kisumu township, she would prove she could do it for five hundred acres, and moreover she would make it as beautiful as his acres were.

For a few days she was so busy she forgot to be frightened, until a leopard got into the kitchen after supper and her cook came running to her. His room was next door to the kitchen and the dividing wall only went up to head level. He escorted her to the kitchen window, his hands shaking so that light from the lamp wavered. Olga, whose hands were also shaking, took aim with Douglas's gun, shut her eyes, and pulled the trigger. She was not surprised that she missed. The leopard took off through the open window, brushing past them, towards the house.

"Cook, I think I left the door open. The leopard may go in. Will you come back with me to hold the lamp while I take aim again?" Cook replied by vaulting into the kitchen, banging the shutters to, and she heard the thud as he jumped down from the partition wall into his own room. Gun in one hand, lamp in the other, Olga walked back into the house alone. Her dogs were still asleep beside her bed. Dogs have good reason to hate leopards, and would certainly have raised the alarm. Yet as she searched the house and locked the doors, she wondered if she was locking the animal in. The doors still did not fit very well, and even Olga could force them by pushing hard – a leopard would have little problem in escaping. That night sleep did not come. Olga lay remembering all the things which frightened her; firearms, leopards, Africans, snakes, making a fool of herself in front of the partners, falling ill, nasty tropical diseases and the countless bugs. Douglas had told her one must learn to conquer fear, but how? Could any one ever stop being afraid?

She decided to fill every minute of the twenty-four hours with activity. Like other farmers, she went out early to set the labourers their tasks. Douglas used to go out every two hours to see if they were still working. Olga found this tedious, and if a man did knock off early she had no way of forcing him back. Why not try piece work? The next day she went through the different jobs one by one. She took a hoe and weeded for exactly one hour, and counted how many coffee trees she had covered; then she took a panga and cut grass for one hour, and again measured exactly how much she had cut. She would have to wait until after the rains to time her pruning. She multiplied the work she had done in one hour by six, and the next day she set each man so many rows of coffee to weed, so much digging or road making to do, so much time spent herding. When she explained this system to her workers, twenty of them refused to work.

"That's all right, I do not need so many workers! I will pay you your wages now and you may leave."

By 11 o'clock the next morning, the forty workers were back in their houses, more work completed in four hours than sixty men completed in a whole day before. Each man worked faster than Olga could hope to work, with her awkward clothes and untrained muscles. She lengthened the daily task gradually, until only the fastest worker could do it in five hours. The work went so well that, when they had cleared the new twenty-acre field, there were not enough coffee seedlings in the nursery to fill it. The November rains promised to be good. What to plant temporarily in the carefully tilled soil? Olga went over to MacFarley's and asked his advice.

"Also I want to keep pigs!" she said, "to help feed the troops."

"Pigs never pay, too many illnesses!" said MacFarley. "But if you really want to keep them, why not plant barley? Should do well in this climate!" The short rains had come and it was a cold, rainy evening.

Olga found she had a large tin of pearl barley ordered from the Army and Navy Stores. She had used a few spoonfuls to make Douglas lemon barley water when he was ill, but there was plenty left. The next day she set about planting the seeds herself in the furrows. Days of sunshine followed the rain, but not a seed sprouted. Olga walked over to MacFarley again.

"And what seed did you plant, Mrs Thompson?" he asked.

"I had a tin of pearl barley left over from the Army & Navy Stores." Funny, the man seemed to be choking on his drink. The next day a messenger brought her a tin of oysters, with a little note asking if she had considered planting an oyster bed. Even Olga could not be surprised that no one was prepared to take seriously a woman farmer.

Now that the daily work was finished so early, both the men and Olga needed something to do in the afternoons. She decided that that something should be football. Cook wore football boots, which he had won at his mission school. So she bought a football, made Cook the trainer and herself the referee, and recruited two teams of footballers. The other players thought it was unfair of Cook to play in boots, so he wore them round his neck on the foot ball field, on his feet at all other times.

Sometimes the absurdity of the scene reached her. She was writing a Christmas letter to Miss Edwards, her old house mistress at the Godolphin school. How could she describe the scene, 22 naked men, their skin gleaming with sweat, running about on the coarse African grass, Cook, fatter than the others, had his football boots clanking one against the other on his chest as he ran about shouting orders. And in the middle of them all, herself clad in breeches and tunic with a boy- scout whistle clasped to her lips. Cook could not remember the rules of football so they played by hockey rules.

Christmas was going to be lonely. Douglas wrote that he would not get leave until January. Back in Austria her mother always gave a party for all the villagers who served her during the year;

butcher, baker, grocer, shoemaker, tailor, plumber, carpenter, mason, and all their families. From an early age Olga had taken charge of the children, organizing games and competitions for them. Now she decided to give a party for all her workers. She used a whole sack of precious wheat flour, now in short supply, to make quantities of sticky buns, another sack of sugar to make sweets.

"What the men want is meat!" said Cook.

"Where can I get so much meat? If the bwana were here, he would shoot some buck, but I could never hit one!"

"No," agreed Cook, "you would miss it. But what about that lame old ox – he'll never work again and he would provide plenty of meat." She had never killed an animal and hated to do it, but early the next morning she ordered the ox to be brought up, took out her revolver, held it to the ox's head shut her eyes, and pulled the trigger. When she opened her eyes, the ox was still standing, blinking at her reproachfully. She replaced the gun to take another shot, and shut her eyes again, when the ox fell on her and knocked her to the ground. The revolver went off, into the air. The workers laughed so much as Olga lay struggling under the dead animal they could hardly summon energy to remove it and rescue her.

On Christmas day Cook supervised the ox roast in the football field and with it went mounds of mealy meal freshly cooked by the farm wives. Next came sticky buns and sweets which Olga had made in her kitchen. This was followed by games which had always been successful among children at home – three legged races, sack races, retrieving a banana first from a bowl of water then a basin of flour.

The workers ate and drank everything in sight, and treated Olga to a mime-show of how she appeared to them, calling her dogs, walking behind the plough, singing one of the few hymns she knew in the tuneless monotone of the tone deaf, giving orders to the cook, shaking as she went to shoot the leopard. They told her her nickname, Agishu, the name of a chief who had lived on a high hill and called out orders and insults to his sub-chiefs on surrounding hilltops.

She had given others a happy day but had herself gone to bed filled with longing, longing to see a friendly white face, to speak her own language, and to lie in Douglas's arms.

Now that the men worked such short hours, Olga decided they needed a school as well as a football pitch. She built a long thatched shelter near their huts, and had benches made from planks placed on lengths of tree trunk. Two or three evenings a week she would go down to teach. A passing missionary supplied her with books for teaching the Three Rs in Luo. Some of the young men were eager to learn all the white man's magic, and turned up regularly for her classes. She rejoiced in their eagerness, in the questions they asked. What was her country like? Was there really a great sea, even greater than the lake? What made the iron snake (the railway) move? How did the telegraph work? Was it true that white men could fly in the air?

Her reputation as a good employer spread and workers from other farms came streaming in asking to work for her, and this at a time when many young Africans had enlisted in the Carrier Corps to support the Army, so there were fewer workers available. Olga had to be firm. It was going to be difficult to pay even forty men, now that her allowance from her parents had stopped. Moreover, the output of each man had increased so much with piece work that she had to plan ahead to keep even forty occupied. There were plenty of things which needed doing, but often she was held up because she had not the raw materials or right tools.

In January 1915 Douglas came back for a week's leave. He was astonished at how much Olga had accomplished in just four months, more than he could have achieved, he assured her. Every thing about the farm looked thriving: the homestead was welcoming and comfortable, the coffee clear of weeds, the quarters in excellent order. The dry weather started in January, the time it was easiest to leave the farm. Douglas took her to Uganda with him, where he was to recruit men for the KAR. They went to Kisumu, crossed the lake by steamer to Entebbe, and spent ten blissful days together, marred only by another attack of malaria.

"You see, Baby, we will have another honeymoon every time I come on leave. Next time I want to hire two ponies and ride round the district, calling in on all the other farms. We could visit that Kitchener chap your father wanted us to look out for. The fighting will all be over this year and then I'll be home again," he assured her as he said good-bye to her at Kisumu station. As the train carried her into the dark African night he stood on the platform waving his hurricane lantern, so she saw the light bobbing up and down long after she could see him.

The weeks passed, there was little work on the farm, and Olga luxuriated in her home, in the little comforts she had made for herself. She was sure she was pregnant, but she would wait until the second month was passed before she told anyone, except of course Douglas. She had always slept well, falling into a dreamless sleep and waking full of energy. But now she had a dream, a terrible dream, a dream that she was alone, that Douglas had been killed, and she had woken sobbing. However, his letters kept arriving and she tried to put the dream away at the back of her mind. How pleased he would be with the news she had sent him.

At the end of March Douglas's letters suddenly stopped. A whole week, then another, without a word. How could it be when she had sent such wonderful news to him. She looked out anxiously across the plains to the lake. The dry weather was coming to an end. Clouds were amassing each evening in the sky, the atmosphere was stifling, still and heavy, but no rain fell. Everyone on the farm grew tense. The drums were beating, beating day and night, going on and on in her head. One day she would move the labour camp further away, put it down near the river, then she would not have to listen to the drums. The understanding she had with the workers seemed to lessen, to be shaky, no one would look her in the eye, fewer came to the evening classes, she sensed they were watching her uneasily.

It was her first hot weather season. She did not realize that the dry weather was the time for building roads. It was so dry all the game came down to the river to drink, and with the game the leopard came back. One night Olga took the dogs out as usual in the evening, and because Bully would chase the game she put a lead on him. Bully did not like a lead, and often tugged hard, sulking and refusing to walk. On this occasion when he tugged, Olga tugged also without looking round. "Damned disobedient dog!" she swore, and then the lead came away so suddenly she nearly sat down. She turned round quickly to run after him, and saw the leopard disappearing, with Bully dragging from his mouth.

That night as she wept for Bully, all her fears came back, not only of predatory leopards and nasty diseases and horrid bugs but of all the other things, new fears which troubled her, something she did not know. Why would her workers no longer look at her? What was afoot? Were they planning an uprising? Why was Douglas not writing, not answering her news? The drums started early, while it was still dark. Thrum thrum thrum - thrum thrum - thrum thrum thrum - thrum thrum - the terrible rhythmic drums of Africa dug not only into her sleep but also into her soul. Douglas's dog, Danny, seized the opportunity to climb on to the bed and started licking her, whimpering now and then to show that he too did not like the drums. What was the message they carried, those strange rhythms beating out through the night? Did Europeans ever come to understand them? Were they really faster, more accurate than telegrams?

A soft light meandered through the windows. Dawn was near. She could hear cook banging about in the kitchen as he lit the fire for her morning tea. Soon he would be by her bedside with the tea tray. It was strange how quickly she had become used to being waited on by men, alien naked men who accepted those parts of her civilization they liked, hymn singing and playing football, and rejected those they disliked, like monogamy and wearing clothes. Douglas had told her they liked to be naked so every one could see their sex, that they were healthy and not diseased, and so that girls could see when they were interested in them. What would she do if ever one showed interest in her, she had asked.

"Oh, they would not do that – you see you wear too many clothes to excite them!" Dear darling Douglas, what a wonderful husband he was, so gentle, so understanding, so loving, so indulgent of her. Thrum-thrum-thrum, went the drums and above them she heard the voice of cook singing – only he was not singing *Onward Christian Soldiers* as he usually did at this time in the morning, but a new hymn, one she had not heard him sing before. She could never identify a tune so listened carefully for the words: "Lead Kindly Light, lead thou me on." Cook spoke deplorable English, but when he sang his accent was excellent. Olga searched her mind for the significance of that tune, but it escaped her. Why did it make her uneasy?

Fortunately the morning was far too busy for the uneasy feeling to win. She dressed quickly, linen chemise and drawers from her trousseau, then the long breeches and loose tunic, Douglas's thick knee-socks pulled up over the breeches, finally heavy lace-up shoes. She combed her long curly hair impatiently, wound it up into a knot at the back of her neck, stuck a battered panama on top, and was ready for the morning's work.

At ten o'clock, with the first round of farm work completed and breakfast enjoyed, she decided to walk down to the little shop to collect her letters, instead of waiting until the afternoon when the cart boys collected them on the way home. There might be something from Douglas. The drums were not playing that day –

what a relief, but as if to make up for it Cook was strumming his harp. Standing naked by the roadside, harp in hand, he reminded her of a huge black angel. Did angels come in black? Could they be hefty, generously equipped young men? She saw no reason why not, it was just that she had never seen an angel wearing football boots and blue garters.

He was still playing the same tune, *Lead Kindly Light,* when she returned half an hour later with her little pile of letters, but this time she did not notice him. She had turned through the letters anxiously as she left the shop – still none from Douglas but one from the Army post office in Kisumu in a hand she did not know. She waited until she was nearly home before she tore it open. It was from Bradley and had taken three weeks to reach her. She was reading it as she walked passed cook. Cook knew what was in that letter and so did everyone else on the farm. The drums had done their job. It was dated March 16.

"I'm awfully sorry about Douglas. He was holding an outpost ambushed on a hill at dawn. He had orders to stay there, so he did just that. He sent a message at noon that the enemy were all round him, and if we had known he was wounded we should have sent reinforcements but we should have had to withdraw our right. As it was we carried the day!"

She walked unseeing back to the house and sat down in the garden under a tree and re-read Bradley's letter, then folded it carefully to put it back in the envelope. Only then did she notice there was another letter in it, a note on paper torn out of a notebook, in writing which she knew but did not know. Her heart turned over. Douglas had written it with his left hand after he was wounded, a few hours before he died. It started as always, "*Darling Baby,"* and ended "*If I do not come back you will know that I have done my bit*!" In between it was a soldier's will, leaving everything to her. Bradley had not known that he was the first to break the news to her. The official telegram she should have received never did arrive. It was only later that she heard what happened. When German troops surrounded the hill which Douglas had been told to hold, they had called on the British to come forward with their hands up. Douglas had been shot in the right shoulder and could raise only his left one. He had been shot.

As she sat on under the tree, dry eyed and miserable, MacFarley rode up. He did not see her where she was sitting under a tree, but dismounted, hitched his horse to a verandah post, and took off his hat revealing his shock of red hair fading now into a mousy brown. Olga noticed every detail of his unprepossessing appearance, his pugnacious jaw stuck out below his overlarge nose, his stocky slightly bowed legs, the way he tapped the steps of the bungalow with his riding whip as he stumped up them. There was no trace of the laughing bonhomie he had always shown before, but then this was no laughing matter. She steeled herself to go and meet him, thinking: "It's good of him to come so soon; it cannot be easy for him to make this visit of condolence. I must be considerate."

MacFarley was calling 'Hodi' as every one did in Kenya, no one had door bells or knockers – and cook emerged still clutching his harp. Olga walked towards the steps smoothing her hair. "Here I am, Mr MacFarley!" she called, "it is good of you to call. You'll have some coffee?"

"Ah Mrs Thompson, I am calling on behalf of the partners, to ask when are you leaving? We will buy your farm now but not later. You have no business here now!" Not a word of sympathy. She wondered how long he had known about Douglas. She had not seen him aggressive before.

"No business on my own farm? What do you mean?"

"As a woman you risk an attack, murder, or even worse than murder, if you understand me. Once that happens in this district it will no longer be safe for our wives!"

"But you are all bachelors!"

"I may get married one day!"

"If I leave, where am I to go? My parents are prisoners of war."

"It is not my business where you go, Mrs Thompson. There are plenty of hostels for young women back in the home country. The point is that we want you out from here."

"I have no intention of going. It would be a betrayal of my husband's work."

"If you stay, you will get no help from us!"

"I had not noticed too much help before!" said Olga, walking over to the sideboard where the coffee which cook had brought was growing cold. She picked up the tin of oysters. "But you were kind enough to send this over. Why not take it back with you?" She handed him the tin. He flushed slightly.

"We've been more help than you know. Just the fact that we are here," he said firmly. "Remember, no more help from anyone unless you go now!"

"Douglas was not too busy to die for you, that you might go on farming in peace!" said Olga from the verandah, watching him mount his horse. Again his face flushed, this time a deep red. So it was true, she thought, he had somehow avoided being called up.

The argument had done her good, she always felt at her best when her fighting spirit was up. She took the coffee tray on to the verandah and sat looking out at her land, at the wonderful view down to the distant blue lake. Clouds were gathering in huge towers and there was a smell of rain in the air. When the rains started she would plant another twenty acres of coffee. Was she really at risk of being attacked because she was a widow? How sad that sounded – a widow at 25. Now Douglas would never know she was expecting a baby, but she would go on planting coffee and looking after the farm for her son, until he could take over from her. She was picturing his future; playing on the grass, going off to school, walking round the farm with her, when small clutching hands round her legs brought her out of her reverie.

She looked down in surprise – it was little Onyango, Anya's son, a great favourite of hers. He was two years old, dressed only in small strings of beads round his plump little tummy and ankles, his skin shiny with health and good feeding. He stood beside her chair and reached up to pat her pockets, looking for sweets. When he found none, he put his fingers in the sugar bowl. Olga clasped his fat little arm, turned his hand over, and filled the tiny pink palm with sugar. The baby licked his hand with satisfaction, smiled up at Olga, and held out his palm again. The operation was repeated until the sugar bowl was empty.

"That's quite enough, Onyango, off you go, or your mother will be looking for you." Satisfied there was no more to be had, the toddler walked towards the steps, and gravely turned round and crawled down them backwards as Olga had taught him to do, then toddled off towards the labour camp. That afternoon she sat on her verandah and read the papers which had come in the morning's post, all bad news about the war. In her mind she suddenly saw how minor her own tragedy was in the context of what was happening in the world, the young men of different countries killing each other. She watched the clouds cluster and grow black over the distant lake, and then the rain, the blessed rain came, with huge drops creating little volcanoes as they dropped on to the dusty earth. It thundered on the tin roof and made a pleasant gurgling sound as water rushed along the gutters and down the drain pipes into the water tanks. It was exactly one year since she had arrived in Africa.

She put an old sack she used as a raincoat over her head and shoulders and went down to give out the rations. The workers were astonished at what a good mood she was in, so they asked for, and received, extra posho and extra salt. Back in her own house, she sat down and wrote the letters she considered most urgent, including an announcement for the East African Standard. Her cart was due to go down to Koru station the next day and the carter would post them for her. She hoped it would be dry enough for him to get through.

The carter was back before eight o'clock. No, it was not mud which had stopped them, but Bwana MacFarley on the road telling him that he could not use it. And no, he had not argued with this angry Mzungu. No African argued with him, he was too fond of the whip. Olga strode over to his house to ask what was happening. His rhino hide whip was parked by the door.

"That is right, Mrs Thompson, I did stop your carters using my road. I have my agreement with your late husband here!" She noticed it was already spread out on his table. "We agreed to share one road for three years, by which time we would each have made our own. Three years have passed. You have not made your own, and now you must do so. There is no reason why you should use mine!"

"But.. but I don't know how to make a road. And I can't build one in the middle of the rains!"

"Quite so, Mrs Thompson! But then you should not be here in Africa alone, should you? Pioneering is not a job for widow women who do not know how to build roads!"

"But you can't do this to me!" Olga shouted and burst into tears. MacFarley looked at her with distaste. He did not like weeping women. Grief had caught up with her. She left his house with as much dignity as she could muster and it was at that moment, she later decided, that the haemorrhage started. There was nothing she could do as she walked the wet muddy half-hour back to her lonely bungalow. And since she had to speak to someone, she sat down and wrote to the favourite aunt. But even to aunts, particularly maiden aunts, one could not mention certain details, not in those days. *"Aunt Grace, I'm a widow and I know there will not be a child. I loved him so, I could kiss his feet, and now I have nothing."*

Olga was not yet 26 years old, it seemed to her that her life was over. In fact it was just beginning.

*　　*　　*

Chapter Four

FROM MATZEN TO KHITARI

This chapter was constructed by using Flo's diary, as well as Olga's "The Adventures of Olivia". Both were vivid writers who used conversation freely.

While the rain fell heavily in British East Africa, in the Austrian Tyrol Spring came late. The day the white telegram arrived from the Red Cross, Flo was in the hunting room, the room Flo and Willie were using as a living room. It was hung round with Willie's prize-winning trophies, and his desk was drawn up to the window. She picked up the binoculars which lay there and peered out to see if he was returning from his morning walk. Now that the thaw had set in, the river Inn was sweeping down the valley in full spate. She thought nostalgically of her native Kent, where green fields would already be covered with spring flowers, whereas here in the Austrian Tyrol the snow was only now retreating, leaving the earth sodden, the grass brown, the fields saturated.

Flo's first reaction when she opened the white telegram was a guilty thank you to a God she did not believe in that it was only Douglas, not her own son Tom, who had been killed. Now she was making a great effort to keep her mind off the news; for if she thought about it, let it penetrate her inner consciousness, she would break down and she must not break down before she had spoken to Willie.

She piled the mail on his desk with the white telegram on top, went behind the green tiled stove in the corner of the room, and thrust some more firewood through the little iron door. The castle was icy cold, the great green tiled ovens ate firewood, and it was proving difficult to buy enough to feed them. Dirty snow lay heaped in the courtyard, while the walls of the spiral staircases glistened with ice crystals. Yet she knew how lucky they were to be allowed to stay in their home, surrounded by their own belongings, even if their movements were limited and normal comforts were lacking. They might well have been sent to a prisoner of war camp or, worse, to two separate camps. As it was, Willie had his writing and his books, she had her painting and her needlework, the coachman and his wife had proved sufficiently devoted to stay with them despite the slurs cast on Willie by the villagers, and they and their family provided all the service they needed.

And what slurs these had been. The worst had been when the local paper had published a letter said to have been written by Willie to Douglas in Africa, saying: "I can quite understand that you have to shoot apes which attack your crops. That is how we should shoot Germans – they too are vermin!" No one had been able to produce the original of the letter, because Willie had never written it, but he had not improved the situation by announcing loudly: "Of course I did not write it; I have far too much respect for apes to liken them to Germans. I agree with Mr Darwin that they are our ancestors!"

Flo could remember meeting Darwin, a distant cousin of her mother, and asking him to sign the copy of *The Origin of the Species* which she had been given by her mother, and how she had nearly been expelled from school for reading passages from it to the other girls. Her day dreaming was interrupted by the figure for whom she was watching. Willie was stumping angrily across the meadows towards the castle, returning from the only walk he was allowed. He, a mountaineer of world renown, was now limited to a radius of one kilometre from his home so that when out walking he looked like a trapped lion pacing its cage and looking for a victim on whom to pounce. She attributed his increasing irascibility to the limits set on his freedom, and feared that the bad news in the post would lead to another raging against their circumstances. It was not easy being prisoners of war.

The news was so bad, and Willie's outbursts so tiresome, that she determined to take matters into her own hands. She had heard that an old friend of theirs, Count Teleki, was now in Innsbruck. He was an influential member of the Austrian war cabinet. As a young man he had explored Eastern Africa and had been the first to report a great lake which he had named Lake Rudolf, (it has since been named Lake Turkana). Teleki had been intrigued to hear that Olga was going to live in British East Africa, and now Flo wanted to plead with him to use his influence to let Willie and herself leave Austria on compassionate grounds so they could join their daughter in British East Africa. Willie would be against asking any favour, and if he agreed that she could make her plea, he would want to accompany her. So she had to persuade Willie to let her go alone and if she was to do that she must not weep. He did not respond to weeping. She heard his heavy footstep on the stairs, nailed shoes ringing on stone steps. His breathing was unusually heavy. She steeled herself, picked up the telegram and stepped into the hall.

She stood holding the telegram as she told him about Douglas. He had sat down and was unlacing and pulling off his boots and remained so silent she wondered if he had heard. She took advantage of this silence to explain why she wanted to go to see Count Teleki the following day, and to go alone. To her surprise he did not argue, nor contradict her, although he swore he would never speak to that man again, since he had done nothing to defend him against that terrible letter.

"Willie, we all know how you feel; the whole valley knows how you rejoice every time England has the smallest victory. But need we be so loud about it while we are in enemy territory?"

"I'm not in enemy territory, God damn it, I'm in my father's country, the country of my birth. It's not my fault if the fools declare war on England, my mother's country, because a mad duke gets himself murdered in Sarajevo!" Willie stumped even without his boots, crossing the hall to take the telegram from Flo.

"Nor is it mine, dear," said Flo steadily, omitting to mention that it had been England who declared war on Germany. She picked up the boots, and holding a newspaper under them, walked across the room and arranged them carefully under the green stove.

"Do we know when he died, or where?" Willie's voice had become gentle, tender.

"No, it just says killed in action last month – it must have been in March. That big affair at Tanga that the German papers were so cock-a-hoop about was last year, if you remember. The message came through the Red Cross – probably through Grace. She was enrolled for Red Cross lessons when we were last in England."

"Poor Olga," said Willie, "Poor, poor Olga. Married just one year. It is so sad." And his voice broke. He sat down at the square table in the centre of the room, put his head on his hands, and sobbed loudly, great dry sobs coming from his chest. In thirty years of marriage, Flo had never seen him cry, not even when his much loved mother had died. She understood that he was crying not so much for his son-in-law as for the pain his daughter must be suffering, alone on an isolated farm in Africa. He had never shown any particular affection for Olga and had often opposed things she wanted to do; go to university, take up nursing, compete in the ski jumping competitions. Olga never took opposition quietly and the two were known for their loud arguments echoing round the castle's courtyards. He must love her more deeply than anyone realized. She sat down beside him and put one hand tentatively on his arm.

"Don't cry so, Willie, Olga will be all right. We gave her so much happiness in her childhood it will carry her through! She has always been such a happy child, so bright, so friendly. I just hope she is pregnant so she has something to remember him by, and something to look forward to. She has always adored children."

"And I suppose I shall have to support her, and it, in the manner to which she is accustomed for the rest of my life. And with this war eating at my savings, I just do not know how I shall manage it."

'That sounds more like your usual self,' thought Flo, but aloud she remarked "I would not be too sure of that – she can drive a shrewder bargain that you do! How pleased your mother was that time she sold you your own jug!" They both managed to smile through their tears. Their daughter was still their daughter, and she would come back to them now Douglas had been killed.

"So you are going to drag your poor old husband out to Africa just to see how your wayward daughter lives!"

"And when you get there you will be blissfully happy, shooting bigger and better specimens of game than any one else has done, and after the war when you bring the trophies back, Matzen will become even more cluttered." She managed another smile, now that he had agreed that she go to Innsbruck, and go alone.

Flo was admitted immediately to Count Teleki's presence. Despite the fact that she was an enemy subject and virtually a prisoner of war, she was received affably, sympathy was expressed at Olga's loss, and exit permits were promised – on one condition. Willie must sign a paper that he would take no action against Austria during the present war.

"What could he do?" asked Flo. "He is sixty five – much too old to join up. The war has affected him badly, particularly his temper!"

"He has a better knowledge of the mountains bordering on Italy than any man I know. He was the first man to climb the Gross Glockner in winter and he has written books about his adventures with smugglers as a young man. Only a year ago, I accompanied him on a shoot to Hintertux and he knew where every track led, where each mountain could be crossed. This knowledge would be most useful to the Italians – I have to make sure they do not get it. He must send his denial, signed and dated, to me as soon as possible and I think I can promise you an exit permit within a month, so that you may travel to Switzerland."

"Thank you, Herr Count, but could our permit be to Genoa, we want to go to Africa."

"Gracious Lady, (this was the normal formal mode of address at the time) there is no way I nor any one else can guarantee you a safe passage over an enemy border. We will not shoot you, but how do we know what those Italians will do? All we can do is to arrange for you to travel over our own border into Switzerland, a neutral country. From there it is up to you to go where you will."

Back at Matzen Willie merely grunted when she told him how helpful Count Teleki had been. "We'll go by Genoa, of course," he said.

"I am afraid it has to be Zurich first – I am sure the Count is right."

"Damn stupid, all that extra travel. Why, I can walk into Italy in a day from here! I am sure I could cross the border, and then we could catch a train."

"I am sure you could, Willie, and be shot as a spy while you were doing it! I am equally sure that I could not, and I have no intention of trying. We shall have permits for Zurich and to Zurich we shall go. We can make our decisions there."

It was in Zurich that decisions indeed had to be made. On the second day, after hours trying to arrange to travel first to Genoa, and then to Marseilles, Willie declared he felt ill and retired to bed It was the first time that she had known him do such a thing. He even agreed she call a doctor.

"Heart disease!" said the doctor, "No more running for trains or buses, and certainly no more mountain climbing! Africa? It is out of the question. The heat would kill him in two days. No, the gentleman must live a quiet life, and be well looked after. And don't let him get too excited – these cases are known for irascibility!"

Flo was torn in her loyalties, a sick husband in Europe, a newly widowed daughter in Africa, but Willie insisted she continue with her original plans and saw her on to a train to Marseilles to await the first ship, while he would cross France to stay with Grace and Maud in Kent. Neither of them knew that "the aunts" had both joined up and were driving ambulances in France, while various other cousins, temporarily homeless, occupied roomy old Boxley Abbey. Willie without Flo was not the Nickalls family's favourite guest, but he was allocated the best spare room, a huge room on the first floor, a large writing table was moved into it, and he settled down to write, working through the mornings, spending long afternoons walking across the fields and orchards, returning each day with a hatful of wild flowers.

He wrote Olga a letter of sympathy chasing the one he had sent with Flo: *"I am sorry I cannot join you, and would gladly have laid down my old bones for Douglas's young ones, but there is no point in making BEA into a family burial ground! I am sending you my greatest treasure – your dear mother, for six long months. Do not keep her any longer, you have no idea of the cost to me. Tom came down to see me, very smart in his uniform but he looked dreadfully tired and thin, poor boy. He has his first command, a minesweeper. He brought a handsome young woman with him, a modern miss driving him in her father's motor!"*

* * * * * * *

Flo waited ten days for a boat in Marseilles, using the long days of late spring to make herself cotton dresses to wear on board ship. The hotel linen room had a Singer sewing machine.

Koru – 1916

At Khitari estate in Koru Olga was out in the rain planting coffee seedlings all day long. She had managed to obtain more seedlings from a nursery but even they were not enough. So she planted five acres with maize and another two with barley – using proper seed this time – and was experimenting where to put the water furrow to run the coffee factory which she would soon have to build.

The details of farming filled her days with activities and her nights with dreams, her physical exhaustion bringing a deep sleep and a satisfaction that she was proving herself. A woman could farm in Africa! Her notebooks came out more frequently and were rapidly being filled. She was not planning articles, she could no longer get what she wanted to say into an article, but a book.

What fascinated her most about Africa were the daily challenges it presented. No two days were the same, one never knew what to expect, so life was never boring, even if it seemed at times to lurch from one disaster to the next. There was for example the deep sadness of the witchcraft incident. One morning, while Olga was dressing, Cook rushed into her bedroom, hardly pausing to knock. "Come quick, Memsahbu, come quick. Ansa's wife says he is dying." Olga finished buttoning her tunic and pushed her feet into her farm shoes, still damp from yesterday's rain.

"How can that be? He was all right yesterday?"

"She says it is witchcraft. Nabba came over – you know, Bwana Lawrence's headman – the two of them have long been enemies. And he is still down there, putting the spell of the eye on him." Olga was ready now, and without touching her tea left her room. Cook picked up the Bible which lay by her bed and followed her: "Take this – it is the only magic which can break the spell". Olga looked astonished. She had hardly read the Bible before Douglas died, but now found the Psalms consoling. Could she really use it to divert black magic? She took it from him and hurried down to Ansa's hut, a big square one with two rooms as befitted the headman. Elsana, Ansa's wife, a large woman heavy with child came out to greet her. In the hut two men squatted on the floor, face to face, staring at each other.

"Jambo!" said Olga cheerfully. "Now what is going on here? Ansa, we need the men to start work!" Neither man shifted an inch, nor took any notice of a new presence in the hut. Olga turned to Elsana:

"How long have they been like this?" she asked.

"Since last night. My husband will die soon!"

"Nonsense!" said Olga, "not with this charm present!" and she waved the Bible, then brought it down gently on the stranger's shoulder. "It is time you went home, Mzee!" she said authoritatively. Mzee means old man or elder, but is a title of respect, not many people reached old age in Africa. However respectfully addressed, the old man showed no sign of moving.

Olga repeated loudly and slowly, "Time to go home!" and pressed more firmly on his shoulder. This time he toppled over to one side, picked himself up, drew his blanket round him, and tottered off on stiff legs as though in a trance, his face blank, pushing past her to get out of the hut but never looking at her, never speaking.

"My husband will die!" wailed Elsana.

"Nonsense!" said Olga for the third time, and went over to him, opened the Bible at the marker, and started reading the psalm: "The Lord leadeth me into green pastures." It was so dark in the hut she could hardly make out the words. Ansa took a deep breath, fell over backwards, gasped and rattled in his throat.

"You see, I told you that Nabba is evil!" Elsana spoke gently as Olga bent over the man to take his pulse, but did not wait for her to say that he was indeed dead. She let out, slowly, deliberately, the high pitched wail of mourning and gradually, from the other huts, answering wails broke out. When the last wail had faded into the early morning mist, Elsana took it up again and again, so crescendos of wailing spun into the air.

Olga felt bewitched herself, fogged as to what had happened, asking herself what should she have done, what should she now do, unable to think against the wailing. She decided this was a case for the police and the doctor. The nearest government station was twelve miles away. She took paper and pencil from her overfilled pockets, wrote a note, walked across the labour compound to where there was a large gong hanging on a tree and banged it hard. It was Ansa's job to bang the gong, the signal to start work. The wailing stopped and the workers gathered round her. She picked one of her fastest runners and gave him the note. When he had gone she said:

"Sadly, I have to tell you that Ansa died in the night; I've sent for the doctor and the police. Now please carry on with your work."

Back at the house she tried to carry on as usual, but at the back of her mind was the nagging doubts, how do I run the farm without Ansa, and more immediately, what do I do with his body? How would police or doctor remove it, and if they did not, what was she to do about it? She went down and talked to Elsana. All the women were gathered together, talking quietly, now and then suddenly breaking into loud shrieks and cries, then quietly talking again. Olga took Elsana on one side. She knew they had been married with a Christian ceremony at the Mission where he had been to school; and that Ansa had paid twenty good cows for her and was paying twenty more since Onyango had been born. And yes, said Elsana, he had promised to remain monogamous. Mind you, she would not have minded a second wife now she was so heavy with child and little Onyango was such a handful. She definitely wanted a Christian burial and a Christian funeral service for Ansa.

Olga was having her lunch when she saw the runner returning. He had covered twenty four miles in under seven hours. He brought two notes but little comfort with him. A scribble on the bottom of her note told her the doctor was out on safari and that it was not the custom of the local tribesmen to bury their dead, while the policeman wrote that he had malaria but reminded her she must bury the dead within twenty four hours. Olga read the notes with disdain. Officials never understood the situation in the field. She rarely hesitated over decisions. Ansa was going to be buried and he was going to have a Christian funeral. Then the lurking truth came home – if there was to be a Christian funeral, she would have to do it herself. Anyone could take a funeral service in an emergency. Cook came in with a cup of coffee.

"Cook, who do you think will help me dig Ansa's grave?"

"You can't bury him!" Cook sounded aghast.

"Why not?" asked Olga

"Because the Luo do not bury their dead!"

"But Ansa was a Christian, like you! And he was an important man on this farm!" Cook cleared his throat ominously.

"Not in here!" said Olga, anticipating the spit just in time. Cook went outside and spat. When he came back she said: "What should we do then?"

"Important men are burned in their houses, but that is a good house, like two houses together! It would be a pity to burn it."

"Certainly," said Olga, "And less important men?"

"We put them out, for the hyenas."

Olga shuddered. "I am burying Ansa this evening under the wild fig tree, and I hope as a Christian you will attend and help me."

"Never! Never! Never!" said Cook. "And if you do, someone will dig him up again. Ancestors do not like burial, they will haunt you for ever."

When it was time for the afternoon football, Olga went down to the assembly place. "No football this afternoon. Now I want some volunteers to dig Ansa's grave." No one stirred. "Will you all stand in a line?" she requested. She walked down the line counting every eighth man. "You four, come with me," she said, and when they reached the wild fig tree, she stopped. "You will all be paid for three days work in return for a little effort now. I want you to dig a hole here where I have marked, and it must be this deep," she handed out a marked stick, "and this wide" There was a second stick. "Now get going!" she handed out spades and big iron basins into which to scoop the earth. To her surprise, they went silently to the spot Olga had chosen and within an hour had completed the work.

Back at the house Olga made her preparations with unusual care. She took Douglas's rifle, cleaned it, and slipped some ammunition into the pocket of her rucksack, she took a hurricane lamp, cleaned and trimmed it, and pumped it full of kerosene from the four gallon tin which stood in the food store. She stood gun and lamp in the sitting room, took the rucksack into her bedroom and filled it with a rug and pillow. She opened her prayer book at the funeral service and read it through twice, slowly, and then slipped it into the rucksack pocket on top of the long smooth bullets. She took the Bible and chose a reading about the Resurrection. She dressed in her warmest pullover and two pairs of Douglas's socks, told Cook to bring her tea with a boiled egg and sat on the verandah, watching the start of a magnificent sunset over the lake, the sky brilliant with reds and gold. As it set, she put the rucksack on her back, slung the rifle over her shoulder, picked up the sacks and the lamp and went down to Ansa's hut and knocked gently on the door. Olga was thankful that little Onyango was sound asleep, curled up on an antelope skin – at least he would not see his father removed from the hut.

"Here, I've brought two sacks. We will put his body in these…" But Ansa lay stiff and cold in the squatting position in which he had died; there was no way they were going to fit that large curled up body into a sack.

"We'll just have to put him on a sack and drag him down." The two women rolled him on to a sack, and tugged it gently through the doorway and with a swishing sound, down the hill towards the fig tree. In the distance hyenas were greeting the evening with their weird cry. It was dark when they arrived at the grave side, Olga lit the lamp, adjusting the wick so it burned bright and clear. Elsana held it while Olga read the burial service, and when they came to the dust to dust, ashes to ashes, they picked up the two corners of the sack and rolled the stiff body in. He would not go in sideways but went neatly on his back, his knees drawn up to his chest. Olga gave a eulogy, saying what a good man he had been and how they would miss him. Then she and Elsana each took a spade and shovelled the earth back in, and they picked up stones and placed them on top of the grave. Hyenas do not like digging through stones. She climbed into the tree, finding a comfortable forked branch where she could lean against the trunk. She turned the lamp wick down and hung it just below her, put the rifle across her knees and loaded it, a shot might frighten away a leopard or a hyena. As she settled herself for a night in the tree, she thought of Elsana arriving at her hut and curling her heavy body round that of Onyango, and she found herself crying, not so much out of pity for Elsana and her children, but out of pity for herself. She had no warm comforting little body to hug all night, no new life pulsating within her. The funeral service had been as much for Douglas as for Ansa, and she cried all night for Douglas as she had not cried before.

The next morning she sat on her verandah watching the sunrise, drinking cup after cup of sweet tea. The weeding team would have to be diverted to collecting the biggest rocks they could find, to pile on Ansa's grave and prevent the hyenas attacking. She would keep Elsana in her house until the new baby was born, and somehow find money to give her a handsome sum and send her back home. Later she was to say that the day she buried Ansa was the bleakest in her life. Olga was an idealist, and for the first time in her life she had seen the forces of evil overcome the forces of good.

* * * * * * *

Her financial problems grew worse every day. The allowance her parents were paying her had stopped with the war, now Douglas's seemed to have stopped also, and she was troubled by threatening letters from the bank, who wanted to call in the mortgage. And once again her kindness had resulted in her being defrauded of a considerable sum of money. A visitor to the farm, a passing vet, happened to arrive just when Olga's monthly money bag arrived. With a long drawn out tale of disaster, the vet asked if she would cash him a cheque for £40, the amount of the monthly wage bill. She could cash another cheque the next day and his cheque would arrive at her bank almost before the debit, so all would be well. So it would, had the cheque not been a dud, had the man had an account, and had he not been using a false name. This extra withdrawal was the last straw for the Nairobi bank manager, who wrote that she was not to draw one more cheque on Douglas's account.

But there was also good news, a telegram from her parents to say they had arrived in Zurich and another, sent a week later saying her mother was sailing shortly. She wondered why her father was not coming too.

Early in May Major Meinertzhagen, who had not heard of Douglas's death, wrote that he had a job for her in Nairobi, and would she please write to him whether she could spend a few weeks there during May or June. She would be accommodated in the Stanley hotel, all expenses paid, and be paid £20 for a month's work. What a wonderful piece of luck. She would be able to see her bank manager, find a solicitor to settle Douglas's will, and see her agent, all without any extra expense. £20 all found was a magnificent salary, more than twice a farm manager earned. She accepted at once for the month of June, asking only that her room be reserved at the Norfolk hotel, the Stanley was too full of memories.

For Nairobi she would need to wear mourning. Mrs Ainsworth had written her such a kind letter of condolence and sent a whole pile of books for use in her school. She wrote thanking her, and asked her to buy twelve yards of black cloth from the Kisumu bazaar. She spent the evenings making black blouses she could wear over her black drill skirts. There was enough material left over to make a wide band to put round her hat, and a square she could drape over her head in Nairobi.

In those days down-trains to Nairobi would stop by request opposite the Norfolk hotel. Olga made the request, and early on a day in June 1915, swathed in her new black garments, she was standing by the door of her carriage as the train drew up. She leapt from the train and unloaded her bag and dressing case and strode towards the hotel, wondering if Meinertzhagen would meet her as arranged. The Norfolk was new to her, and she laughed at its pretentious mock Tudor frontage.

It was still not seven o'clock when she went into the dining room for breakfast. She had missed supper the previous night and was too hungry to be aware that the only other occupant of the dining room, a man in captain's uniform sitting in the far corner opposite the window, moved his chair so that he could watch her.

Meinertzhagen arrived promptly at 8 and took her to a private sitting room where they could talk. Too much military information was reaching the Germans. The job he wanted her to do was to call on a number of people who were suspected to be German but who claimed to be some other nationality, usually Scandinavian. When she called on them, he wanted her to use her maiden name, Grohman, and pretend to be German herself, and not to wear widow's weeds. Her story should be that she had fallen on hard times and needed help. She refused to change her name or her clothes, and told him that it would be difficult for her to act the part of a German woman, her demeanour lacked the necessary meekness and her spoken German was too Tyrolean for an educated woman. Better to say that she was the Austrian widow of an Englishman, and because she was Austrian the English would not help her. With that alias she could wear mourning, a fact which would win her sympathy.

Olga liked to speak out the truth as she saw it – the very idea of spying made her feel queasy. She took the list of names reluctantly, and set out in a rickshaw to call on them. Some were bachelors and it was not done for a woman to call on a man unless she took her husband's card, so she had to think up some excuse to call. The coffee Douglas had planted in 1911 would soon be bearing, and she would pretend to be trying to sell coffee. Perhaps the Scandinavian gentleman concerned could help her export her coffee to a neutral country and so get money to maintain the farm? Finding her first quarry was not at home, she asked the servant if she could rest in the sitting room, and then asked to use the bathroom. By looking round the house she was convinced the family were Germans – German books, German letters, an address book of German names, and no toothbrushes in the bathroom. Olga always insisted that young German men never used toothbrushes. She discovered that it was easier to learn about people by looking at their possessions than by talking to them, and she covered several houses that day, calling when people were most likely to be out.

Meinertzhagen had asked her to have a drink with him at Nairobi club, where she could report on her day's spying. Women were not allowed in the bar, but he took her to a corner of an upstairs room set aside for ladies. She noticed all eyes on her, in her dusty black clothes, as she sat in a corner with this dark, good looking man. She was breaking conventions. Young widows did not appear in public unchaperoned with a married man. Afterwards he escorted her back to the Norfolk in his rickshaw, and gave her a large suitcase which he asked her to look after for him. She thought it was a very strange thing for a man to do, but took charge of it unquestioningly and asked the porter to put it under her bed. She unpacked her own case, hung up a white blouse, black skirt, and another black cotton dress she had made, and looked round the shoddily furnished room. She poured some water from an enamel jug into the washbowl and washed her face. She found the prospect of occupying a double room alone almost too daunting. When loneliness hit her she tried to ward it off by talking to Douglas.

Darling Douglas, why are you not here? And he replied comfortingly: *Be brave, Baby, be brave. Go down and enjoy a good dinner.*

She was the first person into the dining room, and the head waiter – an impressively broad man from the Coast dressed in a long white robe with the embroidered cap and waistcoat of a well-to-do Arab, seated her near the door. She understood the message at once. An unknown young woman by herself did not merit a better table. It was the first time she had ever dined alone in a hotel and she did not like the sensation. She bent over the soup, tasteless brown Windsor soup, and tried to focus on what her parents might be doing at this moment. Her mother would be with her within a month. Why not her father? Had her mother started yet? Where was Tom? What was going on? At home she would be thinking about the farm. Here she was thinking about the world, she felt alone, deserted, friendless, and tears were dangerously near. Soon an army captain chose the table next to hers. When two ragged pye-dogs slunk in after him and settled under his table, she looked up and smiled. He had very fair hair and a high forehead above piercing blue eyes, strange eyes because round each iris was a ring of blue. His nose was long and straight, his chin firm, and his moustache so fair and well trimmed it was only just visible in the lamp light. He was as handsome as a Greek god and had an air of decision about him, a man accustomed to giving orders. She listened with admiration to the fluency of his Swahili as he joked over the menu with the head waiter.

"How long did it take you to learn such excellent Swahili?" She leant over to his table. He was very friendly, introducing himself as Captain Watkins. What a luxury, to have someone to talk to at last. It was while talking to people that Olga worked out her ideas. She hated bottling things up inside her. Because the neighbours had been so hostile she had not spoken to a white person for two months, except for a certain vet of unhappy memory. For his second course, the captain had his place moved to her table, and then accompanied her from the dining room to the lounge, and Olga found herself pouring out her problems and asking his advice on all kinds of matters – how could she make her cook wear clothes before her mother arrived? How could she get Douglas's will proved and get her pension started? How did she set about building a road which would be weather proof?

"I do not know why I am asking all this to a complete stranger! I feel I must have met you before," she said suddenly.

"You very nearly did!" he replied, "when you visited your friend Eileen Hayes in Oxford in 1907. I was a friend of Eileen's parent's neighbours and was invited to escort you to a dance! I am afraid I was foolish enough to refuse, but I had not met you then."

"How do you know? How did you know my maiden name?"

"This is a very small community. Everyone knows everything about everyone else!" It would be a long time before he told her the full story.

The following day Olga went about her work, visited another five households, found only one woman in, and once again Meinertzhagen debriefed her and returned her to the hotel at dusk. This time she bathed and changed her clothes into one of her serge skirts and the white cotton blouse. Widows did not usually relieve the full austerity of black with white until the second year, but she did not have another pretty blouse. She redid her long hair with great care, and found she was looking forward to seeing Captain Watkins again. He was so helpful and kind, and seemed to know everyone and everything. What a pity that she could not tell him how she had spent most of her day visiting German households. This evening they were given one of the best tables in the room, from where they could see all the other guests. Captain Watkins seemed to know many of them. She had plenty to tell him about the two hours she had spent on her own affairs in lieu of a lunch break. A clerk at the Army Pay Office said they had not heard of her husband's death and refused to let her see the officer; her agent had not kept his appointment with her; and her solicitor had left a note that he was too busy to see her. No one took seriously a woman trying to do business.

It was late when she returned to her room but she remembered to check on the suitcase. It was not under the bed where she had put it. Carrying her hurricane lamp she searched everywhere, in the wardrobe and above it, under the washstand, under the bed again – it had vanished. How could a whole suitcase vanish into thin air? She lay awake for long hours wondering what had become of it and what Meinhertzagen would think of her. In the morning she was downstairs at six calling for the hotel manager in an alarmed voice. Captain Watkins came down to breakfast a few minutes later, and when she told him what had happened he said: "Why not telephone Major Meinertzhagen?"

The telephone was a new gadget and not one to which Olga was accustomed but Captain Watkins made it work as if by magic – all mechanical gadgets were magic to Olga – and in two minutes she was speaking to the Major himself.

"That's all right," the Major replied, "I had it removed. I was just testing your reliability in reporting it!"

"How could you? How could you do that to me? I lay awake all night worrying about it," she screamed down the telephone, and burst into tears. Captain Watkins was standing just round the corner.

"You are working for him?" he asked. She nodded. He looked round and lowered his voice, leading her into the deserted lounge and shutting the door.

"I wouldn't advise it! If you associate with Germans you will come to be considered a German, and if you do get picked up he cannot come to your rescue without blowing his disguise, nor can you announce what you were doing!"

"I have already been picked up as a German!" Olga told the story of the German prisoners of war, then added: "He did pay me a good fee, for the time I had been detained, and my foot recovered with two days enforced rest!"

The Captain smiled, he could envisage the young policeman and the junior magistrate wondering how to deal with her. But he sounded serious when he said: “We must talk about this, Mrs Thompson,” he looked round again, “but not here, not now!”

That evening he took her out for a walk, and on the way back, leaning over the bridge crossing the Nairobi River, Olga wept as she confessed how confused and awful the last eight weeks had been, how she had quarrelled with her neighbours when they wanted her to leave her farm, and how during the last week or two she had found herself screaming at her workers and even hitting one of them when she found him lighting a fire under an ox which had collapsed to make it get up on its feet.

“Of course, it was not his fault, but that of the wretched Boer farmer who taught him to do it,” she said. Now she was getting edgy with Meinertzhagen. “I suppose it will not be his fault either,” she commented in a flat voice, “but mine for being such a fool as to work for him!”

“I have an idea,” said the Captain. “Do you know how many people Meinertzhagen wants you to meet?”

“About fifty households! So far I have visited fifteen but will have to return to some! It will take me at least another fortnight!”

“Well, if he organized social gatherings of some kind, and asked the people he suspects, several at a time but other people as well, do you think you could pick out the Germans?”

“Immediately and at once!”

“How?” asked the Captain.

“By the way they stand, the way they walk, and the way they speak, particularly to a woman.” Olga found herself describing the Prussian on board ship.

“Well, tell Meinertzhagen that it would be a cheaper and quicker way for him to get the job done.”

Meinertzhagen was difficult to convince, and when he at last agreed to give the first party he said: “I will bring the suspects over to you and introduce them.”

“No! Let them come over and make their own introductions if they want to. I'll pick them out all right. Not more than thirty people at a time, and only ten suspects.”

“Really, Mrs Thompson, I do not see how you can tell the difference by just looking at them, in a room full of strangers?” he demanded.

“By their manner and the way they talk, particularly the way they react to a young woman. Watch for yourself. Every German will come up to me because I am in mourning; most Englishmen will not come for the same reason. I shall carry a handkerchief in my sleeve. When I take it out, it means the man who is talking to me is suspect."

Soon after the party began, while guests were still arriving, Meinertzhagen sent one of his aides to her with a message. This man was not a suspect – he was a Norwegian, and Meinertzhagen had taken him on because he spoke good German. Meinertzhagen was horrified when the handkerchief came out. He was even more horrified when a check-up proved Olga was quite right, not only was he German by nationality but an established agent who accounted for the leaks from his own department. Overall, she had selected all ten suspects and found two others as well. Everyone of the suspects turned out to be German, although of course not all were spying, mostly they were leading false lives because they did not want to go into detention for the rest of the war.

The new way of work gave Olga more time during the day for her own business. She made several fruitless visits to the bank manager who had remained adamant; no more money until the will was settled, and he would have to foreclose the mortgage within a year. Widows could not hold mortgages. He strongly advised her to sell at once – no woman could farm alone in Africa. Her agent and solicitor both remained elusive. She could hardly extend her visit any longer and Captain Watkins promised to visit them for her. He borrowed one of Nairobi's few motor-cars to drive her to the station. Up-trains did not halt at the Norfolk.

"You know, I would very much like to be your friend, the person you could rely on to do things for you!" he said, as he helped her out of the car. She pushed back her thick cotton veil and looked at him. She could see the admiration in his eyes, even while her own filled with tears as the import of his words sank in.

As the train pulled out Oscar stood there waving. Olga had already got out paper and pencil and was sitting in the train writing a list of things she wanted doing in Nairobi. Head of the list was "Send up a carpenter." Those doors on the bungalow still did not fit properly. He replied promptly.

"Dear Mrs Thompson,"

"I was so pleased to get your letter. It seemed years since I had heard of you. I know so little of you that your absence makes me feel almost a stranger again. Until I got your letter I did not know even the name of your estate. If I were going through and wired to you to meet me, how long ought I to allow for the wire to reach and

for you to reach the station, and would you come? I am trying to get you carpenters. It is harder than I thought. Your agent has been kind enough to give me an appointment in his office at 9 a.m. sharp. He appears to be thinking of doing a job of work, by way of a change. I hope things are going well on your estate. I hate to think of your having to be violent or forcible. Please do not do it more than you can help. One has to find time occasionally to remember that one's existence is an educational period and not the end of all. The recurrence of moods of any kind, depression or hysteria or violence, inevitably shapes character. Good-bye, and do for heaven's sake let me know probable movements before hand. I should hate to miss a visit to Nairobi. Would you like me to come to Mombasa with you? It could be arranged."

The deeply religious man who knew the forces of evil were always threatening, always around, had met up with an irreligious idealist who believed that if only one showed goodwill, the good would always prevail. It was going to be a passionate partnership.

* * *

Chapter Five

THE START OF A LOVE AFFAIR

July is a lovely month in the Highlands of Kenya. The damp chill of the rains is gone, yet it is cool enough most of the day to enjoy walking. Oscar Watkins was addicted to walking and as he climbed the hill to Khitari estate he found the conditions ideal. Tiger lilies were pushing their great stripey blooms through tangled grass, there were black-eyed susies and blue and white convolvulus winding their stringy stems over everything, and, as he approached Olga's farm, the scent of coffee blossom rose gently above the other forest smells. Some trees seemed to be alive with weaver birds building their astonishing nests. He mimicked the monkeys chattering in the trees with grunts which they apparently mistook for insults, showering him with twigs and leaves.

He used solitary walks to work out his problems. Here he was courting this beautiful widow. He had been in love twice before, but this one topped them all. But she was a settler, a farmer, and to be an official's wife she would have to become a completely different sort of person. John Ainsworth, an officer senior to him in the administration and whom he much admired, had married a missionary's daughter and they both remained devoted to the African cause, living serious, simple, unostentatious lives. John did not like, had never liked, white settlers; he found it difficult to respect the white aristocrats who seemed intent on making Kenya their playground. Oscar agreed with John.

It was up to the Administrators, appointed by the British Government, to protect the local inhabitant from having his land occupied or his labour exploited. Government had of course to cover many more things; the introduction of the basics of civilization, law and order, roads and railways, literacy and learning, preventive medicine, hospitals and hygiene, and the creation of sufficient wealth to support all these things. Beyond all, they had to set up and maintain *Pax Britannica.* A country where there is no law and order, where every tribe is intent on capturing its neighbours and selling them into slavery, is not a happy country.

What sort of farm was Olga running? Would it prove an obstacle between them? The train had been punctual and Oscar was a fast walker, but Olga was not out on the farm when he arrived.

He liked the little prefabricated bungalow she had brought out from Harrods. She had painted it white and the corrugated iron roof green; had used the packing cases to panel the walls, and had placed a rectangular dining-table in a corner with a bench round it, Austrian style. There were chintz curtains at the windows, a Welsh dresser gleaming with pewter plates, two wicker arm-chairs by the fire place and heaps of magazines everywhere. It was a bright, happy room, neither fussy nor over furnished, somehow conveying an air of inconsequential untidiness. The guest room was the usual banda, a round African hut with a thatched roof, standing in the garden; an excellent idea as it gave privacy to both hosts and guests. The breakfast was well set, and Olga announced proudly that everything on it except the coffee was home-grown, and next year she would be producing that too. In fact, she had bought flour to make the bread and sugar to make the marmalade.

She said she would show him round the farm while she did her normal round, and lithe and lanky in her recently designed outfit of a long tunic over breeches tucked into long socks, led the way out by the back door. Two churns of milk were being unloaded from a donkey who eey-ored loudly when he saw Olga. "This is Jacky," she said, rewarding him with a carrot from the food store. Beyond the donkey stood the milk parade, a row of a dozen or more children, naked except for the beads they wore round various parts of their anatomy. Each had a mug or an old tin in his hand. Olga filled a jug from the first churn, and walked down the row filling the mugs, talking to each child as she did so, inspecting them for cuts and bites and bruises. She put the rest of the churn to stand in cold water in her food store and sent the other churn, still loaded on the donkey, down to the shop.

As he followed her around the farm, Oscar became more and more amazed at what he saw. He commented on how well her work force was housed in properly built mud and wattle huts with windows and doors; some of the huts were square. “A far more useful shape if it is to be a comfortable home with beds and tables,” said Olga, “but not popular with many of them.”

“Yes,” he said meekly. He had not noticed that other settlers had comfortable homes for the labour high on their list of priorities.

“We did the good housing right at the start,” Olga was saying. “These men come from the plains around Kisumu, and here, 2,000 feet higher, it is much colder at night. Unless they have proper houses and beds, and each man has two blankets, they fall ill.” He could hardly believe it. Three years earlier, in his report on labour conditions in this area, he had given the cold nights in the highlands as one of the reasons the local inhabitants did not like coming out to work. This woman had never heard of his report, which had been circulated before she arrived, but had recognized the same fact and done something about it.

A group of men stood outside a long low building, its front open to the air, but it had a neatly thatched roof with a huge open fire-place in the middle. He was surprised at the cheerful, almost intimate, way the workers greeted her, at the number of women and children there seemed to be about the place, and at the spotless state of the area.

“What is this building for?”

“It’s brand new, finished since I was in Nairobi. I put it up so I have somewhere to teach in the evening – they love coming to the classes. Mrs Ainsworth got the Mission to send me some books to teach reading in Luo.”

“And you teach them?”

“At the moment, yes. I’m not very good at teaching reading in Luo but I hope to employ a clerk one day and then he can take over the *a b c* bit. Some of them can already read and write their own names. Now the shed is up, it is used for other things. The young bachelors cook there, two or three cooking together; visiting missionaries and doctors can hold their gatherings there. And when it rains the children use it as a playroom."

"How do you keep the area so clean?" he asked. He himself was employing some thousands of young Africans as porters in the Carrier Corps and knew just how difficult it was to make young men keep the rules of the most basic hygiene.

"Oh, that has been quite easy", she replied. "I employ one woman, a senior one with several children, to see that it is clean."

"And she can make them sweep and not spread litter everywhere?" he asked.

"Well, I give out rations three times a week, and I don't even open the store until the place is clean." This sounded unacceptable to Oscar's code of behaviour.

"And do you have to hold back food often?"

"So far once, for half an hour. A couple of new arrivals had not used the latrine. The entire work force led them out and made them clean up after themselves. It has never happened again!"

"You have a great number of women and children about!"

"Yes, I prefer to employ married men, and I like them to bring their families."

"And you find enough men who want to do that?"

"More than I can employ, I turn away several most months. They seem to like the way I run things. Why are you surprised?"

He did not tell her how totally unexpected her outlook was. Here was this woman, a new settler, proving John Ainsworth right. John had said again and again that unless the settler could offer better conditions than men could expect at home, they were unlikely to go out to work, whatever their pay. And he, John, was not going to persuade them. And now Oscar had found a settler who was providing better conditions, and attracting more workers than she could use, proving John right. Settlers were needed as they had the skills and the capital to make the economy work, and settlers like this one might be able to do more for the African than the administrator could, building a sound agricultural basis for the economy and a deeper understanding of the local people. An administrator was moved inevitably from place to place as his career developed, a settler remained in the same place, employed the same people, and became a pillar of an evolving agricultural economy.

It was a long morning. Olga checked that the weeders were using Dutch hoes and not the ubiquitous long knife, the panga, they all loved to use. She went down to a spot where ten young men were digging a furrow. “This is to take water from the river to the new coffee factory. We shall only use the factory in the short rains so in the dry season they can use the water for their vegetable gardens which will be in that triangle between the furrow and the river. That will give them fresh vegetables all the year round.”

Later that day she took him down to the rations-shed and he watched the workers with their baskets and tin bowls line up for their rations – two pounds of maize meal, a handful of salt, a mug full of sugar.

“I'm always worried that the rations are inadequate, or rather that they lack variety. They don’t get enough meat now – only about once a month when I have to slaughter an animal. Before, Douglas shot quite a bit of game.”

“Is there game on the farm?”

“Yes, plenty. Everything from baboons, colobus monkeys, leopards, zebra, plenty of antelopes of different kinds. We are trying to get rid of it because of the disease.”

“Would you like me to shoot a buck this evening?”

“Would you? The workers will be delighted – and we could have some for dinner too.”

“I'd have to borrow a gun!” said Oscar, avoiding saying Douglas's name.

* * * * * * *

After steaks of unhung venison so tough that they could hardly chew them and vegetables from the garden boiled soggy, Oscar looked at her seriously, but not because of the food. This was another thing they had in common, neither noticed what they were eating – there was always something more important, more interesting to talk about. He produced a plain khaki folder labelled: *Mrs Thompson.*

“Now we have to talk business. I saw your bank manager, your agent and your solicitor. The situation is not good. Your husband's pay has stopped and it will be at least three months, perhaps longer, before we can get his pension sorted out. We think it will be around £120 a year. The bank manager did not want to talk to me; he says the mortgage cannot be extended and on the contrary he should foreclose now.” Oscar paused, he did not want to say that he had himself guaranteed it. “Eventually he agreed to let you carry on as you are, and he will give you three years without having to pay interest, although it will all have to be paid back in the long run. This gives you a breathing space to see if you can make the farm pay. And your agent was no use whatever; he said that when a holding was bought jointly and one man died, the land should be offered to the other holders at the original price, regardless of improvements, if they wanted it. And he said two of the three had already told him – they do want it!"

"Of course they do. They have already arranged to sell it at a much higher price because of all the improvements we have put in. They tried to threaten me out the very day I heard about Douglas!" Olga's voice was tearful with indignation.

"Well, if you want to keep the farm, you will have to be very careful financially. Do you know how much the farm costs you to run? How much is it bringing in?"

"No, Douglas did all that. It is not bringing much in at the moment, not until the coffee comes into bearing next year. And I have to put in a coffee factory before then!"

"May I see the farm books?"

"Books? What do you mean?"

"Account books – how much money you have to spend each month and how much you have coming in?"

"I have not got it written down anywhere. It is all in my head, except for those bits of paper there, on that desk!" She pointed to an old oak kneehole desk which stood in one corner of the room, so piled with papers you could not see it was a desk. "I draw money on Douglas's account but the Bank Manager does not even want me to do that in case it belongs to someone else!"

She sat in a wicker chair darning her farm stockings. She was wearing a long, dark blue house gown with a wide lace collar. Her long dark hair was brushed back in a knot at the back of her neck, wispy curls escaped in a halo round her face bent over her sewing.

"Do you mind if I look through it – I may be able to help?" Oscar took one of the oil lamps and moved over to the desk. The papers were completely unsorted. There were, as he had feared there would be, a number of bills she had not paid, and a surprising number of bills she was owed. There were some very impolite letters from the bank asking her what she was going to do about her overdraft, and any number of personal letters. He stacked them in neat piles, while asking her questions:

"What is this cheque?" He held up a slip of paper for 600 rupees, a lot of money in those days, more than he earned in a month.

"Oh, that is the cheque a vet bounced on me. He was passing through, he said, and wanted to sleep here. Then the post boy brought up the leather post-bag with the wages in it, and he asked if I would cash him a cheque as he was short of money to reach Kisumu. I said I would as I could send for more money the following day. His cheque bounced."

"He will pay up when he hears," comforted the captain, "it is surprisingly easy to make a mistake."

"No, he did not even have an account on that bank. He had pinched the cheque-book from his previous night stop! And used a name not his own."

"What a delightful character! Has anyone else set out to cheat you since your husband died?"

"Yes," said Olga, "including one of our partners. And nobody tried anything when he was alive!"

"How much did you say your wage bill was? And how much for rations? How much have you spent on tools over the last year? What about your household bills?" He was jotting things down. "Got any red tape?"

"Red tape? Good heavens, no. What should I do with red tape – here take this." She threw over a ball of darning wool, which he retrieved from the floor and started to unravel.

"The trouble with this stuff is that it will cut into the paper!"

"Do you mind if I go to bed?" It was ten o'clock, well past her normal bedtime. She could never do without her sleep.

"No, of course not." He stood up politely as she left the room. "Shall I lock the door behind me?"

"Yes, and give Cook the key in the morning when he brings your tea." They shook hands formally. He noticed there were tears in Olga's eyes and before he could stop himself he had thrown his arms around her; she did not draw away but rested her head gently on his shoulder. He did not try to kiss her, sensing it was too early for that, but whispered:-

"You know how I feel about you, and I hope one day you will come to feel the same about me, dear Mrs Thompson." She nodded and moved slowly to the door, where she paused and turned to him.

"Good night, Oscar!" It was the first time she had used his Christian name. She had signalled acceptance of him. When she came into the sitting room in the morning the desk was tidy. On a shelf above it her letters were neatly tied up and labelled. On the desk were three little piles of papers weighed down. One pile was labelled: “Save yourself trouble by paying these at once!” Another one said: “Pay these when you can!” One piece of paper had all the incoming money and outgoing expenses neatly listed in two columns. There was a deficit of £500, the precise amount of their joint allowances. Douglas had planned their expenses meticulously. On another scrap of paper was written: “I am leaving by an earlier train. Goodbye for now. We shall meet in Mombasa.” She knew there was no earlier train, he wanted to save her from another good-bye to a man going to the front. He was on his way to inspect his Carriers in the same area where Douglas had been killed. She stood staring at the desk; never again would she let her financial affairs get into such a state. She sat down and wrote to Nairobi to order two account books. The partnership between Oscar and Olga had begun.

A few weeks later they stood at dawn at the seaward point of Mombasa Island watching the SS *Matiana* being piloted through the reef. For once Olga was silent, and Oscar guessed her thoughts. Only fifteen months ago she had arrived on that same ship and Douglas had met her. And here she was, hand in hand with another man. He determined to divert her.

“Tell me something about your mother?”

“She will like you.” Olga as always jumped straight to the point of a question. “She always …” she paused, seeking ways of not mentioning Douglas – conversation between them was still full of potential pitfalls. “She always wanted me to marry a strong man, an interesting man, I think a man who would keep me in order like she does.”

“So she keeps you in order?”

“Oh yes, for example, when I see her I shall probably want to cry, and she will say ‘Pull yourself together, Olga. No time for hysterics now!’ “

What Olga really feared was that her mother would take in the situation at once and say: “Nonsense, you can’t be in love again already.” Yet her mother knew, as no one else did, that she had not been in love with Douglas when she married him. It was after marrying him that she had discovered the strange fact that dull men often make good husbands and wonderful lovers. Douglas had bought the farm in Kenya to satisfy her longing for adventure, and had shown himself so attentive, so loving, that she had grown to love him. Sex was not mentioned in those days, even between mother and daughter, but Flo had understood how successful the honeymoon had been.

"Let's not tell her at once!" she said, as the ship passed the lighthouse and they turned back for breakfast.

"As you like! But you haven't told me much about her."

"You'll have to listen to her interminable stories, she tells them well, but again and again! She makes even the most commonplace event sound like an adventure."

"As long as they are about you I shall not mind!" he replied.

"No one ever leaves the castle, the chimney sweep, the man who empties the cess pits, without sharing wine and cake with her, so she has a huge number of stories, from the stone mason's sister-in-law's difficult pregnancy upon a mountain high summer pastures, to Count Teleki's latest explorations, Roosevelt's determination to set up game reserves, and the problems the parish priest has in casting our local passion play."

Oscar took a deep breath – so that was where the unstoppable flow came from. He dropped her hand, for there were more people about now and they were near the District Commissioner's house where she was staying with his old friends, Geoffrey & Mrs Northcote, while he went to the Nairobi club. In those days it was up to the man to see that no breath of scandal touched a woman he wanted to marry. They must not even stay in the same house. Now it was time for him to do a morning's work.

"You know, the very first recruitment camp for my Carrier Corps is here in Mombasa and I have to inspect it. The Carriers only started last August with 100 men; now there are 10,000 in ten different depots. I'll be early at the club for lunch. The train leaves at 3. Load your mother's luggage at the docks, and try to find the number of your carriage."

After breakfast Olga packed her bag, put on her terrai hat and walked a mile down to the docks, rejoicing in how much cooler it was in Mombasa in June than it had been in April when she arrived. The steam bath atmosphere had quite gone and a cool breeze blew in from the north. She stared out across the lagoon where the *Matiana* had already dropped anchor and the lighters were crowding round the companion ways. When at last she caught sight of her mother, as the motor launch brought her across the water, she perceived her for the first time through grown up eyes.

This well preserved, well set up woman in the dark linen skirt and stiff lawn blouse was an attractive woman, the sort of person she would pick out as a friend if it had not been her good fortune to have her for a mother. Although it was only just over a year since she had seen her, Olga noticed how she had aged, the fair hair was streaked with grey, the grey eyes had a new depth to them, tinged with sadness. Poor mother, her favourite brother and three of her nephews already lay buried in Flanders; her son-in-law in Africa, while her only son was at sea and another half dozen brothers and nephews were on active service. Her own family and her husband's stood on opposite sides of the fighting line. It was an unhappy predicament for any woman.

There were two stations in Mombasa in those days, one in the docks to meet the boat train, and one in the new town, an easy walk from the club. When Olga went to the docks station to load Flo's trunks, she asked the booking clerk where their carriage was. Mrs Thompson, Mrs Baillie-Grohman, not a trace of either on the booking list. The train was full, as it always was when a boat had arrived. "You'll have to wait two days," said the booking-clerk. "You are not on the booking list!"

"I am sure Captain Watkins booked them for us?" Olga said. At that moment the stationmaster, spotless in his white uniform, came into the ticket office. He took over:

"Captain Watkins? You must be Mrs Thompson." The station-master, spoke with a sing-song Indian accent "Yes, he booked two compartments. You and Mrs Baillie-Grohman are in a four-berth, and he has a coupé in the same coach." The station-master looked at Olga attentively, then accompanied her to the train and himself helped her stack her luggage where she wanted it. He locked the compartment and said he would see them at the other station in the afternoon.

"Who is this Captain?" demanded Flo as soon as they were out of earshot, looking for the tramway that would take them back to the residential part of the town. Little carriages were pushed along the tram-lines by Africans, understandably languidly when it was both uphill and hot.

"We are lunching with him at the club," said Olga, "but first we have to have coffee with my hostess and say good-bye."

"Who is this Mrs Northcote who is putting you up?"

"Her husband is the District Commissioner." Olga did not want to explain to her mother how she happened to know a government family six hundred miles from Koru. "Look, that is Fort Jesus, the old Portuguese Castle where the Portuguese were besieged and massacred. It is now used as a prison. We get out here."

When Mrs Northcote had made them welcome and the coffee had been brought in, she turned to Olga and said: "You are lunching with Oscar at the club, aren't you?" And Olga realized that this easy use of a Christian name had told her mother the whole story. If Mrs Northcote had not been aware of familiarity between Olga and the strange man, she would have referred to him as Captain Watkins.

* * * * * * *

Nor had it been necessary to take all the elaborate precautions of dressing the household servants. Olga discovered with some surprise that it would take more than naked men to shock Mother. She had followed Oscar's suggestion to offer Cook a khanzu, the long white robe worn by Swahili and Arab gentlemen and increasingly worn by servants in European households.

"Cook, would you wear clothes if I got you some?" Olga had opened the debate as soon as she knew for certain her mother was on her way.

"Clothes on a black man are dirty. I don't wear clothes because I am clean!" he said firmly. "That is why I left the mission. They said clothes or go, so I went."

"But you wear football boots and garters?"

"Because I won them for playing football, and they would get stolen if I didn't wear them!" he had replied. They had had the same argument many times before. She had returned to the attack some days later.

"My mother is coming out and she is not accustomed to men without clothes. If I got you a nice white khanzu like the Arabs wear, would you wear it? You know the stewards in all the big hotels wear them."

"I will try one," he consented, "for the old lady!"

Olga went down to the local Indian tailor to order khaki shorts for those workers whose jobs brought them frequently to the house and long white robes for the house servants. The tailor had one cubby-hole in a row of cubby holes called shops. He sat on the concrete walk in front with his sewing machine, running up anything asked of him. He had little idea of time, and Olga's order was not ready when she left to meet her mother, but the tailor promised to send them up to the farm so all would be clad when Mother arrived.

When Olga and Flo arrived back at the farm, tired after two nights in the train and the five mile walk from the station, the three house servants and the new headman were lined up to greet them on the door step. Cook was magnificent, his sturdy six foot three frame in a flowing white robe with a beautiful lace border, which Flo at once recognized as the table cloth, lovingly trimmed with hand-spun lace by the sisters-of-charity for Olga's trousseau. He was a strong man and had split both the tailor's khanzus trying to struggle into them. Impressed by Olga's insistence that he must be dressed when her mother arrived, he had taken the tablecloth and cut a hole in the middle for his head and belted it round his waist with one of Olga's stockings. The farm hands who worked round the house had donned their new shorts in accordance with her instructions, but unaccustomed to such clothing, they put them on back to front. This was particularly unfortunate because when they bent down the cheaply sewn-on buttons below the waist had all flown off, so although they looked respectable from the front, the gaping back bulging with well muscled half moons was distinctly unconventional. When Olga noticed her mother was struggling to keep her face straight, she decided not to interfere with local custom in future. This decision was re-enforced when she found that the kitchen toto, the lad who helped in the kitchen, was keeping his drying up cloth in the pouch in front of his shorts. Soon everyone was naked again, except for Cook who liked his khanzus, now replaced with larger ones; they signalled class, his superiority to the other workers.

*   *   *   *   *   *   *

Douglas's dog gave them a warm welcome, bringing tears to Olga's eyes as he sniffed round looking for Douglas. After supper she took him out for his usual walk, keeping the lead shorter nowadays than she had with Bully and Flo accompanied her. She had not been told about the leopard – no good frightening the old lady. There was a strange laughing noise loud and close.

"Really Olga, you should not accommodate the farm workers so close to your house," Flo scolded.

"That's not men, it's hyenas," replied Olga, "they are very good scavengers and come round most nights." Flo had been walking slightly behind her, but when Olga glanced back, she was not there. Her heart lurched, had Mother suffered the same fate as Bully, and vanished into the African night? At that moment a piercing shriek, more of fury than of pain, reassured Olga – it was definitely Mother and not the hyenas, and signified that she was nearby and very much alive.

"Where are you?" Olga called.

"There's something biting me. Ouch!"

Olga held up the hurricane lamp. "If you must leave the path, what do you expect? I carefully avoided the stream of ants on the way out."

"I didn't like the sound of those hyenas so thought I would take a short cut back to the house."

"Go inside and take your clothes off and I'll come and de-ant you in a moment." Olga followed her indoors, scooping embers from the fire-place into a dustpan and spreading them carefully across the threshold of both outside doors. "Those ants are serious trouble. They can kill young livestock! Sometimes they invade the house so that in the middle of the night we have to get up. My word, you have got a lot. Are they in your hair yet?"

* * * * * * *

It was two months before Oscar could get time off to visit them. He took Flo on one side and told her he adored Olga and wanted to marry her, but not until the end of the war. By 1915 the High Command in British East had at last understood that it would have to capture the central railway in German East Africa to bring the East African campaign to an end and preparations were going ahead for the attack. It would be a short, sharp, hazardous affair, and Oscar would be in the vanguard, for the army could not move without porters and he believed he must lead his porters from the front. Between them Oscar and Flo hatched a plan that she would take Olga back to England for six months to get over the shock of Douglas's death, to see the Thompsons, and to sort out the property problems. By the time Olga was back again, the whole East African campaign should be over and they would get married.

The only trouble was that Olga would not hear of it. "I cannot leave Oscar in the middle of this war!" she declared. After he had left she became nervous, fidgety, and started writing endless letters, mostly scribbled in pencil in old exercise books. At least one fat letter was posted every day although the post only went twice a week. Although she did not tell Flo that she had written “Please come at once, I am going through absolute hell!” she did not succeed in hiding her anxieties from her mother, how depressed she was if there was no letter from Oscar among the tide of condolence letters which only now was beginning to flood in, the bitterness towards her neighbours, and her increasing irritability with her workers. She was in no state to be left alone. Flo knew she should stay with her, but in England she had a sick husband. Olga was not concerned about her father, only about Oscar. He and the farm were the only subjects she would discuss.

“Don’t you see, it would be better for Oscar too if you came home with me for a short time. He could get on with his job with a quiet mind,” Flo pressed. She thought her mother wanted to separate them.

“You don’t think he is the right man for me, do you Mother?”

“He is a good man, he will be honest and upright with you, just as I am sure Douglas would have been. And I shall appreciate his learning and knowledge as much as you do, and I am sure your father will too!”

“Do you think father will like him as he did Douglas?”

“On the one hand, your father will enjoy the company of a man who plays an excellent game of chess and who knows so much about old books and ancient history. On the other hand he is in for a shock. Shooting has been his passion since he was nine years old. Now he is going to acquire a son-in-law who lives in one of the world’s most exciting big game areas, is a Bisley shot, and yet declares he hates killing animals. This behaviour will seem inexplicable.”

“It’s not inexplicable to me. I hate shooting, even when I had to aim at the leopard and then had to shoot the old ox, I hated it. But you are not entirely happy about him, are you Mother?”

“If you can accept that he is ten years older than yourself and accustomed to authority, that he is very much a career man and that you will not be able to wear the trousers as you did with Douglas, then I think you can be happy. Good men are not always easy to live with.”

“How do you mean?”

"Well, suppose you want to go to a dance, Oscar wants to give the money – has possibly already given the money – to a charity and wants to spend the evening working. Will you feel resentful? You want to go to some society picnic or meeting, and he thinks you should both be looking after some poor friends or acquaintances. These things can be difficult in marriage."

"There is something else, isn't there?"

"Well, yes there is. You are a favourite throughout the English family, as you well know. One of the sorrows of my life has been that your dear father has never been popular with my brothers and sisters, too foreign, too uppity, too bookish, they say. Oscar will be just as unpopular but for different reasons, too quiet, too unassuming. Guy and Vee will be snubbing him just as they snub your father, without even knowing they are doing so, and unlike your father Oscar will just sit there and take it and you will feel unhappy. So your welcome in England will be different."

"But we shall be living out here."

"And you should think very carefully about your life out here. It will be very like living in an army cantonment, where your man's rank affects your whole life. It is such a relief to meet another woman with whom you can make a real friend. Yet even that can have repercussions. If her husband is senior to yours, people say you are sucking up; if he is junior, that you do not know your position. As Oscar is ten years older than you, your fellow wives will be older, possibly plainer, certainly duller and certainly jealous of a younger, prettier woman."

"What you are saying, Mother, is that Oscar will make me a good husband but that I may not make him a good wife?"

"Let us say that you are dealing yourself a difficult hand. Give yourself time to think things out. Your father was 38 when I married him, the same age that Oscar is now, and very set in his ways, accustomed to pioneering, and living rough. It does not make a marriage easier, particularly during those first few years. You were lucky with Douglas, the two of you fitted so well together, but I feared you might outgrow him. You will want to go on to bigger things and Douglas would have held you back. With Oscar you will have to grow at once to keep up with him. The first years will be difficult but with patience and luck they should challenge you to grow together. Remember that the poor man will always have one severe handicap!"

"What handicap?"

"He will grow old and ill and crotchety as we all do, and in your mind there will always be the comparison, with that other man who will never grow old, who will always be at the honeymoon stage of marriage. It is a hard test for any man. You must get over Douglas first. You must come back to England with me!"

"I hate to leave Oscar in the middle of a war!" repeated Olga.

"You are not fit to marry any man at the moment, and you have much to sort out. The Thompsons deserve a visit."

Preparations for the journey went ahead. Willie, safely ensconced at Boxley Abbey in England, was asked to find a farm manager for Olga. There was a double coincidence. The man he chose, with the name of Smith, was the brother of one of Douglas's partners, who had joined up to become a Carrier Corps officer under Oscar. Smith the farm manager hoped to manage both his brother's farm as well as Olga's.

Oscar, afraid always that she might meet someone else, besieged her with letters, more letters than he had ever written in his life before. When she was near to him, he referred to the farm as his hated rival but the further away she was, the more polite he became, writing:

"Why stint the farm for lack of pay and posho. If 100 or 150 rupees a month are any use to you, you know where to get them. Your farm is a very good investment It is a lucky man who is allowed to put some money into it."

However, when in March 1916 he found time to visit Khitari and check the books, he saw that the farm was still costing £500 a year more than it brought in. Whereas he could help her at the moment, this amount was as much as a District Commissioner's annual pay, the pay he would get at the end of the war. He was rash enough to point this out to Olga.

Olga wrote back furiously. The farm brought in nearly all it cost when it was properly run. The deficit must be because of Smith's inefficiency. Oscar replied:

"My darling Spitfire, after two months of silence an avalanche of letters, a whirlwind of instructions, a tornado of indignations. I simply love you. I came back from Moshi with some fever and tummy, and a head buzzing with quinine."

He sometimes found space to mention the war. When the invasion of German East took place at Dar-es-Salaam, the carriers had to land first to repair the docks for the troops to land. Oscar went with them and was the first ashore, with the Germans still sniping. His only comment to her on this operation was when he was awarded the D.S.O. : "*I am afraid there is another medal for you to scratch your dear face on.*"

*   *   *   *   *   *   *

On board the SS *Matiana* once again, the bell rang to warn that the pilot would soon be leaving ship and with him the mail bag. Olga hurried to finish her letter to Oscar from whom she had parted just three hours earlier. "*The main problem for wives is to be there when they are wanted and keep out of the way when they are not!*" It was the sentiment of the day, but it was one she was going to find it hard to live up to. "*Lots of love, dearest,*" she scribbled and rushed out to drop the letter in the still open bag by the Purser's office. The pilot's boat would take the post back to Mombasa and Oscar. She would not see him again for six months. Would he survive? Would she? How she hated these war-time partings.

So did some other passengers. On deck, there was a bevy of miserable school children watching the pilot leave the ship; with him went the last contact with the country where they had grown up. *Going Home* for them meant a long and tedious journey in the care of strangers, years of separation from their parents, attendance at terrifying boarding schools they had never seen and for which they had not been prepared, and guardianship by relations whom they had never met.

Olga surveyed them with dismay and turned to her mother: "Do you think it is worse for the mothers or the children?"

"The mothers!" said Flo firmly. "The children will be quite happy in a few hours but the mothers will be weeping for days. Go and organize a game for them now, to cheer them up, like you did at our Christmas parties at home."

Olga's heart was heavy with her own parting, but she forced cheerfulness into her voice. "Come on, children, let's go down to the end of the ship and have a shouting competition. I will give a chocolate bar to the one who can shout loudest!"

Her ruse worked like magic. The noise was so loud that other children emerged from the cabins and corners where they had retired for a quiet weep and went to join her. In ten minutes she had all the children laughing and playing, and the Purser's Shop quite sold out of chocolate bars. For the rest of the voyage she was like the Pied Piper of Hamelin, followed everywhere by gaggles of children. "What are we going to play now, Olga?" they would roar, and in those days children did not address grown ups by their Christian names, nor did they call out to them. If she did not appear on the lower deck on time, two of the older girls would sweep round the upper deck asking: "Where is Olga?" and the oldies would murmur about how disrespectful the younger generation were.

Now she no longer had the distraction of hard physical work or the responsibility for her workers, her thoughts fell into a terrible confusion as she tried to make sense of the last eighteen months. It was such a short time since she had arrived in Africa, a young bride so full of hope and happiness. She was returning swathed in the heavy widow's black clothes her mother had bought in France, cumbersome garments designed to make her an object of pity. She did not want pity, she wanted action. But what action? Why wear them when she was already engaged to another man? She scribbled away at her book 'Olivia'.

She had not yet come to terms with the changes within herself. She had arrived in Africa determined to devote herself to her husband; she was returning as a fully fledged farmer in her own right, a woman who made decisions and conducted business. She had a vocation. She carried responsibilities. She had, in modern feminist parlance, found herself. In those days, few women made that discovery, but hid behind their husbands all their lives. Olga was not sure she liked the self she had found, and for the rest of her life would argue with that other self, often out loud. Later, when we lived in England with no servants, visitors would ask who was talking in the kitchen, and my father would solemnly reply: "That's the housemaid arguing with the cook!"

Did she really want to tie herself to another man in Africa? It was the other way round. Africa had entered her blood so much that the new man provided an excellent excuse to stay, to continue with the life of adventure, in the country of the unexpected. Had he lived in England, he would not have proved nearly as attractive. She was surprised that she had already adopted something of his outlook, she was proud to be among those bringing good things to this part of Africa, law and order, schools and clinics, ploughs and pens, hygiene and medicine, needle and cloth, roads and railways and wheels to run on them, where none of these things had been known before. If she stayed on in Africa, one day she would have to pay the awful price of Empire, the parting from her children at the age of ten or twelve, the parting she was observing on this ship.

"Mother, you will take my children for me, when the time comes to send them home, won't you?" she asked.

"Olga! You are impossible. You are not even married yet. Just remember that board Oscar has hung over your desk!"

Don't Worry, It May Not Happen! Olga quoted, conjuring up the slightly crooked lettering on the raw wood board. But she wanted it to happen, more than anything she wanted Oscar's children.

Travelling in wartime is always tedious, with unexpected delays, many boring life-boat drills, overcrowded accommodation and none of the usual amusements. The Mediterranean was in the danger zone for German submarines sailing from the port of Trieste. All the men on board were divided into watches for look-out duty, scanning the sea with field glasses hour after hour for any tell-tale signs of a periscope. Just before they reached Marseilles, on their early morning walk round the deck, Olga leant over the ship's rails.

"Look, Mother, oranges and deck chairs scattered over the sea!"

"Must have been that explosion we heard last night! Come and have breakfast, Olga, I'm getting cold."

"I can't bear it, Mother – look, there is a teddy bear. It means..." she put her head on her hands on the railings and started sobbing.

"Olga! Pull yourself together! War is terrible, but you have a future to look forward to. And you are not setting a good example." In Flo's mind it was very important, in everything one did, to be a pattern others might follow.

* * * * * * *

Boxley Abbey was a grey cube of a Regency house dumped down among the ruins of an old abbey. The aunts had lived there for five years since their mother, Emily, died. Maud had found a splendid Kentish gardener and applied her gardening skills to create a water garden in the remains of the abbey church, and a walled fruit garden among the dormitory ruins, while Grace had arranged the inside of the big house with wit and originality, making the whole top floor into large nurseries. The two spinster sisters bickered as happily as any married couple while providing wonderful hospitality for their thirty-odd nephews and nieces. The house was constantly full of young people, and with the war the frequency of visits had increased.

Willie was ensconced in the biggest first floor bedroom, where he had moved a large writing table. He was delighted to see Flo but was gruff with the constant flow of cousins, some on leave, some convalescing, some visiting London, others parking children or picking them up. Soon after arrival, Flo opened one of Maud's letters, as she had been asked to do, and announced: "This is a request to Maud to cook at a makeshift hospital at the mansion down the road. She must have applied before she knew she was going to France. I am going to offer to go in her place."

"You can't be a cook, Mother!" Olga said, horrified at the idea.

"Why not? I did the cooking in British Columbia for the work camp!"

"But you've always had a cook!"

"Yes, I have been lucky. I hope to employ one again after the war, but if I cannot, I shall be proud to do my own cooking to a professional standard."

"Why don't you cook here and let Maud's cook go to the hospital?" suggested Olga, when the maid had left the room.

"Two reasons. First, I do not think the girl is up to cooking for forty sick men. Secondly, Grace and Maud are paying her and we must keep her on. Also I think educated women have got to lead by example, to get away from silly snobberies. If the country needs cooks, then we must show that we can cook."

"Yes," said Olga, "I see!" And she did see, only it was not her mother in a cook's apron at a nearby country house she saw, but herself back in British East in a nurse's uniform, tending wounded Africans. If BEA needed nurses for African soldiers, then she must nurse. She too must set an example.

On the anniversary of Douglas's death she went up to London to visit the Thompsons. She felt more hypocritical than ever as she wrapped herself in one of the Aunt's thick black coats and adjusted her widow's veil over her hat. The Thompsons lived in one of those rather dreary houses in Marloes Road in Kensington. Colonel Thompson was watching for her from his study window and came to the door himself. He kissed her warmly, and led her into a sitting room heavy with dark furniture and dim with half-drawn blinds. Dolly and Mrs Thomson, both dressed even more blackly than was Olga, received her silently and started weeping as they embraced her. Douglas had been the only surviving son; an older one had been lost in some skirmish in India before the war.

"Now don't drown poor Olga before she has even taken her coat off." Colonel Thompson's voice was barely steady as he distracted himself by peeling off her long heavy coat. "Olga, I need to take you into my study to sign some papers before lunch."

Once in the study, a dingy little room lined with volumes of regimental history and photographs, he cleared his throat and said: "You must forgive Dolly. She only heard a week or so ago that her young man has been killed. They were going to announce their engagement on his next leave. It all happened while you were at sea."

He seated her at his immaculately tidy desk. "I'll just get Emily to witness your signature, my dear." Emily was the parlour maid. His absence gave her time to think. She had planned what to say, to tell them about Oscar, but this, the anniversary of Douglas's death, was not the right time to say anything. Dolly's loss had clearly re-opened the wound and increased their own pain. She would have to ask her mother to tell them later, when she was back in Africa. That way they need never know how soon she had committed herself to another man.

"Now the farm is yours," Colonel Thompson said as Emily left the room. "We promised Douglas an allowance for five years when he married, and that five years is not yet over. So we want to transfer the allowance to you. It was a mistake that the bank stopped it the moment they heard that Douglas…" his voice faltered. "It must have made matters very difficult for you!"

"No," said Olga, "it is most kind of you, but I can well manage without the allowance – I have started to sell vegetables and eggs and all kinds of other things. Are you sure you want to transfer the farm to me? We were married such a short time. I could repay you slowly." Silently she decided that, as soon as she could get a good price for the farm she would sell it and pay back the money.

"What good is the money to us – we have lost both our sons, and our prospective son-in-law. We are old people, and Dolly will inherit this house and such money as we have. It is you we are concerned about, alone and in Africa!"

"I am most grateful to you," she said as they both stood up. "I love that farm. It has so many memories." She went to him and kissed him. He put his arms round her and she started crying on his shoulder. He spoke to her gently:

"We are both so thankful for the happiness you gave him! He adored you and he never looked at another girl. You were so brave, to give up your comfortable life in the Schloss, and to go off with him to British East. You write so well, your letters made it so vivid for us." He stood back from her and took her hands. "Now I want you to promise me something, Olga. Life can be difficult for a woman on her own, and I want you to promise that you will come to me if ever you are in difficulties or need help! We think of you as a daughter, a beautiful and gifted daughter, and we want you to have as good a life as you possibly can. Please, please remember that." His voice broke.

"I will," said Olga, "I will." She tried to smile despite eyes still brimming. Had Douglas grown old, he would certainly have looked like the taut, grey-haired military figure in front of her.

"You know," she said, "It was because I hoped Douglas would grow old like you that I married him!"

"That's quite enough flattery from you, young woman," his voice was normal, military and crisp. "I think we both need a glass of sherry!"

* * * * * * *

Life at Boxley Abbey was scarcely suburban but Olga found it restricting and yearned for her farm. In one short year, *home* had ceased to be an English country house or an Austrian schloss, and become a bungalow on an African farm. She took her notebook into the sunny morning room and started sketching out the book she had in mind. She had already written three chapters and could now see where the book was going.

"What are you writing there, Olga," Willie asked tetchily at lunch. He never quite trusted her since those articles of hers had appeared in Titbits and Home Chat.

"I'm writing a book about British East Africa!" said Olga.

"That's a good idea, but you don't go shooting ..." As a sportsman it was difficult for Willie to see East Africa from any other viewpoint.

"No, it's about farming."

"But you don't know anything about farming. You have only had a year on the place."

"Nearly two years," said Olga firmly. "It is about women farming. I want to stress that they can farm on their own."

* * * * * * *

Tom had married the previous year while Flo was in British East and he brought his new wife to meet Olga. Evelyn was as tall as herself, stunningly beautiful, with a kind of china doll beauty, fair hair, blue eyes, picture-book complexion, and dainty clothes, which sometimes seemed amiss on a six foot frame. Flo was out cooking, and at lunch Olga did the honours. As soon as the coffee had been served, a bit too soon to be polite, Evelyn said:

"Do you think I could have a jug of hot water for the car? I'm sorry but I have to get back home now. I have to drive Father on his rounds this evening!" She turned to Olga, "You see, Father is a retired GP but has gone back to work because so many of the younger doctors have joined up. He only let me take the car on condition I was back punctually. Our chauffeur joined up too so I'm the driver."

They went outside and there was the car, a gleaming open-top monster. Evelyn buttoned her long thin body up in a trench coat, then went to the radiator of the car and unscrewed the cap, took the jug of hot water from the maid and poured it down. "Tighten that for me, Tom, but not too tight!" she said as she tied on a large hat with a veil, put her hands into huge gauntlets and climbed into the driving seat. Tom stepped neatly over the door into the front seat. Olga watched the look of intense concentration on her face as she turned one switch, then another. The engine backfired twice and then puttered gently into life. She reversed expertly and steered neatly through the gates, even taking one hand from the wheel to wave.

"What a handsome couple they make!" Olga said to her father as they went into the house.

"Silly young fools to get married!" growled Willie.

Olga was quite taken aback. "Why, Father, you seemed quite pleased when I got married!"

"Yes, that's just it; and now, my poor dear, this damned war has put you back on my hands, and if the same thing happens to Tom as to Douglas, I'll have two of you to look after! I am glad the Thompsons have made a decent settlement on you. I won't be worth anything after the war."

"I'm not on your hands, Father!" she remonstrated. "I have a farm and I am going to run it. Shall we wait for Mother for tea?"

A couple of weeks later Willie asked: "What are you going up to London for, so often?"

"I'm learning to drive!" she announced proudly. "There wasn't a driving school in Maidstone so I've enrolled in one in London!" In those days there was no driving test but unless one had a motor at home, it was considered wise to take lessons before purchasing one.

"What nonsense, my dear. Motors can't last, once we get back to normalcy. They frighten the horses far too much and they'll never last in Africa." Olga held her peace. She knew Oscar would not be applying for as much motor transport as he could get for his unit unless he thought the vehicles had a future there.

"Also I am looking for new coffee pulping machinery."

"New what?"

"Coffee grows as a red cherry. The skin is removed by a machine and I need to install one later this year. Everyone planted coffee at much the same time and there is a shortage of pulping machines out there."

"Who is paying for all this?"

"I've found I can take out a mortgage, now the farm is mine. I know it's wise to develop it. Demand for coffee will shoot up after the war. I have not been able to find the machine I want in London. They are sending up north for a different model. It won't be here before I leave. Would you inspect it for me, before they ship it? I will type out the minimum specifications I need – I just want to be sure they ship the right one!"

"I cannot think what has got into you women these days! Taking out mortgages, running coffee farms, cooking at hospitals, driving ambulances, buying machinery, going out to work without a by your leave!" It was his irritable tone, but when he looked at her he softened. "Yes, I'll go up and look at your coffee machinery for you! What are you writing this time?"

"Only a letter," said Olga, and turned the page quickly, afraid his long sight might have been able to read the word "Darling." She went on writing her description of Evelyn: "*Beautiful as a china doll, cold as ice, and winds Tom round her little finger. But she is able, she dresses beautifully, and you should have seen her handle that car. Poor father very upset by all the changes the war has brought.*"

It was Easter, time to make her first visit to Oscar's parents in Oxford, always referred to as the old people. Olga had always found Oxford an intriguing place when she had visited her friend Eileen Hayes. Now it looked lovelier than ever. The portly cleric, her future father-in-law, was waiting for her at the station and walked her back to the grey stone vicarage next door to the Saxon church of Holy Cross. Both garden and churchyard were awash with daffodils. She enjoyed the aesthetic way of life, the shabby furniture, the affectionate understanding between the old couple. She knew their income was less than a quarter that of the Boxley Aunts, yet their life somehow had a depth, a serenity, that was lacking in most other homes.

She loved the way they sat down to a game of chess before supper every night, the way the old man was always up early in the morning to write for two hours before the first service of the day. She was amused by the muddly way the old lady went about her household tasks before she too went over to the church. She was the dreamer of the family, he the organizer. She could see how delighted they both were with her – at last their favourite son was going to settle down. Olga, always swift to make judgements, decided there would be no misunderstandings with her in-laws. She felt so confident of her father-in-law's support that she told him that she intended to get married as soon as she returned to Kenya and then enrol as a nurse to nurse the carriers, something she would not have dared mention to her own father.

"Quite right, my dear, quite right," he said, "The sons of Ham are human beings and we are equal in the sight of God! You should certainly nurse them. I think that Oscar is a very lucky man!"

At that moment Olga felt reassured about Oscar, at the wisdom and love and goodness that had gone into his upbringing. She wanted only to be back in British East.

Where Olga met Oscar

* * *

Chapter Six

THE CHIEFTAINESS

The sons of Ham were going to have to wait. Olga's boat was late arriving in Mombasa and Oscar, who had returned from GEA to meet her, had to continue to Nairobi before she arrived. He left a letter; he wanted to meet her in Nairobi to discuss their future. In Nairobi he told her that the Central Railway in GEA had not been totally captured, and he now had to follow the troops slowly up the line. It would be better to postpone their marriage once more. Meanwhile he wanted Olga to sort out her finances before he married her. Once he had to take on the expenses of running a house, he could not take on the expenses of the farm as well. After two days each went back to their solitary lives. Oscar had sent a letter ahead to greet her.

"*I have been picturing you returning to your farm. The first appearance of the new bicycle taking a hungry lady up the hill. And was there not a drizzle. There ought to have been. The chieftainess has regained her crag and summoned her vassals, and is already no doubt hurling defiance at her ancient foes. War broods once more over Koru. My salaams to your friends and condolences to your foes – beware the internal hun!*"

The chieftainess was indeed suffering from the internal hun. The conditions she found brought out the worst in her. The house was dirty, the garden littered, and as Olga set to work with her usual energy, she discovered that things were even worse than they looked. The books had not been kept up, many of the workers said they had not been paid, some of them had left, and reports came from all sides that Smith had spent most of the time over at his brother's farm, and Olga's house had only been used for occasional visits. She wrote outpourings of her discontent to Oscar who wrote back that she must not blacken Smith's reputation since he was the brother of an officer under his command.

As the war took Oscar down south as far as Portuguese East Africa visits to the farm became a thing of the past. He wrote to John Ainsworth in Kisumu asking him to keep an eye on Olga. In those days administrators spent much time visiting their tribesmen, sitting round the camp-fire at night talking to the chiefs but occasionally dining with settlers and listening to their problems. This was the way a man kept in touch with his district. Ainsworth had heard so much about Olga's farm, for he had heard that she was attracting labour when no one else could obtain it, that he had already decided he would like to visit her. He gave her two days' notice before he arrived with his wife, two of his junior officers, several tribal chiefs, and two young settlers who had come to him seeking labour. He wanted to show them an exemplary farm before they started up on their own.

The safaris in those days proceeded in Indian file along the winding African paths, each of a dozen or so porters carrying a 60lb load on his head. Olga saw them coming from the distance and walked to the bottom of the hill to meet them. She had cleared some grassland, down by the river, dug three latrines at suitable distances one from another and put grass screens around each.

"You'll come up to tea?" she asked her visitors, and turning to the chiefs picturesquely clad in skins and beads, "and you'll come too, of course?" she added in Luo as she shook hands with them. They grinned with pleasure. John Ainsworth gave her full marks. Not every European woman in those days would have invited two naked African chiefs to tea with such aplomb.

"I have not had time to get the farm back in order yet." she kept repeating as she showed them round. Then two of her workers who had left under Smith's regime arrived back with their families. Everyone laughed when the children ran squealing to welcome Olga, the younger ones trying to clamber up her legs to see what she had in her pockets. Mrs Ainsworth had brought more books from her parents' mission and said they were still looking for a literate African who would be able to keep farm records as well as run the school. Ainsworth pronounced himself extremely impressed with all that had been done for the workers' welfare and comfort, and kept private his opinion that a woman as independent and dominating as Olga would make a difficult wife for a senior administrator. Members of a small service in a distant colony had to work as a team and accept team discipline. Discipline was the last word which came to mind when contemplating Olga. He recognized that everything she had accomplished on the farm demanded hard work and imaginative thinking. The colonial service gave wives little outlet for either of these abilities.

No visit goes off without a hitch, certainly not one to Olga. The Ainsworths were very fond of kippers, and had brought their latest consignment from England with them. Oscar's dog, Angel, who had been left with Olga, also developed a taste for them and removed them from the frying pan outside their tent at breakfast time, two days running. Mrs Ainsworth laughed heartily at the sight of her husband clad only in his shirt chasing Angel round the compound; John was not amused. Then one of the chiefs went down with a fever. Mrs Ainsworth went to attend to him and discovered he had strange spots reminiscent of the smallpox epidemic she had witnessed twenty years earlier. She called in Olga, who had never seen smallpox. The doctor at Kisumu was informed and telegraphed back that everyone was to stay where they were until he arrived.

"We have no food," said Olga, "and the shop has run out of everything!"

"Nor kippers!" said Ainsworth stiffly.

"We'll go shooting!" said the young settlers, looking at Olga for approval. Later that evening two large eland buck were delivered to her house.

"You can have one of them!" said Olga, to the farm hands who delivered the animals.

"We have been given three already, and the Bwana D.C's camp has one. These are for you!" Olga went to bed wondering how Cook would handle them, and how they had found five young bucks so quickly. Before long she was roused. The doctor had arrived on the night train and wanted to know where the spare room was. No, he had nothing with him, no bed, no bedding, no lamp, no food. Olga gave him a lamp, drinking water, a banana, and directed him to the guest house, which she kept always ready. The next morning he declared it was not smallpox and everyone could go home.

Olga stood outside her house to watch them leave, Ainsworth in his long khaki trousers and bush shirt, a great Wolseley helmet on his head, a map held in his hands, led the column, closely followed by his gun bearer with a loaded rifle in case they disturbed big game on the way. Next came Mrs Ainsworth riding her mule side-saddle and holding a parasol over her head, then a donkey laden with things which they might need during the day. Two settler farmers and the line of African chiefs followed the donkey, and a dozen porters and two more donkeys carrying the camp equipment straggled after them. Finally came two tribal policemen carrying rifles. The two junior administrative officers had been sent off earlier in a different direction. Travelling this way each safari would cover about fifteen miles a day. As Olga watched them, she felt she was watching her own future. There was just one thing about which she was sure. Never, never, would she ride a mule side-saddle nor would she carry a parasol.

The doctor had decided that he would return by train rather than walk and so he was with her until the evening. She showed him her little clinic and he checked her medicine cupboard for her. In the afternoon she started the long process of mincing boiled eland meat. She packed the mince into glass preserving jars, covered the meat with a layer of eland fat, and sealed the jar with a glass lid. She filled all her preserving jars and went on to use the empty glass jars left over from the cases of food she had bought at the outbreak of war. The method worked, the meat lasted for three years, until she left the farm.

About three weeks later a strange African came to the farm, arriving after dark. He stayed in one of the huts and fell ill during the night. He had a high fever and cried out for water. It was morning before she was told about him. She hurried down to see him. His hosts had deserted him.

"Did you take him water?" she asked.

"No, of course not," they said, "he might put his spell on us then we would die too!" He was indeed a very sick man. Olga had him carried on a bed to the little clinic, where she had a room put aside for very sick people. Three times a day she took him food and drink from her own kitchen. He did not speak, and would not eat, but he drank milk or warm sweet tea gratefully. Olga crushed aspirin into the tea and the fever abated. On the third day, just when she thought she saw signs of recovery, he died. He too had sores on his body. Was it smallpox? Olga sent a note to the doctor, but nobody came and that evening she buried him under the tree where she had buried her head man. Some days later she herself felt feverish and discovered she too had some spots. Did she have smallpox? Was she going to join those two men under the tree? Had she enough energy to fight a major illness, here alone on the farm? It was a long itchy night, and when Cook came in with the morning tea, she said:

"Cook, I think I may have smallpox. Will you stay with me and look after me if I am ill? You should not get it as you have been vaccinated."

"You have been vaccinated too!" he reminded her, "But if you do get it I'll stay with you, and I'll bring you food and water." Then he looked at her severely: "but there is one thing I will not do for you. I will not bury you. And this house is too good to burn," he added, "so it will have to be..."

"I know," said Olga, shuddering, "the hyenas!"

When she sat down that night to write her daily screed to Oscar it was difficult not to mention the smallpox – she always found it difficult not to mention what was foremost in her mind at that moment. But she wrote a cheerful letter all about the Ainsworths' visit, "a glimpse of a great empire at work", and wrote up her fears of smallpox in *The Adventures of Olivia.* The mysterious fever disappeared and so did the spots. The incident served to strengthen her determination to nurse Africans.

1916 was a rare kind of year when it rained too much and at the wrong time. It rained throughout the autumn. Floods cut off communications for weeks at a time, making Oscar's letters erratic and increasing her feeling of isolation. The buildings for the new coffee factory were washed away and she struggled to rebuild it in the wet. The young trees were so heavy with the hard green cherries that when at last the sun came out and the berries ripened she needed two shifts of workers to pick them, and she had to run the factory 12 hours each day. The engine she had bought in London sat in its own little shed chugging slowly and spitting out the red cherry skin on one side, the olive green coffee beans covered in a thick sticky white coat on the other. This stick had to be washed off, so the coffee was routed into yards of cement channels where it was stirred with huge paddles, left to soak for three days, then washed again in fresh water. Little gates of different heights were fitted into the channels, so that all the lightest coffee floated off the top, then a lower door was fitted and the next layer of beans floated off. At the bottom lay the heavy coffee which did not float, the grade 'A' coffee, which was carefully shovelled on to stretcher-like trays and laid out in long lines to dry. The trays had to be carried into the sun in the morning, and brought back under shelter at night. There was so much of it that Olga had trays on the verandah of her house. After that the coffee was packed into sacks. In peace time it would have been sent off to the coffee mills in Nairobi to have the outer husk rubbed off and to be graded for shipping. In war time each farmer had to look after his own, packing his own sacks, arranging the shipping himself, and when shipping was impossible, building his own granaries in which to store it.

Oscar wrote that despite the stock-piles of coffee, he could not find any roasted coffee to supply his officers' messes. His organization now had more than 150,000 men, of whom 1,000 officers and NCOs might each drink 3 cups of coffee a day – 26 tons a year, more than her total output. Olga promptly set up impromptu roasting machinery. First the husk has to be rubbed off. She recruited the farm children to use flat stones, like their mother's grinding stones, to rub the rough beans. The children loved it, as she paid them the money direct, ten cents for each debbie filled with milled coffee beans. When the harvesting season was over she lit log fires in the cement washing channels, and when they burnt down she set the metal coffee trays spread with green beans over the hot ashes, and the farm hands used long wooden paddles to stir the beans as they heated. It took two lots of fires to roast them an even, nut brown. It was convenient work, in that the raw beans kept well and could be roasted all through the year as orders came in and as other work permitted. Soon she was supplying not only the Carriers but also hotels in Nairobi and some Army units as well; no one else had thought to roast their own coffee in quantity, although many households roasted enough for their own use. She was also sending baskets of vegetables and eggs up and down the railway line to hotels and hospitals.

Sometimes she was working so hard she did not see another white person for weeks on end. She wrote to her mother: "*Solitude is strange. For the first two weeks it is quite pleasant, in the third week any visitor is welcome, and by the fourth I could kiss the postman!*"

Oscar knew she still suffered acute fits of depression, and asked various women of his acquaintance to visit her for a week or two at a time. One Mrs McClintoch, an Oxford classicist, wrote to Oscar after her visit, comparing Olga to the goddess Diana. "*The resemblance is most striking, but I gather that the problem of finding a husband for Diana was found insuperable even in the factory where all marriages are made. My logical training compels me to point out that it is only by destroying Diana that one can hope to attain the desired result.... I don't think I ever met anyone so out of tune with her surroundings as Olga.*"

Oscar wrote to Olga: *"Mrs McC loves you and likes me, but I am not sure that she thinks we shall run well together. We are both accustomed to rule. Are you sure you are ready to be ruled, because I am not*!"

Another recommended guest was so adept at helping with the farm that Olga took on a neighbour's farm five miles away for a few months and earned £20 a month, an elevated sum because she needed neither house nor keep. It kept her bank manager a bit happier.

That same year, the year of the great rains, she wrote to her mother: "*The mill will grind tomorrow. The fundi (artisan) says this pair of stones will grind 15 loads today, and another pair for which there is both water and room would grind the same. The mill sluice is taken through the banana plantation and it is now the ideal place to grow vegetables in the hot weather.*"

That Christmas Oscar arranged that Olga should stay at a little hotel, Brackenhurst, high in the hills north of Nairobi. She enjoyed it because there were a number of army wives there with their children, and she played with the children. She also made a firm friend of the proprietess, one Mrs Hudson Cane, who like Olga was a widow who earned her own living.

Back at the farm, in the dry weather, there was a forest fire. Olga took off her long socks, tied one round her mouth, gave the other one to her head man, and with him led her entire labour force as fire-fighters. They had to beat up-hill first, and then across the hill diagonally, and down. It took them three hours to bring it under control. Wisely she had the perseverance to make every one work a fourth hour to extinguish it.

Early in 1917 Oscar telegraphed for her to join him in Nairobi, where they were invited to dinner at Government house and Oscar was singled out for special treatment. They went to a concert and the Governor himself came down to escort them both back to his box. This gesture augured well for Oscar's future. The further away the pursuit of the German army, the more porters were needed, and the more difficult Oscar's job became. In order to attract more workers into his Carriers, he had inveigled John Ainsworth to join the Carriers at a rank above his own. Ainsworth had just been appointed to a newly created post, Chief Native Commissioner, but nevertheless agreed to Oscar's request and joined up. He was widely known and respected by Africans, who would be assured of fair treatment with him in command and would be more likely to join up themselves.

In August that same year Oscar telegraphed her again, to meet him this time in Kisumu. They then went to Nairobi; where Oscar had a motor to drive him on an inspection of a camp south of Nairobi. The road was so bad that Olga said it was like being thrown inside a milk churn. She looked so ill he insisted she see a doctor immediately, and on the doctor's instructions took her down to Mombasa. Going down to sea level was considered a remedy for overwork at high altitude.

On September 8th she wrote from Mombasa: "*We are being married this morning, and I am very, very happy. We had such a rush. Oscar arrived in Kisumu where I met him. 6 hours there, then two days on the farm, five days in Nairobi with work all day every day. I went ahead to the Coast as I was supposed to get down to sea level, and when Oscar turned up after doing an inspection at Voi we heard his ship (back to Dar-es-Salaam) would not be coming for another week, which gave us a whole week to the good. So today at 10.a.m we are being married very quietly. Mr Northcote, the D.C., is to give me away and Mrs Northcote will come with me to the church...Mr Paterson, the new manager, has arrived at this precise juncture of course.*"

September is one of the pleasantest months in Mombasa. The rains are over but the northern monsoon still blows fresh from the north east. Ali bin Salim, later Sir Ali, the Liwali (Arab administrator) for the Coast, lent them his house for their honeymoon. It was an old house built of coral rag in the Arab style, three stories high with each floor surrounded by wide cool verandahs to catch the monsoon from whatever direction it blew. The views over the old harbour were entrancing, and Oscar called it "My fairy palace," and the time they spent there as "an enchantment." For Olga it was a disappointment. Oscar was a totally inexperienced lover, and an exhausted one. The ghost of Darling Douglas lay heavily beside her. Olga's lack of sexual satisfaction lasted a long time, and at an early stage in this marriage she insisted not only on her own bed but her own bedroom. It says much for their mutual understanding of one other that their love continued to grow and neither ever looked at any one else.

On the morning of their wedding, the new manager recruited by Willie arrived. Right from the first meeting Olga doubted whether Mr Paterson was the kind of person she wanted as a manager. Oscar reminded her that for the salary she was offering she could not expect too much. Challenging discussions about farming were always to interrupt the time they spent together. She never needed to relax and found it difficult to understand why others should want to do so. She saw him sail for Dar-es-Salaam with a heavy heart. She was going to be separated from both the things she loved, the farm and Oscar, for she had promised that once the coffee picking was over she would leave the farm to the manager, and live in Nairobi where she would be on hand when he visited. They had agreed that the farm should be sold as soon as the war was over. Down at the quayside she saw the sick carriers who had arrived from Dar-es-Salaam being loaded into the train for Nairobi. She suddenly realized that she was now free to nurse them. And as Oscar's wife no one would prevent her.

Back on the farm she found she distrusted her manager even more than at first sight. She wrote to her mother: "*Mr Paterson has gone to Kisumu to get his hair cut. He is very dour, very silent, and very imbued with the idea of the amount of work here. He does about five hours a day and like all men makes awfully heavy weather of the intricacies of farming.*" She knew Oscar would be furious if she sacked him, and left the farm with a heavy heart. Why did no one, not even Oscar, understand how she loved the farm, how she and Douglas had created it, how wonderful it was to wake up on crisp cold mornings to see the mist swirling between her hill top and the great lake, and then to see the sun's rays on the mist, dispersing it. She loved the way the red laterite soil somehow made the green look so much greener. She loved the healthy herds, well kept farm buildings, the neat rows of coffee trees with their shiny leaves translucent in the sunlight, the branches white with flowers or red with berries. How was she going to manage without the farm, cooped up in a little tin bungalow in Nairobi?

Yet she knew Oscar was right, the farm was too full of ghosts, it was Douglas whom she remembered walking up from station, Douglas who seemed to sit with her on lonely evenings and talk to her. And now it was to Douglas that she built a memorial in the garden, a stone cross which is still there, a monument that would stand long after the bungalow had fallen into decay. She had carved those words inscribed in her heart: "If I do not come back you will know that I have done my bit."

Douglas had promised to take her on a trip round the district, calling on all the farmers round about. She decided that she would do this trip now, with a friend, one Miss Hervey. Oscar had bought her a horse to save her walking ten miles every day while she was running the second farm, and now she and her friend, who had brought her own horse, rode around the district, dropping in on farm after farm. Everyone they visited offered generous hospitality. At Koru there was a man trying to plough 1,000 acres with a steam plough. The plough plunged out of control, the driver was unhurt but hysterical, and his employer was now looking for a new man to train as a driver. At Kibos she found a government farm run by: "a nigger" from the West Indies. *"He speaks better English than many Englishmen, has perfect manners, and has all his meals with white people. Everyone does here from the lowest to the highest."* (The word 'nigger' was in no way derogatory, it was used to distinguish black Americans from indigenous Africans.) She was even more amazed at how many women were running their husbands' farms, and how they had all adopted the same sort of dress as herself, some kind of loose smock or tunic worn over long shorts or breeches tucked into knee socks. When she commented upon this, each replied:

"We heard about you, Mrs Watkins, and knew you to be a steady woman, so we followed suit." One Mrs Wilson had just fifty acres of well cultivated, clean, tidy coffee, she sang beautifully, but was an ineffectual sort of person, though very kind. At Fort Ternan she met a Miss Lepine: "*I did not like the look of her, she wears long earrings and low necks when the rest of us are in overalls, and is the sort of person who adores everything.*" This was her good-bye trip, to Koru, to the farm, to Douglas, to what might have been.

In Nairobi, Oscar had arranged for her to stay with friends of his, the man was away in the war, his wife, Madge Pedraza, was alone with small children. Although Olga became a great friend of Madge's and indeed god-mother to the next child, she was far too restless a person to live in anyone else's house for long. And there was her ambition to nurse Africans. By early December she had made a new start, writing to her mother:

"*I have been made senior sister of the lower hospital. Today the senior sister of the upper hospital being off, I am orderly sister for the entire hospital, 1,500 beds. I have twelve wards of thirty to forty beds each... yesterday 340 patients arrived, then three doctors. In all there are five sisters and two padres here. Within two hours of arrival each patient has had a dose of quinine and been assigned to his ward – each patient has four meals a day, three rounds of drinks of water, three rounds of medicines. There are three diets, one consists of brandy, arrow root, and milk; one of slops, milk cocoa, rice, cooked bananas and sugar cane; the full diet includes rice, meat, veg, cocoa, and posho (maize meal flour). The different diets are marked by coloured disks above the beds... of course those on the starvation diet get hungry and steal food from those on full diets. Orderlies take the food around – each ward has two orderlies and a sweeper. I mess with the doctors."*

Oscar did not hear of her enrolment as a nurse until later, because of postal delays. He wrote: '*it was a dear thing to do but I give only partial approval. A commandant's wife should not put herself under orders from one of his officers'*.

Oscar came up for Christmas and they stayed in the bandas Olga had built in the hospital compound. She had thought it a brilliant idea to provide her own accommodation where they both worked. Oscar said the last thing he wanted was to be accessible to all the depot officers while he was on leave. He needed a complete break. After Christmas she went up to the farm to see how it was getting on. She gave Paterson notice and wrote to her parents to find her yet another manager. All the time she was running a battle of words with her father who thought she was spending too much money on the farm – she was always asking them to send things out and somehow there was never the money to repay them immediately.

Olga had hoped to set an example to other women and encourage them to come out and nurse too. What she had not anticipated was the opposition from the older wives. In the colonies in those days social life was very formal, the mantra being: *We must keep the standards up*. A bride or new arrival setting up house would be called upon by other ladies who considered themselves of equal or superior rank. The new arrival would be expected to return the calls, and this would be followed by an exchange of invitations, first to tea, and later to dinner. During these visits the new-comer would be told all the local customs which grow up in a new settlement, how to treat her servants and people of other races, how to dress, whom she should know and whom it was beneath her to know. The last thing Olga wanted was *to keep up the standards* of suburbia in the midst of a war in Africa.

A bevy of hatted and gloved ladies travelled by rickshaw the long dusty road from the Hill where the officials lived to the

Carrier hospital on the race course near Muthaiga, to call on Olga in her bandas. The sentry pointed out the neat little white-washed huts to them "My dear, almost African," said the senior and most aggressive lady as they crossed the grass. Olga's servant was sent to find her. Inside the bandas were cool and comfortable, chintzy curtains on the windows, pretty watercolours painted by the aunts on the wall, and on the round table in the middle of the room stood a beautiful blue china bowl. "Majolica," said Mrs Aggressive, picking it up and turning it upside down, "Italian, I think. Must be from a good family!" She put the bowl back and each lady dug out her cards, one for herself and one for her husband as protocol demanded. Each, in order of her husband's rank, placed them in the bowl, one corner of one of each pair of cards turned down, to signify the husband had not been present.

Olga arrived in her extraordinary dress. She was wearing a white doctor's coat belted in to her narrow waist. It only reached her knees, not long enough for propriety, so underneath she wore khaki shorts to below the knee, with khaki knee-high cotton stockings. On her feet were sturdy farm shoes. Dark curls escaped wispily from the white muslin square perched on her head; her hastily washed hands were held out at waist level in front of her to dry. Her eyes were friendly and questioning, her smile welcoming. She was sure that here at last were women coming to offer their services at the hospital. Why, she wondered, did they look so grim.

"Mrs Watkins, do we understand that you are nursing black men?"

"Indeed yes, I am nursing Carriers, men serving under my husband."

"We think it an unsuitable occupation for a lady!"

Never at a loss for words, she retorted: "That's what they said to Florence Nightingale in the Crimea!"

"But she was not nursing black men!" said the second lady, her double chin wobbling with anger.

"Possibly not, but I don't expect there were black men fighting with the British forces," she replied.

"Well, we warn you, if you persist in this foolish behaviour, we shall none of us call on you. Seeing black men naked and ....and doing things to them puts you beyond the bounds of society."

"I am in good company with the Catholic sisters!" said Olga.

"Catholic sisters do not set the social tone!" Mrs Aggressive retorted.

"A pity," said Olga, then added: "It is probably just as well. I am so busy that I should not have time to return your calls. If you will excuse me now, I have to supervise supper for 700 men."

The first lady turned round sharply to face Olga. "You mean you are choosing them and not us?" she asked.

"I am choosing to nurse sick men fighting our war." Olga stuck to her guns.

"In which case, Mrs Watkins, you will be ostracized." Following their leader's example, each lady picked her cards out of the bowl, again in exact order of each husband's seniority. It took some time as Mrs Aggressive's cards were at the bottom of the bowl. The ladies trod out of Olga's mud hut delicately, as if shaking the dust off their feet. Olga was already supervising the supper, so many jugs of soup for each large tent, so many saucepans of rice. It was only later that night that she realized how rude she had been. She had not asked them to sit down nor offered them tea. Tea would have taken so long with only a primus stove, for she had no kitchen, no running water, few comforts in her bandas.

Oscar arrived early in the New Year and after two weeks working at the depot and continuous discussions with Dr Kauntze, the medical officer at the camp, he took her to the Blue Posts Hotel at Thika for a few days. Olga found this break even more disastrous than the honeymoon. Oscar was wearier and more distracted than before. The only relaxation to which he was accustomed, and which he now claimed, were long walks morning and evening on his own. On one occasion he did not return for supper until two hours after dark, and Olga had imagined him eaten by a lion, or gored by a buffalo, a hundred times before he eventually appeared, quite unaware that he had sinned. She was not one to hide her feelings.

When they went to the farm things went rather better. Olga was in charge on the farm, her routine was the one followed, and it was easy for him to get the exercise he always craved while she was busy on the farm. But she was fretful, irritable and seemed to lack energy.

"What's up?" he asked, "You are not your usual self!"

"I think I'm pregnant!" she replied.

"We must go straight back to Nairobi, and you must stop working!" he said, "I don't want you to have another miscarriage."

"I can't do nothing all the time, and you won't be there to look after me," she wept.

Oscar sat up later than usual that night thinking out domestic strategy. He had a terrible year ahead of him. Six months after the central railway had been captured the East African campaign showed no signs of abating. On the contrary, it seemed to be more challenging than before. The Germans had not surrendered but had instead vanished into the vastness of Southern GEA, crossing the border into Portuguese East Africa when necessary. The British generals had decided to chase them. Oscar thought this decision a waste of effort and lives, for the outcome of the war would be determined in Europe. As it was, each of four military commanders had charge of his own force and conducted his own chase. Oscar's problem was that units of his men had to be attached to each of these forces, and often the officers concerned had no idea how to look after African labour. His men had to work harder than the soldiers, carrying heavy loads long distances in appalling conditions, building their own roads and bridges as they went. It took him every ounce of his ability to see that these hundreds of thousands of men scattered over 1,000 miles from Mozambique to Burundi were fed, housed, clad, doctored, paid, recorded, and discharged – no man served more than two years. Olga, who had suffered so much in this war, needed him and he had no time for her. He considered reapplying for the house he had been offered and which Olga had spurned, but then thought again. The ladies she had offended would not make good neighbours. He wrote to Dr Kauntze, asking him to look after her while he was away.

Kauntze let her continue nursing until April. It was now that the folly of building the bandas in the depot became apparent. Olga had lived in them for about six months, but once she stopped nursing she could no longer stay in the grounds of an army hospital. Nor did the doctor think the environment was suitable, surrounded as she was by sick men, many with unknown diseases. Oscar had arranged that four kind invitations to stay would arrive, and Olga had no alternative but to accept them. She hated living in other people's houses, hated having to fit herself into their routines. However the first invitation was from Madge, and here she could devote herself to the children from the orphanage whom she was already visiting. Even while nursing, she had taken on two families, five little girls in all, took them out on Sundays, gave them treats, celebrated their birthdays, made clothes for them, and told Oscar she wanted to adopt all five. After the war most of them would return to relations in England. He asked her why she was always running out of money – he was sending her a good allowance, but he knew it was all going on the children. She also set about making a layette, sending the list to her mother: 6 binders, 6 long flannels (petticoats), 6 white robes, 6 night-gowns, 4 dozen nappies, masses of petticoats. She adds that: *"I am not getting a big outfit of long clothes because washing is so easy out here...and a baby is short-coated at three months. I have made six plain little silk frocks for boardship wear."* For herself she had provided two maternity skirts, several jumpers, a dress, and ten night-gowns.

It was not an easy pregnancy, Olga suffered several minor illnesses, had constant backache, and the months seemed to drag by. She moved from the Nairobi household to that of the Graham Bells, South Africans who had a big coffee farm and market garden about eight miles from Nairobi. The family had befriended Oscar in the Boer War. She got on well with old Colonel Bell, adored his grandchildren, but complained in her letters that the house was dark and depressing and the Colonel's daughter-in-law, who ran the house, was gloomy and grumpy. From them she went to the Northcotes, who had moved to Kiambu. This District Commissioner's household was the centre of interesting activity which would normally have fascinated Olga and have introduced her to life in the Administration. She felt restless and miserable, wanted her own house, her typewriter, and beyond all her farm.

Meanwhile, Oscar knew that the senior officer in Nairobi needed leave urgently and arranged to do his job for him during October, when the baby was due. Olga, who had conquered her fear of living in Africa alone and would sit up all night in the African outdoors to guard a dead body, was terrified of childbirth and was very tense; the labour was a prolonged one but unusually for those days Oscar stayed with her throughout. When she heard she had a daughter she could not stop weeping. She had so wanted a son. She longed for her mother, but mother was 3,000 miles away.

A month later the war was over. John Ainsworth resumed his 1916 appointment to the new post of Chief Native Commissioner in Nairobi and asked for Oscar to be his deputy. This was big promotion for Oscar. There were sixteen men above him on the list and now he was to be senior to them all. Houses had been allocated to both men and Oscar moved Olga and Pella (Penelope) into the new house before returning to Dar-es-Salaam in November 1918.

Olga became dangerously ill with inflammation of the breasts and had abscess after abscess. She took on a Seychellois nanny to look after the baby and once again Madge came to the rescue, taking all three into her own house so she could look after her.

While Olga was still recovering, she heard that various disasters had occurred on the farm. She packed up Penelope, asked one of Oscar's colleagues to accompany her, and set out for Khitari. At Koru station Penelope was placed into a tin bath and carried up the long road to the farm on the head of a porter. Olga looked round the farm, sat down and wept, hardly able to believe how much the place had deteriorated in the eight months she had been away. The farm workers crowded round her. No, they had not been paid, and a number of those whom she asked for by name had left. According to them, the new bwana stayed in the house all day drinking and was bad tempered if anyone took a problem to him, or reported machinery broken or tools lost. Olga sat on a tree trunk to think out what to do. Cook came looking for her. He was no longer wearing his blue garters and football boots, nor his fine white kanzu, but grubby trousers and a torn football shirt, cast out by Mann. He said the Seychellois nanny wanted her at once. Penelope was ill.

Olga ran up the hill and found nanny trying to change the baby, who was wailing a thin little scream. The baby's bottom as well as her face was an angry red colour, she had bad diarrhoea, and Olga could see she was dehydrating fast. Nanny said she had changed the baby so often, she had run out nappies.

"You mean, this started while we were in Nairobi?"

"Oh yes," she replied.

"Why did you not tell me?"

"Because you seemed so tired and so busy." Olga looked sadly at her first-born. Her Great Ormond Street training came in useful. There was nothing else for it, farm or no farm, she must go back to Nairobi that night. She would find a new manager in Nairobi, meanwhile she telegraphed Doctor Kauntze to meet her at the station the next morning. He was standing on the platform accompanied by one of the new VADs who had come to join the hospital as the result of Olga's example, and the girl carried a large towel and a baby's bottle of water mixed with salt and glucose. Kauntze had a car to drive them back to the camp. He confessed later that he did not think that Pella had any chance of survival, and it was Olga's care which had saved her.

In Europe peace was declared with the surrender of Germany on Nov 11. The surviving German troops, hidden in the wilds of Portuguese East Africa, had no communication with the outside world and did not hear. Oscar was leading his carriers in hot pursuit. When he returned from Lindi, in Southern GEA, to Dar-es-Salaam he had to wind down the Carrrier organization before he could take up his new job. He had 64,000 men in GEA and another 10,000 in British East. He had to make sure each was properly recorded and rewarded before he could take up his new job. He had also to search for many missing men, to try and determine whether they had survived or not, and to record what was owed to their dependants. All this was made more difficult by the occurrence of the flu epidemic. He lost several of his clerks on whom he relied, two doctors, and dozens of men.

When at last he returned to Nairobi in January he had to start again, closing down his depots in Mombasa and Nairobi and writing a report of the whole campaign. He tried to persuade Olga to go back to Europe before him, to see all her relations and family before he arrived, but she would not hear of it. A wife's place was near her husband and she would stay with him. She waited impatiently, feeling lonely and neglected at the hours he worked and the amount he travelled. She was sure it would all be better on board ship. It was a whole year later, January 1920, before they at last set sail. And it was not any better, but seemingly worse. Olga was one of those women who become extremely touchy when they are pregnant, and she was pregnant again.

The leave was a disaster, and influenced their future lives.

* * *

Chapter Seven

THE DIFFICULT YEARS

In these days of swift and easy travel it is hard to imagine the tedium and discomfort of those long sea voyages. Before the days of air conditioning, tempers as well as skin became prickly in the damp heat, collapse from heat stroke was a real and ever present danger. No sooner had the hot weather been left behind than it was rough and cold, too cold to sit on deck while the lounges and libraries became unbearably stuffy and cigarette smoke invaded every part of the ship, even the crowded little cabins occupied by non-smokers. British social snobbery was at its worst in the dining room where seating took place according to the head waiter's understanding of the husband's rank and with little regard for individual choice; even a handsome tip could achieve little more than a change of place, rarely a change of table.

Since no babies were allowed on the first class deck or in any of the public rooms, Olga had to spend her time on the nursery deck with the nannies and small children. She listened once again to the usual tale of woe from the stewards and stewardesses, long hours, low pay, poor food and other shortcomings. She wrote: "*We are building a hidden torrent of hatred against the system.*"

Olga disliked other social results of the British system. She resented the fact that Oscar found a bridge four and a chess partner more entertaining than joining her on the babies' deck, and that she saw him during the day only at meal times when she persuaded a nanny to watch over Pella. Throughout her children's childhood, Olga, like many modern mothers, was pulled two ways. She wanted to look after the children herself, and yet at the same time she resented the curtailment they imposed on her freedom, even greater then than now in that there were so many places where you could not take a baby. She resented even more the social demands which made employing help almost a necessity. She was right to make a fuss; for she and her generation changed the conditions for us, the next generation. When thirty years later my turn came to travel with children, nannies were a thing of the past and I could hand the children into an equipped and air-conditioned nursery every day and for a few blissful hours follow my own pursuits. I could eat my meals with them and put our cabin on the baby sitter list in the evenings.

It was a relief to disembark at Genoa and to take the train over the Brenner Pass to Innsbruck. Willie and Flo had returned to Austria in 1919 and immediately started The Tyrolean Famine Relief Service, harnessing Flo's Quaker friends in England and Willie's wealthy American contacts to provide food and clothing. It was heart breaking to see men as hard working and independent as the Tyrolean farmers looking for handouts to keep their children alive. The only people disappointed when Olga arrived were those villagers who – when they heard she had remarried in Africa – were expecting a fine up-standing African. An Anglo-Saxon with red-gold hair who looked like a university professor and was possessed of the retiring habits of a hermit was definitely a let down. Oscar loved the old castle and the history which lay behind it, the chapel with its beautiful crucifix, the opportunity to take long walks into the mountains. He already admired his mother-in-law; and now grew to admire Willie. The old man was putting his rapidly declining energy into feeding the hungry. He was still irascible, and Pella summed him up by calling him *No! No!*

It was a short visit – Oscar was impatient to reach England. He had not seen his own parents for eight years. They went straight to the Oxford vicarage, where Pella brightened her grandfather's services by standing up in the pew when he processed into the church, waving at him, calling out Grandpa, and then imitating his every gesture. She was a good mimic. In the vicarage she would stand at the top of the stairs, wrap a white towel round herself, and practise intoning her nonsense baby syllables.

Oscar at once took off for London to present his various reports and claims for the Carriers to the Colonial Office. He wrote to his friend Keble Martin with whose family he had spent so much time as a boy and a young man when his parents were in India. Keble was in Yorkshire and it would be difficult to visit him. Keble asked him to look out for another member of their old set, Dora Iremonger. She was just back from India, had two daughters and a shaky marriage. Oscar took her to dinner and the theatre, then promised to help her educate her daughters should the need arise. He mentioned this casually to Olga some days later, to let loose a volcano of bitter invective.

"I never went out with a man to dinner, all the time I was in Nairobi alone!" she wept.

"Why ever not?" replied Oscar. "I would not have minded!"

Oscar could not believe that any one could distrust him or even suspect he could do anything dishonourable. This argument developed into a rift which took time and effort to repair. Olga removed herself from the vicarage to the shelter of the Aunts at Boxley Abbey; she was in any case finding social life in Oxford less than exciting. She then had to go through the ritual of introducing Oscar to all her other relations. There were plenty of them. She was by now very pregnant and Oscar could do no right, which meant that the cousins thought he was a weak man whom she had married in a moment of despair. What sort of a man spent all his leave running round government offices in London when he should be giving his poor wife a good time? Were the needs of a handful of pagans in a distant country sufficient reason to neglect his wife? Olga was feeling far too ill to want a good time, but she did feel neglected.

When he went back to Kenya he was alone, leaving Olga to have the baby in England. He was careful to stress in his letters how he was avoiding female company, how he had chosen a table at which there were only men, how he had made a bridge four the same way, and the only women he mentioned were those who collapsed with heat in the Red Sea and blamed their husbands for bringing them out at that time of year. On the boat also were Sir Edward and Lady Northey, the new Governor and his lady. On July 24 half the British East, as the Protectorate was known, had become the brand new Colony of Kenya. Uganda would remain a protectorate, and the Coastal Strip as a complicated leasehold from the Sultan of Zanzibar. Oscar reported that a great deal of social jockeying and currying of favour was going on and he was careful to steer clear.

On arrival in Nairobi he took possession of their old house. Like all government houses, it had been occupied by a junior officer in their absence. It had been left dirty, half the furniture had disappeared and the other half was damaged. Both his car and his rickshaw were unusable, and even Jacky was referred to as "that man-killing donkey of yours." Apparently Jacky had nipped the five year old daughter of the occupant, who considered the donkey could no longer be considered safe, and had sent him off to the veterinary farm.

When John Ainsworth retired in August, he re-iterated his view that the African was not lazy, it was the European who lacked understanding. It was a heartfelt statement, but a tactless one for the unpopularity would fall on his successor. Oscar wrote to Olga: *"Poor John! He leaves here criticised for being a negrophile, and when he arrives in his native Manchester will no doubt be equally criticised as a slave driver. It is an unjust life."*

Olga remained in Boxley Abbey for the birth. Here she was given the treatment she had always had, the best room, her favourite food served at the right intervals, a nanny to look after Pella and a nurse to look after herself. She was the centre of the household, petted and fussed, and enjoyed every minute. Veronica was born on August 30, and was once again greeted with tears for not being a boy. Oscar wrote: "*My Darling, It is ripping to think that you will be back here in two months as the pace of ships has improved so much. I had not realized the weight that was on my mind until it was lifted. You must be very careful what you say about the Northeys as just now there is a general cry of favouritism, and people are rather currying favour, so they say, by carrying tales of what so and so said. I always say that everybody is charming. My problems with the Public Works Department (over the state of his house) have grown into a full scale row and I am threatening to take it to the Governor."*

His next letter said: "*It is our third wedding anniversary next week and we have spent less than a year of that time together. It will be nice to have you back. You know I am quite happy if you give me congenial work and a restful home without any frills at all and there is a big and interesting position for you if only you can take and fill it but we both have to grow to it and go slowly while we do. I do hope you are going to be a nice girl and help me with my Legco (Legislative Council) work by not grumbling at seeing very little of me when you first arrive."*

Olga was kept flat on her back for three weeks, as was the custom of the day, and three weeks after that was on the boat to Mombasa. Nanny and both children shared her cabin, and the four weeks' voyage was not enhanced when it was discovered that Nanny was an even worse sailor than Olga, while Pella, an active two year old, remained unaffected by the rough seas and had of course to be watched every moment of the day.

On arrival in November 1920 Olga found herself once again mistress of one of the biggest bungalows on the hill, with a wonderful view of the plains where Wilson airport now lies, in those days still a wilderness occupied by huge herds of game. Jacky, liberated from the veterinary farm, would go off to join the zebras when he felt like home comforts. The moment he saw Olga, he eey-ored with ear splitting delight, munched his carrots, permitted the new baby baskets she had bought in Rye to be strapped to his back, and willingly accepted his new role of perambulator.

The other wives played bridge, golf, and tennis, organized musical evenings and kept up an endless round of coffee mornings. Olga read the papers with the many letters about inadequate African housing and walked two miles down to Pangani to see for herself what was going up in the way of new housing for African labour. She was horrified that only 'bed spaces' for bachelors were being provided – no housing for families, no room for wives, no proper washing or cooking arrangements, just dreary dormitories each for eight or more men. This was not bringing civilization to Africa, this was exploiting the workers, and introducing them to new, and dangerously deprived, living conditions. She would have to do something about it. These sentiments undoubtedly made her more supportive of Oscar in his efforts to achieve good administration for the whole colony but her determination that she must herself do something did not make his life easier.

Nor had poor living conditions escaped public attention. In fact the newly established Municipal Council of Nairobi had been set up precisely because the town had out-grown being administered by one District Commissioner. There was now a white population of 2,000, but only 491 voters were on the council role. More than double the number of Indians had yet to be given the municipal vote. As a new institution the Council was feeling its way. Throughout 1920 the weekly newspaper, the *Leader*, published articles and comments about it, how it had "*expressed a unanimous desire to have the simple title of 'Chairman' changed to 'Mayor'*". It also listed the matters which had come up for attention, *the leakage of public finance, lack of organization in running Nairobi, the need for street islands in the great wide streets, unattended vehicles, street nomenclature, casual native labour, building plans, town planning, the need for a YMCA, and the presence of a telephone post in the middle of Government Road. Volunteers were needed to form a fire brigade.*" Olga set her sights on becoming an elected member of the Municipal Council.

The fact that Kenya had become a colony altered the position of settlers who now expected the same powers of local government that they would have in their home countries. The only, but all important, difference was that they assumed responsibility for the Africans in their midst. Several letters written to the *Leader* deplored African and Indian housing conditions, pleaded for segregated and well organized housing for the different communities, and for a municipal franchise for the Indians. On Christmas day this theme was repeated with the urgent need for improved African housing. At this point in time, what we would today call the culture clash was too great for housing not to be segregated. The British and other Europeans were 100% literate and mostly from the professional classes; and the women considered themselves people in their own right; the African was 99% illiterate, unaccustomed to the discipline needed to live in large communities, and considered women as chattels. The Asians were more a cross section of India. There were a few professionals, doctors and lawyers, a handful of immensely rich and very efficient business men, and a large mass of the poorer castes, the men were mostly literate, but not the women who lacked both the education and the wish to be active outside their homes.

Olga was already a member of the East Africa Women's League which had been founded during the war, intended as a support group for white women who too often fell into difficulties in a pioneer country, particularly with their men at the front. The League had achieved full voting rights for white women – in England men could vote at the age of 21 but women had only just acquired the vote and could not use it until they were thirty. In Kenya women had equal rights with men from the start of Legislative Council as an elected body.

At the League's AGM in early 1921 Olga failed to interest the members in better housing for Africans, but she did manage to interest them in providing a place of safety for European children bereft of their parents, either temporarily or permanently. There were some tragic cases, father in prison and mother dying of malaria; both parents alcoholics; or simply father away on safari and mother suddenly taken ill. Sometimes the children were taken in by a neighbour – Olga's own nursery was always filled to overflowing with other people's children – but a permanent place of safety was needed. The old lady who had made a large bungalow into an orphanage which Olga had so often visited during the war had now closed down, and some place of safety for young children was urgently needed. In Olga's view it should not be a long stay orphanage, the very few children who were not reclaimed by their own parents or by relatives should be returned to their own countries, but it could take time to make the necessary arrangements.

There was also a quite separate need for a crèche in central Nairobi where younger children could be parked for the day. Within two months of arriving back she was asked by the League to represent them on the new Municipal Council to press for immediate provision of a crèche. The League already had a splendid site in Sixth Avenue and needed only official backing and some assistance with funds. This scheme could go ahead quickly and cheaply, and later they could provide the longer-stay home. There was near unanimous support for this plan of action, but one important dissention. That was from Lady Northey, ex-officio chairman of the league. She resigned in protest – the League should not take part in politics.

This is not politics, this is childcare, women's work, declared Olga, not to be put off by a carping governor's wife. *"Nor,"* she said firmly, "*am I a candidate for the EAWL, a non political body. I am standing as someone who wishes to see women and children represented on MunCo. I am chiefly interested in housing, and in the welfare of all the women and children of Nairobi."* She stood for Municipal Council and was elected, only to be immediately disqualified because her seconder was not on the municipal role. The council went into session, and nominated Olga as a member to represent women's interests.

There were photos of Olga in the paper, and interviews as Personality of the Week, all of which gave her the opportunity to speak of her experiences running her own farm for four years and her conviction that better African housing was essential. Lady

Northey was not amused. The crèche was never achieved, but the Lady Northey Home for Children was built just below Government House and remained in use for at least fifty years.

Municipal Council debates were not going to set the world alight. Indeed, some of them were intended to achieve the opposite effect – how to organize a volunteer fire brigade. Olga was adamant that Africans should be included. They had shown great courage during the war and would continue to do so in peacetime. And then there was that time-honoured subject – sewage. When a motor cyclist collided with a night-soil cart, to the detriment of both, though no one, not even the donkey was hurt, Olga said that the carts must have lights at night before a worse accident occurred. When she looked into the matter, she found that estimates for making the carts were much too high and suggested that prisons and reformatories, as well as private contractors, should submit estimates for making night soil carts. The private contractors said carts made by the prisons would be inferior, and she suggested some be made by each institution and their performances compared with those of the contractors. She also thought the dog-pound badly run – a dog she sent there that morning had returned home hours later minus its chain. She thought that Africans should be allowed to continue bathing in Nairobi River at Ainsworth Bridge until such time as better washing facilities had been provided for them. She was put on the special committee for council salaries but was not able to suggest any economies. In January 1922 she resigned owing to ill health.

Oscar had decided that anything was better than having Olga publicly voicing all kinds of opinions rubbing up the backs of officials as well as settlers. He felt considerable sympathy with her views but her strongly worded expression of them did his public image no good. He decided she must have a farm, and as soon as Khitari had been sold he took her farm-hunting on his motor bike. Distances were long, roads were bumpy, and a miscarriage threatened. She recovered temporarily, only to loose the baby later.

The settlers were already challenging Oscar's suitability to take over the job of Chief Native Commissioner. He was much too pro-African. He had made many enemies in the war, when he had condemned much food supplied by contractors as unfit for human consumption. Before he left Kenya in 1920, Governor Belfield had told Oscar he was confirmed in his job of Deputy CNC. It was widely assumed he would then walk into John Ainsworth's shoes when he retired. On Jan 29 when Mr Rodwell asked in Legislative Council who was going to be appointed to the post of CNC, the Governor said he could say nothing at the moment. He had already declared that European interests must be paramount. He had in fact already written to South Africa and found two inspectors of labour either of whom he considered suitable to take over Oscar's job. Fortunately this proved too much for the Colonial Office. It was Sir Edward Northey, not Oscar Watkins, who was recalled on June 24 for talks with Winston Churchill, then Secretary of State for the Colonies. Sir Edward never returned.

* * * * * * *

Leave was again due to them and at the end of 1922 Olga had reason enough to go back to Europe before Oscar. On November 27 her mother wrote:

This morning your dear father passed away suddenly, so suddenly I can scarce believe it is true. He seemed so well these last days, the headache which had worried him as well as myself had gone. This morning he was rather restless and asked me why the girls were so late in bringing the water and waking us. I said "It's Sunday." He got up, then came back to bed very cold and I told him that he would catch cold if he walked about without a dressing gown. When we were called, he got up first, had his bath and said I was lazy and must get up too. However when I was dressed he said he did not feel very well and would take one of the tablets the Doctor gave him in case he felt an attack coming on. He did not feel breathless, came down to breakfast, and said "Oh, I don't feel like anything!' so I poured him out a cup of tea and said: "Take just a little!" but noticed that he did not, so I took hold of his hand and felt his pulse. It was very strong and jumpy but has been so for long. I said "It is jerky but not more so than usual." I then poured a cup of tea for myself, heard a slight noise, looked up and saw that the end had come. He breathed quickly a few times and then no more. A lovely quiet death. Poor dear, he worked all yesterday and the day before at those blessed bills and audits. Much too much for him, but he could not leave it. He really died in harness, looking after other people's families for nothing."

Her brother, Tom, also begged her to come back as soon as she could as their mother needed her and he felt *such a booby in the face of such grief.* Tom confirmed the work his father was doing, the mountains of paper work and piles of audit sheets. Nor was this their only bad news. Oscar's father had developed diabetes and insulin had yet to come into general use. One of the more disastrous results was that they would have to leave the vicarage and had made no provision for such a contingency. They had nowhere to go; nor were their children well placed to help. Lawrence in India and Oscar in Africa had each a growing family to support, while their sister Dorothy was in a convent. With the collapse of both parental houses, Olga determined that she must buy a house in England. It was going to be a busy leave.

Flo gave her the warmest of welcomes; conditions were recovering in Austria, although she had herself packed some 152 Christmas parcels and was now planning ways and means of distributing food and clothes to distant mountain hamlets. Olga left Nanny there with the two children. In England she went at once to the Oxford vicarage where her father-in-law was already so doddery that he would lose his place in the middle of a sermon. Soon he would be unfit to take any service at all and the vicarage would be wanted for the new man. She found a small house for them in Winchester Road in Oxford and put down a deposit on it. She booked builders and plumbers to install gas fires, gas cooking, and hot water, planning out each room of the house to make it as labour saving as possible for the one maid of all work they would be able to afford. She showed an extraordinary foresight into the demands of old age, making the two downstairs rooms into sitting rooms, one as a study for the old man, the other a sitting room which the old lady referred to as *my boudoir*. The dining room was put in the basement, an unheard of idea in those days – it doubled as the maid's sitting room and saved her from carrying trays up and down stairs. Olga knew the sensible thing would have been to buy a larger house in Oxford and to divide it into two so that both sons' families could keep an eye on the parents when they were over on leave, but such was her feeling of hurt from her last visit she could not bring herself to do this.

Instead she then went house-hunting for herself in Kent. She found an old inn at Four Throws near the village of Hawkhurst; on the weald of Kent, an easy bus ride from the Aunts at Maidstone. It was a roomy old house with plenty of outbuildings and five acres of fields. Flo offered a mortgage. Olga started workmen on both houses, in Oxford as well as Hawkhurst, and then escorted her parents-in-law on the long journey to Matzen. Oscar met them there on his way back from Kenya. Flo entertained them all nobly, the old vicar celebrated the Eucharist every day in the Castle's chapel, Tom, Evelyn, and the boys joined the party, and the four grandchildren thrived with the attention centred on them. When Oscar brought the old couple back again it was time to install them in Winchester Road. Each wrote individually to thank Olga: "*Fancy, hot water and gas fires on demand! We have never had such luxury before,"* wrote the old lady, and the old man added: "*How clever of you Olga, I have almost enough room for all my books. I never expected that in so small a house. And it is hardly further from the Bodleian than the vicarage was!"* Within the next seven years, they were both to die in that house.

At this point Olga received a letter from the War Graves Commission – they wanted her consent to move Douglas's remains from where he had fallen in Tanganyika Territory, as GEA had become, to a war cemetery they were setting up at Mwanza, a little town on the southern tip of Lake Victoria Nyanza. "Let him lie in peace where he is" said Olga, and burst into tears.

"My dear, you should consult his parents, and I think probably he should be moved." Oscar remonstrated. "Otherwise his grave will disappear."

"You do it" said Olga, and after a pause: "They must put on his gravestone the words *'If I do not come back you will know that I have done my bit'*. Oscar wrote to Colonel Thompson and persuaded Flo to take Pella to see the Thompsons and to keep them up to date with Olga's activities. He put the War Graves Commission on his list for his next visit to London. The Thompsons always refused Olga's offers to repay the money she had received for Khitari, but they longed to keep in touch with her. They had no grandchildren of their own and wanted us as proxy ones. Olga would not, could not, reciprocate. The very mention of Douglas's name could produce unexpected tears.

At Four Throws, the old Inn and its out buildings were in poor condition, but she loved to do them up, undertaking much of the work herself as well as supervising everything else that was going on. She was due to return to Kenya at the end of the year and was planting fruit trees in the new orchard when she felt a great pain and realized that she was starting a miscarriage at a much earlier stage than the time before. She was put to bed for a week. Miscarriage threatened a month later, when she was again working in the garden. This time she was put to bed for three weeks and told she must not travel. Oscar went off alone, with her instructions to put down money on farmland they had seen just before they left.

After three weeks in bed she decided the maids' sitting room needed painting and new curtains. She painted it herself and was hanging the curtains when trouble again started. This time she was warned that if she wanted the baby she must stay on her back for the remainder of the pregnancy. It was only January and the baby was not due until June. Her mother had come over for Christmas and promised to stay. Olga's nerviness started again. She felt alone and deserted upstairs in her room, so had her bed brought down into the dining room where all the family could gather around her. When they did, she wrote to Oscar how irritating she found each and every one of them, including her mother. She also wrote that approaching child-birth was like *going over the top* for a man in war-time. She was nervous at night sleeping alone and had Nanny move her bed down stairs as well. This meant she had to take on another nurse to look after the children. Nanny sent for her younger sister, Mary. Mary was not yet fifteen but she proved a Trojan worker and was wonderful with children. She loved her job, and having a bed to herself for the first time in her life.

Olga was running a large household. Tom and Evelyn were off to the Persian Gulf and Flo had promised to take their two boys with their own Nanny. Olga adored the boys but the two nannies did not get on. Other Kenya parents heard Olga had a large house and staff and found it an ideal place to park their children while they enjoyed 'home leave'. She could never say no, but resented intensely two teenage girls who would lounge about her room doing nothing all day. Flo thought it was wonderful to have a house to which she could ask her English friends and relations and they all flocked down to see her. Olga found she needed a cook, two housemaids, a kitchen maid, and a gardener, in addition to the two nurses, and even then was always short handed. Oscar sent every penny he could but it was never enough, and when he remonstrated that she was getting much more than most wives, she said: "We are not extravagant; I always buy margarine instead of butter."

The months dragged by. Spring came and she ventured into the garden, usually in a wheel chair, and supervised outdoor operations. From her sick bed she had purchased a cow and chickens and the gardener, a man lamed in the war, ran a flourishing dairy. She was now impatient to build a tennis court. She herself did not play games and it would be a long time before the children did, but Olga insisted it would add to the value of the house. Oscar replaced lunch at the club with a sandwich and rationed himself on the whiskey and pipe tobacco he so much enjoyed.

At last, on the morning of midsummer's day, 1923, the baby started. After a six-hour labour Olga greeted a third girl with: "*Take the little frog away!*" Nanny did so.

"*I have a lovely surprise for you*!" Nanny said to Pella and Veronica as they came in from playing with Mary in the hayfield behind the house.

"Is it a kitten?" asked Pella hopefully.

"No, look, it is a darling baby sister!" Nanny squatted down so they could see the baby.

"I'm Baby, I'm Nanny's darling," screamed Veronica, promptly throwing a terrible two's tantrum.

"Of course you are!" soothed Nanny. "We'll call her Tiny Wee, shall we?" Tiny Wee I remained.

The doctor and Flo both wrote reassuring letters to Oscar that the baby was both beautiful and healthy. Flo said she had never seen such a storm of tears as that with which Olga greeted a third girl and the doctor that he had never attended a case where the mother was so overwrought and highly strung, and advised strongly against any further children. This was confirmed when Olga started to resume her farming operations – and developed thrombosis in the left leg. Once again she was put to bed and could only go out in a wheel chair. One of the god-mothers drove the old vicar and his wife from Oxford to Hawkhurst to take the christening. It was nearly three months before Olga was ready to pack up, let the house, and set sail for Kenya.

In that time Nanny heard that her mother was dying and felt she must go back to Scotland to nurse her, but her family could spare Mary to stay with Olga. Olga knew that Nanny was genuinely disappointed at having to leave, for she had left her heart in Kenya with a young man at the Scots Mission there. She decided she would take Mary as she was keen to travel, but she was too young and inexperienced to take full charge. The midwife, Nurse Austin, applied for the job even before Olga advertised it, and was engaged.

Oscar wrote asking Olga if she was sure she could manage with only two nurses for three children, as he could if necessary pay for a third girl to help out. The financial relief of no longer having to keep up Four Throws would be enormous. It was part of the job that he had to maintain a large house in Kenya and do much official entertaining. With all the family under one roof finances would no longer be a problem. But they would not be under that roof for long, not now Olga had another wild piece of Africa to cherish.

* * *

Chapter Eight

WISPERS FARM

The *Llandovery Castle* passenger list for October 1923 included the names: "Mrs O.F.Watkins with three daughters and two nurses." Oscar met them at Mombasa, delighted to have his family back at last. In Nairobi Jacky greeted Olga with his usual exuberance and introduced his new girlfriends, two conspicuously fat zebras grazing round the garden. She was happy to include baby 'zonkeys' in her menagerie but fat lazy zebras without their herd to defend them might prove too attractive to lions. Nurse Austin announced "I wasna' trained for that," that being Olga's instructions on emergency tactics if lions did appear on the scene, and she started to look for a passage back to England.

Olga was brimming over with energy at the excitement of planning the new farm, frustrated only because the process of buying was so slow. It was August 1924 before she could write to Flo:

"*We have bought 140 acres 6 miles from Nairobi. A delightful situation with four roads of access, two through beautiful forest. At first we started clearing it from Nairobi but it rapidly grew beyond twice-weekly visits and we got a not very comfortable but cool house within three miles from my work. Oscar goes into Nairobi daily and I turn out at 6.30 a.m. and remain on the farm until 12.30, ploughing, cross ploughing and harrowing ninety acres of land. I hope to get the whole planted up by the next long rains and to that end am working hard. We took up some capital for the farm and £850 for a small house. We must run it on Oscar's screw and whatever I may be able to earn with transport, etc. In four years the coffee will start to pay, just when O may go on to pension. If we get a good price any time after next year we shall sell out, I expect. In the meantime we have a good proposition but one which is draining us of every scrap of income. The house is starting this week. I have had to cut all the stone for the foundations in a quarry we found in the forest two miles off, then I had to set to and make a road from the quarry which took twenty men 4 weeks. It will be a brick house with a tiled roof, very plain. I have got a store built already and the labourers' thatched houses are going up – we hope to give them stone quarters soon.*

We have got a ram (water-pump driven by water) installed that takes water to the house. We have seven acres of swamp which is now being cleared and is one of the toughest jobs I have ever undertaken. The water is ankle deep in some places, and in others knee deep. The soil is thick mud. The grass is well over my head, in some places papyrus 15ft high. The swamp should be valuable for market gardens and we are near Nairobi so we must clear it, ditch it and drain it out."

A new farm, but what to call it? Olga decided against having a local name, such as Khitari, which people found difficult to remember. She decided to call it Wispers. Her grandfather, Tom Nickalls, had died when she was 11 and her grandmother with her five unmarried daughters had moved from Patteson Court to a smaller house, Wispers, in Sussex. Olga had spent many happy holidays there and she loved the name. Oscar said:

"Wispers is misleading, it ought to be shouts!" It was not for nothing that at Khitari she had been nicknamed Agishu, after the legendary Luo chief who lived on a hill and used his loud voice to summon his minions when he needed them. Oscar was given a week to think of a better name, but he was pre-occupied and Wispers it remained.

Olga worked out her own development plan and budget. She had taken up all their capital, £3,000, to buy it. This was to be divided £2,200 for the land, £700 to build the house, and £200 to start the running expenses of the farm. It was at this point that Olga took complete charge not only of the farm finances but also of the family ones, keeping detailed accounts of all expenditure. Few men in those days would have handed over both their entire salary and their capital to their wives, but Oscar did, keeping only his allowances – about a quarter of his salary – for himself. From this he paid for the family car as well as club subscriptions and such alcohol as they needed for entertaining.

She was always an economical housekeeper, her household expenses were low and the cost of living even lower. Light (kerosene oil for lamps) for the entire family cost £1.00 a month, milk £3.00, vegetables, £1.00, stationery £1.00, groceries and meat £15, and minor repairs £2.00. She employed a huge household, governess and nurse, white farm manager, five house servants and forty men on the farm. Although she budgeted carefully, she usually overlooked a number of vital items in her budget so it never ran according to plan. The main leak was their extraordinary generosity to everyone, providing hospitality to strangers and help to anyone who had fallen on hard times. Oscar was proud to be able to indulge her by supporting the farm, and the many lame ducks she liked to help. He found Wispers a welcome refuge from an increasingly hostile work place. Most senior civil servants lived next door to each other on the hill, frequented Nairobi club, their proximity to one another fomenting gossip and intrigue. Why was X invited to Government House for tennis and bridge, when Y, who was two years senior, was not. At Wispers discussions were more down to earth. How could Olga persuade a doctor, any doctor, to come out to Wispers whenever she needed one at the little hospital she had set up, or how could she find a job for some unfortunate young woman who had been sacked.

Olga was still susceptible to blood poisoning and yet would often disregard minor wounds. In our childhood in those pre-antibiotic days, I can hardly remember her without some portion of her anatomy bandaged. An eye shield, a finger shield, a boil dressing, an arm in a sling, a bandaged foot. In December 1924 she developed blood poisoning sufficiently severe to demand hospitalisation and as there was no suitable hospital bed available in Nairobi she was sent to Mombasa. She and Oscar wrote to each other every day, he reporting that she had missed Tiny Wee's first steps, she describing her fellow patients with a humorous pen. He had been trying to get her a bull-dog puppy for years, now at last he found one and bought it to welcome her home.

Olga started the New Year, 1925, with a huge effort to earn some money. Only a mile from Wispers was a brick works owned by a Cockney, Tom Young. He and his wife had at once befriended the entire family and supplied her orders ahead of any one else's. The brick-works were the only neighbours within easy walking distance and soon became a favourite place for the children to visit on afternoon walks. They were always given lumps of clay to play with and allowed to leave their creations for firing in the brick ovens. Jacky always accompanied the walk and Ronny and Tiny Wee travelled in comfort on his back.

Olga now had access to convenient quarries for stone, sand, and murram, well trained oxen and herders to transport building materials, a work gang who regarded her sufficiently to swarm down from Victoria Nyanza 300 miles away the moment they heard she had a new farm. She took on a Seychellois mason, Meriton, and his friend the carpenter, with whom she would have long conversations in French as they laid the foundations and made the fittings for the new house. She now advertised that she would deliver stone, murram, and sand, and would pave drives, build garden walls, garages, and servants' houses in the wealthy Muthaiga suburb. She would also supply raspberry canes, watercress roots, farmyard manure, mulching grass and hard-wood fencing posts. She would harrow or plough land, or bring a team of 25 African labourers for a day's supervised work. In the morning she would appear at some wealthy Muthaiga house in her farm kit and complete whatever task was on hand, sometimes being offered a hot drink on the verandah when the lady of the house might exchange a few words with her. No one knew quite how to treat this extraordinary woman but she did good work at a low price and was far less intimidating than Asian contractors who often spoke little English and did not understand what was wanted. In the evening the same householder might well meet her at some social function or at Government House. Olga said that not one of them ever recognized her despite her height and distinctive looks, though many looked at her as if they were wondering where they had seen her before. She had only two evening gowns, a formal black taffeta one which lasted at least thirty years, and a brocade which Flo had designed for herself for her coming out parties in the 1880's. Flo had outgrown it but Olga never did, and later handed it on to Ronny who looked marvellous in it.

At Government House seating was formal, and Olga had often to go into dinner with the new Chief Native Commissioner, a man brought in from Fiji to do the job which was to have been Oscar's. He was short and stout, and unkind observers nicknamed them beauty and the beast. He always took over the conversation, telling her how they did things in Fiji, and soon he was known as Wee Wee Fiji. Olga was a useful guest, in that she had command of several languages; once an important Frenchman was asked to take her in because he spoke no English. They had an amicable conversation for a few courses, when suddenly he turned to her and said: "Tell me Madame, how long is it since you left the Seychelles?" She had picked up the accent from Meriton, her stone mason. Seychellois French is to French what Jamaican English is to English.

She still wrote and the result of one article was the offer to become the editor of a new magazine at the salary of £250 a year, about what a new administrative officer earned. She wrote to her mother that she would much rather be a magazine editor than a building contractor, but as a contractor she could earn far more and also make her own hours so as to be available for us children. In 1925 and 1926 she earned £600 a year, more than a District Commissioner's pay, and a great help in setting up the farm. The contractors said she, a senior administrator's wife, was taking work from them and could only offer lower prices because she was subsidised by her husband. The criticism became aggressive when she won the contract to build the new electricity booths every mile or so along the Muthaiga road. Olga's friends congratulated her and nicknamed the square brick huts with tiled roofs *little Olgas.* She charged £100 for each *little Olga,* the same amount as for a garage with double doors or a servant's house. Her other speciality was building outdoor conveniences, as the long-drop lavatory in the garden was called. There were still no sewers in Nairobi, night soil was collected in carts; in the suburbs householders provided their own cess pits, and most households had at least one long drop in the garden – a deep hole with a packing case rough cut above it. As these lavatories were re-sited fairly frequently they were often built with mud walls and a thatched roof. On one occasion someone visiting Olga asked her how much such a lavatory would cost. Olga took the man out of the back door at Wispers, pointed to our own long drop of mud and thatch, and said: "You can have that one as it stands for £10." A voice from inside said: "Thank you!" Oscar always said he was the only man to have been sold by his wife for £10, with a lavatory thrown in.

Flo's weekly letters to Olga were mostly full of her own activities, the castle which needed continual care and repair, her stream of visitors in the summer, when she often had nineteen to meals and rarely less than five houseguests, the problems of heating during the winter, and her visits to various relatives in England. As her income spiralled down with world events during the twenties she found it difficult to adjust. The five servants she employed during the summer were second generation employees and considered part of the family. When the coachman reached retirement age she did not replace him or his wife, and gave up the horses, writing to Oscar: "*Won't it be nice when you retire and can drive me round in your car*!" He could think of other ways to spend his retirement, but eight years later that is what he spent much time doing.

Flo's letters were also full of concern for Olga and the children. Pella had had typhus fever, Ronny had been ill, and Tiny Wee had malaria. Flo felt sure she should come out, collect the children and take them back to England with her. Africa's climate was, she said, too difficult for delicate children. She was always acutely aware of her own children's shortcomings and was full of good advice to them on marriage and on everything else, but she never criticized their spouses and frequently expressed her gratitude to them for making her children happy. Olga was instructed that she must not appear everywhere in slacks, men like pretties, frillies and muslin. "*It is always the picturesque rather than the capable woman who attracts a man.*" As Oscar's wife she must also be sure to appear smartly dressed in public, with her hair combed.

Olga built a good spare-room in the garden and invited Flo to visit. She came in 1927, and wrote to her sisters that she was glad Olga had at last installed reasonably civilized living conditions, but that she would wear trousers all the time, and that there was an immense amount of mending for Flo to catch up on. When Oscar was away with his car, the farm cart visited Nairobi once a week and did Olga's shopping for her, the carter taking a separate shopping list for each shop and handing it in, and then picking up the post before he did a second round of the shops to pick up the orders.

Almost as soon as she had moved to the farm Olga built a long low building with four rooms and an open verandah at one end.

The Hospital

This was the hospital, with eight beds for in-patients while the dispensary was held in the open verandah. There was a tiny room off it where examinations were made and wounds dressed. The Government hospital at Kiambu had not then been built and Olga dealt with anyone who came, even with such illnesses as smallpox and a deadly flu virus still circulating in the colony. As soon as an ambulance service was set up in Nairobi the very sick could be sent to hospital for proper medical treatment. Olga had no medical training beyond the two year's nursing in Great Ormond Street hospital, but she had worked under excellent doctors at the Carriers' Hospital during the war and could sort out the very ill patients from those who needed first aid. She was only too conscious of her shortcomings and wrote:

Even if my little hospital is not doing good medical work, it is worth while over and over again for it has become a link of good will between the white and black races, between employer and employee, and most particularly between the women in modern civilization and the untutored African.

She loved the maternity cases and told the story of one woman who was having a very prolonged labour in one of the villages in the forest near Wispers. The African midwife was called in, and, when she could not help, an old African witch doctor who cast his spells and performed all the rites of throttling a goat and cutting out its entrails while it was still alive so that as it died it would take with it the evil spirits. Even so, the agonising labour continued and the midwife suggested *White man's magic.* A man was sent to find Olga, who was at that moment wading to and fro through the river, directing the placing of beams across the supports she had built for the new bridge. She went at once to the hut where the poor girl lay on the floor crying out with pain – it was very unusual for an African to cry out in childbirth. Around her sat, in solemn silent gloom, nine older women. Olga hurried to the nearest phone half a mile away at the brick works. Two doctors said they could not come, both said they had an appointment that afternoon. So they did; to play golf with each other. She tried two more, getting ever more frantic, and managed to persuade one to come out. She hurried back to the hut, only to discover that four men had set out to carry the patient slung in a blanket to Wispers. Olga caught up with the porters balancing with their patient across the beams newly laid over the river. The patient seemed to find the swinging motion soothing – or was she getting too weak to cry? By the time the doctor arrived with his merciful chloroform she was installed on a bed in Olga's hospital. As Olga came out of the room in her stained overall carrying the baby wrapped in a towel, she found a crowd of Africans had gathered to hear the outcome of this drama. The African midwife, a small woman bent with carrying great loads on her back, peered at the baby approvingly, touched the tiny hand, then reached up to put her hands on Olga's shoulders and said: *"Your magic is greater than our magic, and your magic has come to stay!"*

My own earliest memory is of climbing out of my cot early in the morning because I heard a noise in the sitting room, directly opposite my room. My mother and an African woman, our headman's wife, were kneeling on the floor on opposite sides of an arm chair. Both of them were crying. In the chair, supported on a cushion, lay the headman's son, a toddler the same age as myself. He had just died of malaria. Her eight previous children had also died. She went on to have eight more children. Olga insisted that the parents did not take these children back to Kisumu until they were five years old – for in Kisumu malaria was much worse than in Nairobi. All eight children lived. Once Olga had cleared the swamp she was able to keep the occurrence of malaria at Wispers to a minimum. We did not have to sleep under mosquito nets.

Olga never thought of charging any patient either for medicine or for any other care, and as a result the Kikuyu tribe living around her, on neighbouring farms or in the forests, provided food for any patient resident in the hospital. Chickens, baskets of vegetables, eggs, and gourds of milk would arrive in Olga's kitchen where the cooking was done. Olga never employed members of the Kikuyu tribe because she did not like the way the men put the women out to do the heavy work, and then came to claim the wages themselves. Nor did she like to see the very heavy loads the women carried, nor the cruel way they were genitally mutilated. However she treated patients gladly, accepted the tribute gratefully, and the patients were well fed. Years later, when the Kiambu hospital had been built, she found the Kikuyu women still came to her hospital.

"*Why do you not go to the new hospital*?" she asked, "*They have a proper doctor and equipment there*!"

"*Yes, but they make the children cry and do not say goo goo to the babies!*" And Olga continued happily day after day saying goo-goo to the babies in her little dispensary.

At Wispers, she was determined to provide for her labour all the things she had wanted to provide at Khitari. Good stone or brick buildings were replacing the mud huts, married men were all accommodated in two-roomed bungalows, bachelors in rooms around a court yard. Clean water was on hand; beds and blankets were issued to everyone, there was a large communal hall used as a school room during the day, a common room at night. All these were unusual luxuries on settler farms at the time. Moreover, her system of piece-work was very popular; most men could complete their day's work in six hours. In cold wet weather work started later, and hot cocoa was handed out mid morning, often by Olga herself. This annoyed her fellow farmers more than anything else she did, "cosseting the natives." Twenty years later she aroused the same spectacular derision when she suggested all farmers should provide showers for their workers!

* * * * * * *

The farm was now running itself, with a young white woman as farm manager, and Olga was ready for new activities. She decided to stand for Legislative Council. When Sir Robert Coryndon, who had replaced Sir Edward Northey as Governor of Kenya, died in harness in 1925 he was replaced by Sir Edward Grigg. Sir Edward had been one of Lord Milner's young men in South Africa and knew Leopold Amery, Secretary of State for the Colonies. Amery had explained his vision of setting up a great East African Dominion consisting of seventeen East African countries from the borders of South Africa to those of Egypt, thus realizing Rhodes's vision of British territory from to Cape to Cairo. Amery may have been an eager imperialist, but he was not a great judge of character. It would be hard to find a man less suitable than Grigg to hold the balance in Kenya between African rights and settlers' noisy claims. Grigg had served in the Army in the First World War and had become very friendly with the Prince of Wales, whose equerry he had later become, a playboy equerry for a playboy prince. Perhaps it was with a prompt from the Palace that he was chosen, and it may also have been the reason he had so many grandiose ideas. He was going to make the wood and corrugated iron settlement of Nairobi into a fine city fit to become the capital of the new East African dominion. The first necessity was an impressive Government House. He had no doubt that he would be appointed the first Governor General of the Dominion of Eastern Africa. There must be another good house at the Coast to accommodate visiting and departing notables. The only trouble with these ideas is that they cost money. The Colony was a poor one, dependent on agriculture. The world was beginning the worst ever slump in agricultural prices. Where was the money to come from?

Grigg not only needed more money for public works. He had married an expensive wife. She was always beautifully dressed, would send forward notice to hard-up officials who had to host them that she liked strawberries and cream for breakfast, silk sheets on her bed, and the opportunity to play tennis. Some wretched official's wife in a distant outpost would have to welcome her guests with an apology that it had not been possible to arrange one or all of these luxuries. Both she and the Governor showed a strong preference for the company of the aristocratic settlers to that of the worthy but dull government officers. This led Sir Edward to Lord Delamere, the settler leader whose party was called the Reform Party because he wanted to reform life in Kenya to resemble the great plantations of the Deep South in the United States before the Civil war. To ensure that administrators appointed by distant Whitehall could not interfere with this potential Nirvana, Delamere also wanted a majority of Elected Members of Legislative Council. The elections were due in January 1926. Oscar had already been demoted to the Education Department but was still centred in Nairobi.

As the wife of a senior official Olga had to apply to the Colonial Office for permission and this was granted, probably because she was considered eccentric but harmless. Her platform was feminist and supportive of small farmers against large corporations investing in farming. She stood in strong opposition to the Reform Party. Her first speech announced:

"I come before you in part as the expression of changing social conditions. Many of us, particularly those who have been out here a long time, perhaps hardly realise how East African Society has changed with the advent of more and more European

women, and perhaps more with the adolescence of those European daughters of Kenya, Kenya born and bred, who are daily entering the business of life. All of these are demanding, and will increasingly demand, representation by their own sex in all those questions which are peculiarly women's sphere. But it is not only as a woman that I am asking for your vote. I have served my apprenticeship on several public bodies including your Municipal Council. My interest in the politics of this country is real. Questions of transport and trade are not, with me, merely exercises of political theory as they might be if I had no stake in this country. I stand as an independent candidate of a fighting spirit in no way committed to any party. My intention is to serve the country as a member of the public who has made Kenya her home. Self-government is the natural political evolution, but it would be premature at the present moment and present interests should in no way be subordinated to the fight for Self-government now. In view of the need for gradual change in the fiscal system of this country, I am in favour of a change in the Constitution when it is generally agreed that the Elected Members have sufficient political experience to undertake this additional responsibility."

In another speech she said that the points of difference between her and her opponent, Schwarz, had not been adequately defined:

"*I agree with my opponent on such matters as daylight saving, the Defence Force, Customs, the Port, Shop hours, registration of household servants, and various other matters. I am however diametrically opposed to the main platform of the Reform party, which is to fight for an unofficial majority in the immediate future, and to subordinate all the other interests of the colony until that fight is won. I will also fight to see the administration of Kenya left in the hands of trained administrators rather than hand it over to the Reform Party. Do you realize that out of eleven constituencies ten are represented by members of the Reform Party, seven of whom are farmers, two are land agents, and one a lawyer. It would be in my opinion a menace to the commercial community and to the civil service to hand over the Government of the Country to an elected majority so constituted. To my mind you cannot disregard two great bodies of electors in Nairobi without directly and indirectly endangering the safety and stability of the whole country. Moreover, all the unofficial elected members are on the finance committee of Leg Co, while only three officials are on it – the*

Treasurer, the Colonial Secretary and the Chief Native Commissioner. Thus the settlers already have almost complete control of finance, which gives them sufficient power for the time being. I pledge to give any support I can to increase the representation of both the civil service and of commercial interests and I shall put up a fight, and a good hard fight, against this government by agreement into which the Reform Party have recently lapsed."

She meant government by secret agreement between the Governor and the Reform Party in which controversial matters would be kept out of public discussion. Since then plenty of evidence has come to light that there was indeed an agreement, by which Governor Grigg would support Delamere in his claims for a settler majority if Delamere would support Grigg in his endeavour to raise expenditure for Government House and increases in his own gubernatorial allowances. In addition Grigg had befriended Martin, one of the very few civil servants widely believed to be corrupt. He was the Commissioner of Lands, who could be persuaded to transfer native lands regardless of previous agreements. He had agreed a particularly generous exchange of land for Lord Delamere. In other words, within months of his arrival Sir Edward Grigg was working hand in glove with the settlers' leader in order that both sides could obtain large advantages without going through the usual channels.

When Olga was asked what her policy would be on finance, would she back Grigg's extravagant building programme and if so where would she look for the extra finance, she replied tactfully that she did not understand financial matters.

Olga was not elected, and it would be many years before she tried again. She always said that the rumour had been put about that if she were elected, she would not be allowed to take her seat because her husband was a senior official with a seat on the official side of the house. It seems to me more likely that her obvious ability as a farmer in her own right was not popular. In the 1920s women with independent minds and the courage to speak out were deplored. Much better to vote for a man!

When the family went on leave in 1926 they established themselves at Four Throws House. Olga was delighted to be in an English home of her own, to see how well the orchard had grown, to improve the garden. She redid the out-buildings, repainted much of Four Throws house, and was presented at Court by her mother. Oscar bought an old car so that he could drive over to Oxford where his father was in the last stages of diabetes. He was thankful that his brother Lawrence was now back from India and living nearby, in Abingdon. Despite the sorrow of facing this fatal illness, it was a happy leave, the first one that Olga was not pregnant.

*   *   *   *   *   *   *

In 1927 Oscar was posted to Mombasa at short notice, to stand in for the Provincial Commissioner while he went on home leave. He had now been demoted back into the Administration. With Oscar at the coast, Olga had to spend much time away from her beloved farm to be a good Provincial Commissioner's wife. She moved a large domestic entourage – there were now three other girls in her care as well as her own three, with Mary to look after them. Then there were the family pets, Olga's new bulldog Bully, and Oscar's young leopard, Chui. Pella's cat, Boda, and pet cock, Cockaloo. They all travelled with the family in the first class compartments, the kind without a corridor. When Cockaloo started his usual lengthy crowing at dawn, the train happened to be at a little wayside station taking on more water, more firewood, for the last run into Mombasa. Heads came out of carriage windows all down the train to see where the noise was coming from, and occupants of the other carriages called out to the stationmaster to shut that animal up. Before anyone could ask him whether the bird was in his compartment, Oscar also stuck his head out of the window and joined in: "Can't anyone stop that damn animal from crowing?"

Olga found herself in political trouble again, this time unwittingly by her activities on a woman's committee to prepare for the visit of the Prince of Wales. The Prince had invited himself, in a private coded message, as the guest of his old equerry the Governor, so that his visit could be private and he need not tour any other countries or attend official functions. Grigg was equally determined to show off his royal friend with his usual conspicuous expenditure. Olga suggested that £5000, enough money to pay ten district commissioners for a whole year, enough to buy and set up two good farms, was too much to spend on decorating Mombasa for one man's arrival, even if he were a prince of the blood royal. The Governor did not agree and once again reported to the Colonial Office that she had shown disloyalty. The Colonial Office in London minuted this complaint: "*Grigg does not get the best out of his officers. He would do better to use Mrs Watkins's undoubted gifts instead of trying to repress the irrepressible.*"

The prince was a difficult guest, always unpunctual, often lacking in manners, and deflected by any passing pretty face. He had wanted a private visit and a taste of some of the goings-on reputed to be found in Happy Valley. Instead he found himself forced to meet people of all races and ranks, spending long hot afternoons with Asian girl guides and members of the British Legion when he would much rather have gone swimming or played tennis with the prettiest women available. When Olga had to entertain him at Mombasa she departed from the usual formal seating which would have put him at a table with herself and Lady Grigg, and placed him with pretty girls and young naval officers. There was dancing to a gramophone on the dimly lit verandah overlooking the sea and Olga insisted that that too should be informal, no duty dances with middle-aged wives. Lady Grigg, who liked the Prince's attention to focus on her own pretty self, was not amused, particularly when the Prince commented at breakfast next morning what a jolly person Mrs Watkins was.

In 1928 Oscar was first offered promotion to the Residency of Swaziland, which he took as a kick upstairs, his promotion to a senior post in a distant country to get rid of him. When he refused the offer he was ordered on home leave a year earlier than he was due. The Colonial Office, alerted by Oscar on his last leave, had instructed Grigg to introduce an act which put all the African lands into a trust so that if there was ever a settler majority in the Legislative Council they would be unable to alienate more land except for public purposes – roads, hospitals, schools, and so on. Grigg wanted Oscar out of the way while the bill was put through, as in his draft he was providing inadequate safeguards against land alienation. Oscar spent the voyage home composing a statement to the Secretary of State for the Colonies, criticizing clause by clause the bill produced by the Governor. There was no airmail then. Oscar's report arrived before Grigg's draft.

Before they left Olga wrote out detailed instructions for Kathleen Armstrong, her young farm manager. The job of managing 140 acres of coffee was no sinecure. The £10 a month, all found, was about three times what the lowest paid white clerk could hope to earn, and her working hours were strenuous. She had to be out by 6.30 a.m. when a large gong was rung and all the workers came up to the house. She would then walk round the farm setting each man or group of men the day's task. Around 8.30 she could take a break for breakfast. After breakfast the housekeeping had to be done, which meant giving out stores to the cook in the exact amounts. It might include mixing a cake, setting bread to rise, throwing out dead flowers, and seeing that the house was clean. By 9.30 she had to be down at the hospital ringing the gong for patients to come. In a normal day there were two or three in-patients and a dozen out-patients to be attended to. Food came down from the farm house, medicines, dressings, and bandages were kept in the hospital and were doled out daily. Careful records of each patient were kept.

From the hospital, the manager must go round the farm again, watching any special work being undertaken that day, such as building or cattle dipping, keeping a look out for any other work which would soon need attention. As the workers were on piece-work some had completed their task as early as 10.30 and this work would be checked. A man had to clean around 30 yards of ditch a day, to prune about 80 coffee trees, or to weed 300. After lunch there was time for a brief rest, but at four she had to be out on the farm again, and three times a week at 5.30 p.m. she must herself give out rations to each worker, and mark on his 'ticket' the days he had worked.

There was a huge list of items for the manager to check as she went round the farm. Olga had divided the farm into twenty different areas, each of which should be inspected carefully to make sure it was free of coffee disease. The cleanliness of both the hospital and of the quarters, particularly the latrines, needed constant supervision, as did the state of the tools and carts, the condition of the buildings, roads, and water furrows. Oxen, donkey, and ponies had to be examined for disease at least once a week, and at the same interval the manager should watch the football games the workers played every afternoon, and visit the school. "*Chat to them and find out who is sleeping where, who is friendly with whom, how many blankets each man has, what sort of saucepans they are using, and where they draw their cooking water. Who has a lot of jiggers and which hut is he sleeping in? What doors have lost their hinges and who took them off? Never tell them off in the evening, but discourage them from using the top bunks as fire wood and then sharing beds."*

It was a very time-consuming way of farming, yet once Olga had changed to women farm managers she was never again short of help on the farm.

* * * * * * *

Down at Mombasa, getting ready to go on leave to England, 10 year old Pella wept bitterly at the thought of leaving her adored pets. She wanted to take them all with her, back to England, back to school. After much discussion, she was allowed to choose one pet to take with her, not Cockaloo, he caused too much disturbance with his crowing in the morning and his lack of house training. What about her grey cat, Boudicca? Olga enquired about the cost of transporting a cat and decided it was too high. Kind friends offered Boda a home. Pella wept every time she looked at the cat.

Olga had an idea. The ship on which they were to travel, the *Llandovery Castle*, was spending several days in Mombasa harbour before it sailed for London. On the evening before sailing, the Captain was going to give a children's party both for the children sailing and their friends in Mombasa. Olga made matching dresses for the six girls in her care, only five were travelling but they looked terrific all dressed the same, and as they all went up the gangway together no one could doubt what good customers the family were.

Pella carried Boda in a lidded basket, and had instructions to keep her from yowling and what to say to the Captain if he approached her. When the children's games on deck started, Pella sat by her basket with one hand slipped through the lid - the whole basket reverberating with satisfied purring. Pella was a beautiful child with very blue eyes which she later used to devastating effect, fair curls all over her head, impressive self-possession and exceptionally good manners. Determination not to be parted from her cat gave her more than her usual courage. The Captain at once noticed the wistful little girl with the big blue eyes and golden curls and her purring basket. He fell straight into the trap.

"Little girl, why are you not joining in the games? What have you got in that basket?"

Pella explained: "She's my cat, I've had her since she was a tiny kitten and now I have to leave her. Mummy says she cannot afford for us all to take our pets when we go away, and Boda will miss me so. Could I smuggle her on board tomorrow?"

"I don't think I can waive the fare. Supposing all the children here asked me?" he said, looking round the room. He noted the surprising number of little girls dressed like Pella. No wonder they could not afford to travel with family pets. When he looked down at Pella again the big blue eyes had filled with tears.

"You know, I think she might work her passage. Is she a good ratter?"

"Oh yes," said Pella, "she catches at least one mouse a day at home."

"The Captain is allowed a cat, and I have not got one. I don't see why Boda should not be my cat for the journey, do you? What is more, then she could have the run of the ship and not have to live in one of those hot kennels. And you my dear will always be welcome on the bridge to visit her." Pella's face brightened immediately, but before she could find words he continued: "Tell me, would it be a good idea to leave her with me now so that your parents don't know about her? And what does she like to eat?" He squatted beside her to hear her instructions. The captain's steward was summoned, and escorted Pella up two steep sets of companionways to the bridge and the Captain's Cabin. He fetched a sand tray from the kennels and placed it in the Captain's bathroom, and Boda was set free. She was quick to notice a coffee tray on the table with a jug of condensed milk and made straight for it. She helped herself daintily, not upsetting a drop, and then settled happily on the Captain's bunk and cleaned her face with her paws. Pella stood by stroking her. It all took a long time.

Meanwhile on the first class deck the party continued. Tiny Wee had drunk too much condensed milk, joined in rough and tumble games, and had been sick. Pella was called back; it was time to go home for our last night ashore. Olga noted with satisfaction Pella no longer carried the basket but nothing was said.

Boda proved a good traveller. Oscar and Olga were seated at the Captain's table. They had been asked not to reveal that Boda was their cat, the Captain referred to her as "That cat of mine". Her adventures were a useful subject of conversation, avoiding controversial topics and petty gossip. On the first day she had cleared his breakfast tray while he was shaving. She had a prodigious appetite, a passion for condensed milk, and seemed to be putting on weight fast. He noticed Oscar and Olga exchange embarrassed glances. Then one day the Captain was late for dinner, an unusual discourtesy for the Captain of a passenger liner sailing in good weather between ports. The purser came over and said he had been delayed by an emergency and the passengers were to start their meal. When the Captain did come down he was somewhat flustered, and fixed his eyes on Olga as he said:

"That cat of mine really gave me a surprise this evening. When I went in to change for dinner, I found not one cat on my bed, but seven, on the clothes my steward had laid out for me." It was Oscar who went up to the Captain's cabin that night, and when he came down there were only three kittens left, all males immediately named Kings Arthur, Ethelred, and Alfred, which was as far as we children had progressed in history since Boda's birth. Oscar was not very good at sexing kittens, and King Alfred matured to produce two litters a year for the rest of her life. When some days later the family left the ship at Genoa to travel up to Innsbruck the basket Pella clutched contained four cats. Now Pella could be with her cat all the time, she had one hand permanently under the lid, stroking hard.

"Won't Granny be pleased!" she said.

"She'll certainly be as surprised as the captain was!" said Olga.

* * *

Chapter Nine

HOTCH POTCH
COFFEE FARMER AND COMMISSIONER'S WIFE

I seek not to challenge the order that is,
I seek but to widen its borders
If the order that is the order of God
Then revolt is part of that order

As a girl, Olga had the words quoted above burnt into wood by a Tyrolean craftsman and hung them above her work table in Matzen. Oscar had been introduced to them on his first visit, two year old Pella in his arms.

"It certainly reflects your philosophy of life," Oscar had commented, "but can one bring children up on it?"

"We can try," said Olga. And try she did.

Although today her ideas would go unremarked, at that time she was often in conflict with more traditional educationalists, properly trained governesses, and now in 1928 her own mother. When in 1928 the family arrived in Austria with two older girls as well as her own three for a visit of six months, Flo was well prepared for the invasion; she had made Olga's old work room into a school room, engaged a qualified governess, and provided warm clothes for all five. At the toy-like station of Brixlegg, she was waiting with a sleigh jingling with bells and piled with bearskin rugs, trophies from their Canadian days. But the children were so excited by the first snow they had ever seen that they ignored her, ignored even the jingling sleigh. They all dashed to the nearest pile of snow and rolled in it like puppies. Pella even deserted her basket of four cats, all of which started yowling as the cold air reached them.

"Whatever have you got in there?" said Flo, quite expecting them to have arrived with a lion or leopard cub. "Goodness, why did you bring cats – we have plenty of kittens in the Tyrol." They drove to the upper gate, where the fir tree immediately in front of the gate was weighed down with snow. The view up the long white valley to the distant Stubai mountains was as breathtaking as ever. Inside the clanking iron gates, courtyards were mounded with snow, the spiral staircase gleamed with crystals of frost, the whole building a giant deep freeze. Three weeks earlier they had been sweltering in the hot season in Mombasa. Inside Olga's rooms in Matzen the great green tiled stoves radiated almost visible warmth, and there was a new warm dressing gown laid out on every bed. I stroked mine lovingly; it was the first time I could remember receiving a new garment, 'just for me' as I put it at the age of five.

We children took an instant dislike to the new governess. I was now expected to join the formal lessons but I flatly refused and as I was expert at creating mayhem I was regularly sent to report to my parents. Oscar murmured "Revolt is part of that order!" and took on the task of walking me down to the local kindergarten every day. I loved the Sisters of Charity in their great starched caps, enjoyed the handwork we were given to occupy us, and quickly learned to communicate without words. I was probably horribly spoilt by the Sisters, for Flo was a great supporter of their charities. It was much better than listening to Miss Rowe reducing at least two of the older girls to tears every morning. She said she had never met such unruly, ignorant children. Olga was stunned; governesses in Kenya, dependent on her goodwill, had always said how brilliant the girls were. Miss Rowe must be wrong.

"I don't think so!" said Flo firmly, and refused to let Olga discharge her.

Boda and her family did not like the cold. Unlike the children, she hated the snow and refused to go out in it. She lived with her kittens under the bench surrounding the green tile stove in the nursery. Here she would instruct them in hygiene. Every hour or so, she would move over to the sand box and summon her family. All three would be lined up with mother, dig their holes, and sit in a row to perform their duties, three little tails and one long one hanging over the edge of the box. Each repetition of this event reduced us children to helpless mirth. The smell was appalling. Miss Rowe sat at the end of the table, a handkerchief held to her nose, her eyes unsmiling. It was much too cold to open the frost bound windows.

* * * * * * *

Olga was involved in more serious matters, selling coffee. She had long noticed that the price to the farmer was under 6d per lb for green coffee delivered to London while the price to the consumer was three times as much. Why should the middleman and retailer make three times as much as she did, while incurring only a fraction of her costs? She had written to her London agent stating her terms and had then asked Oscar, who was in London, to follow up with a visit. He did not record what was said but wrote to Olga: *Next time you ask me to visit a bee-hive you might warn me when you have lit a fire underneath it.*

If the agent would not sell coffee on her terms she would do so herself, and set off for Vienna, in those days one of the main coffee drinking capitals of the world. Her great-grandfather had made his fortune by selling coffee to the Viennese and she would do the same. She visited his old coffee-house, the famous Dams café, who liked the samples she brought with her and put in an order. Other cafes and hotels followed, as did grocers who specialized in *Kolonialwaren.*

Olga was delighted and on her way back to England later that year she visited Zurich and Basel with the same success. She had more orders than she would be able to fill regularly and pictured how delighted her coffee-farming friends in Kenya would be when she shared out the market. Meanwhile, she arranged for all her orders to be filled. Each new client wrote back, that he was delighted with the quality of her coffee and the promptness with which it had been delivered but regretted he could order no more. *"If we order your coffee direct, our suppliers will no longer supply us with the other things we need to import!"*

It was Olga's introduction to the coffee marketing cartel, a much stronger organization than she had realized, designed to keep prices down to farmers and up to consumers. She spent the rest of her life opposing cartels and fighting almost any organization which restricted the free movement of agricultural crops. Long term crops, coffee, tea, sisal, rubber, and cocoa are peculiarly liable to this kind of exploitative marketing, the reason being that the many years it takes to bring them into production makes it difficult to adjust supply to demand. From the small farmer's point of view this can become catastrophic. In a good year the price falls because there is a surplus while in a poor year the farmer has very little to sell but still the price does not go up because the previous surplus has been stored and is released to the market. When he goes broke, the cartel moves in, buys up the farm cheap, puts in a manager, and soon has vertical integration forming a series of oligopolies – in other words a few big firms obtain complete control of the market.

There were two sets of losers in this situation, the coffee consumer who paid more than double the price which Olga thought was reasonable, and the small farmer who was squeezed out of farming by the big plantation companies. Olga considered that the workers also lost out, for big plantations run by managers rarely provided such pleasant conditions as did an individual farmer – smaller farmers had to compete with each other to attract workers. Had Olga been a free agent she would almost certainly have done what the founder of the Swiss firm, Migros, did. Migros is today the Sainsburys of Switzerland. The firm (the name is an abbreviation of demi-gross or half wholesale) was started in the early 1930's by a young Swiss who had lost his job on a Brazilian coffee estate when prices fell in 1929. Like Olga, he realized he could profit from the difference between the price of coffee to the farmer and that to the consumer, and did as Olga had done, going round to hotels, cafes, and grocers to sell his former employer's coffee. When rebuffed as Olga had been, he worked round the situation by buying a van and selling direct to housewives. He did so well that soon he had a fleet of vans, who started selling other imported goods such as sugar, tea, rice, and cocoa as well as coffee, all much cheaper than the village shop could buy from the wholesalers. When he started grocery shops he arranged for direct supplies from the growers. His prices were much lower and in a generation he owned one of the biggest retailing chains in his country.

Olga was not a free agent and had to return to her duties as wife and mother, but from then on she sold a considerable proportion of her coffee through a cousin in Suffolk, who advertised in *The Times*, *The Telegraph*, and *The Lady*, then roasted the coffee freshly and despatched it the next day at 1s 3d a pound, 33% down on the price being fixed in grocers' shops. It provided a remunerative cottage industry for a handicapped young woman, and an outlet for Olga's coffee.

* * * * * * *

In the summer of 1929 the family moved from Matzen to Four Throws house in Kent. Oscar had to go back to Kenya to take up his new post as Provincial Commissioner at Eldoret. Olga had intended to stay in England until Pella went to boarding school but now decided to follow Oscar out to Kenya. While they were in England, Olga had insisted that he had an extensive medical examination to try to find the cause for his loss of both weight and energy. Stomach cancer had been suspected and it came as a relief that it was only pernicious anaemia. In those days the only known way to treat this disease was for the patient to consume at least one pound of liver every day. Oscar was not fussy about his food but if there was one he hated, it was liver. After three months he had to admit that he felt much better and his concentration had improved greatly, but he dreaded mealtimes when he was presented with yet another plate of liver. Olga as usual put her imagination to work, and found that liver cooked hard could be disguised as a breakfast cereal which looked like grapenuts and, drowned in milk, was more palatable.

These were possibly the most difficult years of her life, when she was trying to reconcile the irreconcilable. Oscar, although demoted because of his defence of African land rights, was still the senior commissioner and responsible for a large province. His position made him a member of both the Legislative and Executive councils, and he worked hard to push his ideas at every opportunity. His position demanded an active wife to undertake much entertaining and supportive activity, visiting and inspecting anything from Girl Guides, new schools, clinics, to training centres and experimental small holdings. She needed to be a conservative sort of person, accepting the status quo rather than challenging it.

Olga remained a rebel. Convinced that coffee farming was the best way of life, she also wanted to pioneer better conditions for women, not only white women, but particularly African women. Nor could she resist the temptation to take on unnecessary extra commitments, such as building a house in Eldoret. It was nearly always snatching at opportunity in order to make more money to develop further projects. Somehow they never quite succeeded. The house in Eldoret, built very economically when the building trade was in depression, was built to meet the needs of the growth of the town as a result of Kenya's only gold rush. It was a very short-lived gold rush and the house became another albatross round her neck.

One of Oscar's first visitors in Eldoret, even before Olga came out, was Margery Perham, who described him in glowing terms in her *African Diaries* and reported how he 'burned' at the way he had been treated. He, the most experienced man in African affairs in the colony, had been deliberately sent to a settler area, where he had to spend much of his time on such things as attending jamborees of Girl Guides and Boy Scouts, long sessions with the Land Bank discussing what should happen when settlers could no longer pay their mortgages, and to return to their country of origin those Europeans who had lost everything in the slump. It was a tedious job for any administrator; for a man who had his heart and soul in African development, it was purgatory. Olga understood this even better than Margery and was faced with the dilemma of all colonial wives, having to choose between frustrated husband and growing children. She chose the former and left us in England, Granny, Miss Rowe, and Mary all in attendance.

Worst hit by the slump were those whites who had been encouraged to settle in 1920, many of them knowing little about farming, even less about finance, and with too little capital. Nor was this the only disaster to hit Kenya. The depression was accompanied by drought, the worst one since the legendary drought of the 1890's; African cattle died where they stood for lack of grazing; and the nomads who owned them had stick-like limbs and bloated stomachs. European-owned herds were slaughtered by farmers to feed their workers.

Then came the locusts. Usually after there had been a shower or two of rain, a few blades of grass would come through, and the young locusts, called hoppers, would move in like a terrible cloud darkening the sky, and roll up the new green growth like a carpet. They derailed trains, jammed the windscreen-wipers of cars, stopped traffic. They ate grass, maize, flowers, household linen, old sacks, the dogs' bedding, and anything left around. Fortunately they did not eat coffee trees, but the weight of them resting on the branches broke them. They left a terrible desolation behind them as the dry top soil eroded away, and in the next heavy rains the rivers ran red far into the Indian Ocean. The early thirties were compared to the seven plagues of Egypt, and administrators awaited anxiously for outbreak of some disease or other to follow.

Fortunately none did. The famine was contained by imports of maize from South Africa and America.

Among those settlers brought to financial ruin in the Eldoret area was the second Lord Kitchener. He was the older brother of Kitchener of Khartoum, with whom Olga's father had discussed a new sight for rifles for the British Army. The first Lord Kitchener was killed in 1916, and his older brother inherited the title. Olga had arrived in Kenya with an introduction to this brother. She could not take up the introduction, and when Douglas was killed Kitchener wrote to her father saying that British East Africa was a most unsuitable place for a young woman on her own, Willie must call her back to Europe. As Willie was at this time a prisoner in Austria he did not get the letter until months later. When in 1917 Olga rode over to see Kitchener, he was so charmed by her that he wrote again to her father, this time saying that she would overcome any difficulties and would be a great asset to the colony – she must stay on.

By the 1930s Kitchener was living on his estate at a settlement called Soy, some 20 miles from Eldoret. He lived alone in increasing squalor in a wood-and-iron bungalow, a somewhat pathetic figure. Both his wife and his daughter were buried on his farm. More recently his son had died leaving two young sons. The old man did not get on with his daughter-in-law, Lady Adela Broome. The cause of the quarrel was financial. When Kitchener of Khartoum had died in 1916, his older brother had inherited his title, but a very considerable sum of money had gone direct to this brother's son in order to avoid double death duties. When times got bad the son lent his father some of the inherited money to keep the estates going, then he died in 1928 before his father had repaid him. Nearly all the Kitchener estate had been invested in property and almost overnight property had lost its value. Meanwhile the old man had fallen into even deeper financial problems. Now his daughter-in-law, Lady Adela, had to arrange for the payment of death duties on the money her sons had inherited, including the money her husband had lent to his father. The grandfather got it into his head that she wanted the money because she was a London socialite and like many of her kind could no longer afford her chosen way of life. He considered her very extravagant and wanted to make sure the money would be available for his grandsons. He wrote kind letters to them full of good advice and refused to communicate with their mother. The truth was that the fall in world markets had reduced his circumstances so he could no longer pay anyone anything.

Between them, the Kitchener brothers had owned half a dozen large estates scattered over East Africa, all bought before the first world war and producing cattle, coffee, sisal, and maize. Now only one big estate was left. The others he had sold off in fragments, and had often granted the buyers large mortgages. With the fall in prices, few men could honour their debts. Kitchener, though owed considerable sums, had himself had to forego his pension to meet his own repayments and was now living near subsistence level. Food consisted of maize porridge, African eggs, chickens bought from his farm squatters, and milk from their herds. Few repairs were done on the farm, so water no longer flowed into tanks, roofs often leaked, verandah boards were eaten away by termites, and roads went unrepaired in the dry season and became impassable in the wet.

When Oscar arrived in Eldoret, Kitchener soon called on him. He accepted Oscar's hospitality with alacrity, and within days asked Oscar to retire and become his farm manager, offering him a share in profits. His first visit coincided with that of Margery Perham, who described Oscar as a Greek God and wondered how he could associate with such a slovenly, grubby old man, whom she likened to a decaying mastiff. As soon as Olga arrived in Eldoret she took the mastiff firmly in hand. When he arrived at her house he was persuaded into a bath, was given clean clothes, taken shopping, and visited both barber and doctor. While he was having his check up, his car would be having one also. For two or three nights a clean and tidy lord would eat three good meals a day, play bridge with Oscar and other guests in the evening, and would then return to his farm. When we children eventually arrived in Eldoret, we loved him. The ancient lord could be relied upon to come into the school-room and disrupt lessons at least once every morning, and was full of good advice on how to handle and care for our pony.

In 1930 Lady Broome had still not paid the death duties and as Lord K refused to write to her, she travelled out to Kenya to see him. His solicitors in Nairobi told her that there was only one way the old man would receive her, and that was if Olga Watkins would escort her. Olga was the only person who had any influence on him. Olga at once agreed, but thought it better not to warn the old man of the visit. Lady Broome, a very sophisticated townswoman, arrived in Eldoret and the two women set out on the rutted dusty roads in Oscar's long suffering box body car. The farm house was up a steep hill, and the road had become so bad that it was no longer possible to drive up it. Kitchener's car was parked at the bottom of the hill, so Olga had no choice but to leave her car there too.

"How does the old bwana get up here?" she asked one of the Africans who always appear from nowhere when strangers arrive. At nearly 7,000 feet above sea level they were labouring up the steep track under a tropical sun, Lady Broome was wearing high heeled shoes and a chic little hat as she floundered up after Olga.

"*Oh, he hoots his horn and two of us come and carry him up. He sent me down just now to see if you needed help*!" The old man had recognised Olga's car through his binoculars. He was on the veranda smiling to greet her and Olga was already up the steps when Lady Broome puffed into view. The smile became a scowl and he turned his back: "*Olga, if you don't take that woman away at once, I'll never speak to you again.*"

"*Lord Kitchener, she is the mother of your grandsons and she has travelled from England to see you. Now give us both a cup of tea, half an hour's chat, and we'll be away! I promised Oscar I would be back by dark.*" Lord Kitchener walked into the house. His driver, an African in shabby torn clothes, came to the verandah from within the house, closed the verandah gates in their faces, and bolted them. He shook his head sadly: "*Sorry, memsahib, sorry. The old one is not good humoured these days*." Lady Broome had to travel back to England, mission unaccomplished.

As they walked down the hill, they were astonished to meet a young white woman. She was neatly dressed in khaki slacks with a dark red bush shirt, but was not a prepossessing figure. Her short dark hair hung limply on either side of a round face marred by a broken nose. When she saw them, she called in her mongrel puppy and stood with him firmly clasped between her knees. Olga stopped to talk to her, and as always she extracted her life story, although this girl was so reserved she had to work harder than usual.

Her name was Phoebe Meeres and she had come out the previous year from her home in Kent to be Lord Kitchener's farm manager. She had done a horticultural training in the war and had worked on the land. Lord Kitchener knew her parents, had offered her the job and had paid her fare out. She was shattered at what she had found on arrival. Kitchener had told her he could no longer pay her, nor could he afford her passage back to England, as her contract demanded. No, she never had enough to eat, and her clothes were wearing out. Yes, she would like to stay on in Kenya but not in an office job. She wanted to be on a farm, away from towns. Olga scribbled down her name.

"I am looking for a woman farm manager," she said, *"mine went on working after she got married, but is now expecting a baby."*

"May I have Brennan to live with me?"

"Brennan?" Who was this Brennan – an illegitimate child, someone else's husband?

"Yes, Brennan, my dog. He is only a puppy but I'll keep him well in control!" Olga gave a sigh of relief.

"*Yes, of course.*" It was the only question Phoebe asked. It was the only interview she was given.

Olga shook hands with her. *"You'll be hearing from me."*

"What an extraordinary young woman!" said Lady Broome, as they passed out of earshot. Her shoes were even more uncomfortable going down hill on the rough track than they had been coming up. *"What do you think she is up to?"*

"She will be a treasure to any one who treats her kindly, and the poor girl is hardly likely to marry with a nose like that. I wonder how she broke it." A few months later Phoebe moved to Wispers and although she did eventually leave Olga to set up her own farm at Machakos, she was only thirty miles from Wispers and would come over in any emergency to help out. She came to know Wispers as well as Olga did, and could do the full routine from Oscar's diet to dipping the cattle and pulping the coffee. From Olga's viewpoint her great asset was her ability to understand machines and repair them, an ability entirely missing in herself. Oscar appreciated her silence, her love of dogs and her ability to handle them, and best of all, here was a manager who would certainly get on well with Olga. It is difficult to quarrel with anyone who rarely speaks.

In her old age, back on Wispers, Phoebe told me it had seemed like heaven to achieve her ambitions so easily despite the economic slump. She had wanted her own home, her own car, and an independent career which made no social demands on her and kept her away from towns. These were difficult aims for a young woman to achieve in the 1930s in a man's country. With Wispers as a stable background and a little help from Olga she achieved them all. We girls nick-named her *Woman Friday*. The Africans nick-named her *Kabithu*, the cow which refuses the bull. My father nick-named Brennan Halitosis, and when the dog went out to bay at the moon my father would sing a little ditty.

"*Will you be Mrs Brennan?*

"Mrs Halitosis Brennan?

"For Halitosis Brennan is a first class name!"

Olga had agreed, against her better judgement, to be Lord Kitchener's executrix. When Lord Kitchener eventually died, there was no mention in his will nor its many codicils of this fact. Everyone was surprised, and the other executor distressed, because he had agreed to act only if Olga were also appointed. It was not until three years after the death, when the will had been settled, that the bank found a packet tucked away and forwarded it to the executor who forwarded it to Olga. It was the codicil appointing her executrix and arrived while Olga was away from home. Oscar opened the letter and wrote to the executor: "*The suppression of the will by the bank is probably actionable. My remarks about it certainly would be so I won't make them. I have sent your letter to my wife who will be as sorry as I am to learn that you have found your job so distasteful. Let me know if I can help.*"

* * * * * * *

Back in 1929 in Eldoret Olga wept on Christmas day – missing her children bitterly. Flo was delighted to spend the whole winter in England, mistress of a pleasant house where she ran an extravagant establishment, with the spare rooms always full of her many relatives and the five girls attending all the right parties, dressed in matching blue velvet cloaks.

Miss Rowe and Mary remained in residence, albeit rarely on speaking terms with each other. Granny's Austrian cook ran the kitchen on lavish Austrian lines with the help of an Austrian kitchen maid. There were two other maids, a full time gardener, and a rota of cleaning ladies. The world slump was now felt throughout the world. Oscar had taken a ten per cent salary cut, coffee was bringing in half the price it had been when Olga planted it, the farm itself had no value, as there were so many farms available for sale. Four Throws house would have to be sold.

Four Throws House
Flo and Nanny Mary with their charges.

Olga came back to England for the summer of 1930 to sell the house, and received only £1,000 for it, half the price she had paid seven years earlier. She had lavished so much money and care on it, installing electricity and gas, central heating, a telephone, rebuilding the out-buildings, adding an orchard and a tennis count, and resurfacing the drive. She had hoped to repay the £1,000 mortgage she had from her mother, but as the price was so low the money was needed to save Wispers.

Pella, now twelve years old, would have to postpone her education for another year. The family said a cheerful goodbye to Miss Rowe and Mary, and the two older girls were reclaimed by their family. From now on Olga would look after her own three daughters herself. Just before they left, Boda and King Alfred were taken to live with the Aunts at Boxley Abbey.

"You'll be able to see her there when you come back to school next year," said Olga. Poor Aunt Grace – both cats always found a way into the linen cupboard to have their kittens.

As the slump grew ever worse in 1931, Oscar gave up his whisky and cigarettes and Olga cut her own allowance, but they never grumbled. "Look how lucky we are!" she said to the children, "we have a lovely farm and your father has a good job."

It became her quest to help the unemployed whites, and they streamed through Wispers in an increasing flood. Most of the men were totally uneducated; few had bothered to learn any African language; one man had claimed to be a mechanic but could not change a wheel on the car; another drank everything in sight – including the contents of the Wispers drink cupboard – and then became quarrelsome. When he started a fight with a fellow unemployed, Olga stepped between them and was severely hit in the face, losing a tooth as a result. Oscar said no more unemployed, at least no one without good references.

Olga then concentrated on helping young women. One of them was in financial difficulties despite a private income in addition to an adequate salary. When she came for help, Olga asked her to keep accounts of everything she spent. Quite the largest item was on a patent invalid food, Bemax.

"*Why do you buy so much Bemax*?" Olga asked.

"*To feed Twiga, my giraffe*!"

"*Why do you feed him this food*?"

"When he was a baby, I had to give him a bottle, and it was the only thing he liked; now he is hooked on it, and when I try to give him anything else he nips my bottom!"

Another young woman arrived with three children. Single mothers were not fashionable in those days, indeed many people refused even to speak to them. When Olga asked what happened to the father, she replied:

"*Charlie's father was an acquaintance and I took pity on him and let him stay while he looked for a job. When he knew I was pregnant he walked out, and managed to clear my savings account at the same time."*

"*And the other two?"*

"That was another man. I really loved him and wanted to marry him. Then one night the police turned up. It transpired he was a cat burglar. And that time it was kittens – (twins)."

In Eldoret Olga heard a rumour that some children were being maltreated, and she went out to investigate. She arrived at an isolated shanty where a beating was in progress, the squeals audible above the noise of the car as she neared the house. She entered unnoticed to see a man using his belt on a boy's back. She asked what the boy had done to merit such harsh punishment. The father stopped the beating, said the boy had been found stealing food and what business was it of hers anyway. Olga walked over to him and put her hand on his arm, again raised with the belt.

"*I am the wife of the Provincial Commissioner. It is very much his business to see that we all keep the law. We cannot treat our children like that even if they are naughty. Could you not feed them some more food and perhaps they would not steal?"*

The stuffing seemed to go out of the man. *"Lady, I have nothing left, no food in the house, unpaid workers on the farm, and my wife died last month."*

"*I am so sorry,*" said Olga, but with the boy so badly beaten it was difficult to feel sympathy.

"*Can't say I am. You see, she was always hungry too, and expecting again! We couldn't have managed.*"

She gently removed the belt from the man's hand while he was talking, swallowing the suspicions which were rising in her mind, went out to the car and divided her picnic lunch into three. As the boys wolfed down the sandwiches and hard-boiled eggs she asked: "*Is there anything I can do?"*

"Yes, since you are so interested in them, you can take these drat boys with you."

"*Take them? I don't understand.*"

"*Yes, take them, clear out with them. I have nothing left. No petrol for the car, no oil for the lamps, no food for their stomachs, no soap even. How can I look after three boys?"*

Olga drove home with the boys in the car. As she negotiated the rough drive she heard a bang – was it the car back-firing or something more sinister? Better not investigate with the boys. She had a song in her heart. Here were three beautiful little boys with fair hair, blue eyes, and fine features, a ready-made addition to her family. She would adopt them all and bring them up as her own. She had always wanted boys, and she had always wanted a family of six. When she arrived home, lamp-light was streaming across the verandah. The boys streaked out of the car and into the living room ahead of her. We girls were seated round the fire in our dressing gowns, Oscar was reading to us, and a servant was bringing in our supper, scrambled eggs on toast. Olga walked in, took the plates from the tray and put them on a low table near the boys. They gulped down the lot, using fingers to shove the food into their mouths, pushing each other aside and grabbing from each other's plates. Only I had the bad manners to start crying, as my favourite supper disappeared down the throats of strangers. Olga led the boys off to the bathroom and started to scrub them. When the encrusting dirt came off, their backs were criss-crossed with weals. Some wounds were suppurating. Next day she would take them to the doctor. Their backs alone were evidence enough that they must leave their father. She dressed them in our pyjamas and put them on camp beds on the verandah.

With all six children in bed, she and Oscar sat down to supper and she recounted her adventures. "*What are you going to do with those boys*?" he asked.

"But we are going to adopt them of course," said Olga.

"*No! No! No! I am not going to do any such thing!"* Oscar was not usually vehement.

"Why not?"

"We know nothing about them. After this terrible childhood they will be difficult adolescents, and they will be growing up with our girls. Anything might happen! I think that middle one may be retarded. Then there is the cost! We cannot treat adopted children worse than our own, and we cannot educate six children on my pension! We could not even travel all together in one car! Pella starts serious school fees next year!"

From Olga's subdued manner he knew he had won this battle. He put his hand over hers. "*Sorry old girl, I know you have always longed for a boy, but if we adopt, we adopt a new baby and bring him up as ours, we cannot take on three urchins and start a home for disturbed boys. But we will probably find they are not up for adoption any way."*

He proved right. Their maternal grandparents longed to have them, so all Olga had to do was arrange their passage back to Scotland. Nor was there need to obtain their father's agreement. It had been a shot that Olga had heard as she drove away.

And soon, too soon, it was Pella's turn to make the long sea journey in the care of friends. Down at Mombasa to see her safely on board, Olga remembered her wartime journey and the miserable children on board. And she knew that it was going to be worse for this ultra-sensitive, shy, and nervous daughter than for most children. Here she was, the eldest daughter of a senior commissioner, with charming manners, great blue eyes, an entrancing smile, trained to overcome her shyness to welcome guests and to talk to everyone. But if she made the slightest error, she would go crimson with embarrassment, retire to her room and weep. What would happen to this sobbing child at school in England, her parents far away?

"Don't cry. Darling, this is the price of Empire, and you must be proud of it!" Olga said, her own voice cracking. For Pella the price was too high. What Olga did not know was that Aunt Grace, into whose care she was committed, was already sickening with the cancer that was soon to kill her, and no longer able to offer the understanding and sympathy which she had shown Olga when she was at school. Pella had no training in sport, no music, and had been taught only by a succession of short-stay governesses. The ignorant, backward, uncoordinated new girl from Kenya was focus for all kinds of bullying which destroyed her emotional security for ever. All three of us daughters found the price of Empire too high to be paid by our own children and when our turn as mothers came we managed to avoid, one way or another, long separations from our young.

In 1931 Sir Edward Grigg's five year term of Governorship was over and was not renewed. He had not achieved the creation of the dominion of Eastern Africa, nor fulfilled his ambition to become the first Governor General. Instead he left a legacy of dislike between Kenya and Tanganyika. In Kenya he was regarded as a play-boy, a dangerous play-boy, because he had spent so much tax payers' money on conspicuous building and entertaining. His one contribution to the future of East Africa was the setting up of a Governor's Conference for the three East African territories which later became the East African High Commission, and after Independence a Common Market, unifying taxation, transport, and other services in all three countries. His worst sin, even worse than his extravagance, had been to weaken the Administrative service that John Ainsworth had built up and to destroy much of its credibility in African eyes. Many administrators thought it was Grigg who had sown the seeds for Mau Mau which was to erupt twenty years later.

Oscar spent three years in Eldoret. Every month he had to visit Nairobi and the family usually accompanied him. Olga wanted to attend to her farm; and we children, now there was neither nanny nor resident governess, could not be left. Time had to be built in to each journey for me to be sick; nor was I the only cause for delays. Sometimes the wet roads necessitated the long muddy business of putting on chains; sometimes the car broke down, often the radiator boiled over on the last steep escarpment before Nairobi, and on occasion the swarms of locusts were so thick it was impossible to drive through them. Then groups of Africans would be sitting roasting the locusts by the roadside, and we girls would crouch over the fire exchanging gossip with the Africans. Olga did not like this to happen, but did not want to offend the hospitable men.

"I think you should get back into the car now!" she would say hopefully. "Tiny, you know if you eat any more you will be sick again." And one or other of us would deliberately increase her wrath by looking round, holding her nose African fashion and blowing it expertly into the dust. Most of the time we could get away with murder, climbing trees, playing in the mud, reading in bed, stumping through puddles, even hiding under the long white table cloth which covered the dining room table when there were formal guests. All kinds of unruly behaviour which nannies had prevented over the years became possible under Olga's pre-occupied supervision, but nose-blowing in our fingers she could not tolerate.

The new Governor, Sir Joseph Byrne, wanted Oscar in Nairobi as an advisor on African affairs. Oscar, who had only a year to run before he retired, was transferred to Ngong, about fifteen miles south of Nairobi. The move suited us all. The large, two storied stone house at the North end of the Ngong hills was the most comfortable the family had ever occupied. There were even two bathrooms with flush toilets. There was a first floor sleeping balcony overlooking the garden, and those lucky enough to sleep there woke to a view of the rising sun rays lighting up first Kilimanjaro then Mount Kenya. There were good stables not only for ponies brought over from Wispers, but room enough to accommodate those of friends on leave. Everyone could go riding together into the hills, with panoramic views over the great Rift Valley on one side, and of the suburb now called Karen on the other. When visitors came and we walked, we were always escorted by two Maasai scouts picturesquely clad in short dark blue loin cloths trimmed with red, their arms and necks a mass of colourful beads which jingled as they wielded their spears to show us girls how they would use them.

The area was full of game. When Archibald the giraffe stood sentinel at the bottom of the drive, nobody could pass. Already late for some Nairobi appointment, the family had to sit in the car blowing the horn until Archibald deigned to move to one side. Herds of wild buffalo visited the garden. One day an Irish priest arrived late for lunch, very hot and shaken. He was driving an open baby Austin, a car offering little protection and unable to build up much speed on corrugated earth roads through the Ngong forest. A baby rhino slithered on to the road in front of him. A few seconds later he looked in his mirror to see Mother rhino charging along behind. "*What did you do?*" asked Olga.

"I said three Hail Mary's and promised never again to get between mother and child! Someone heard me. After about two miles the calf slipped in the mud and slid into the ditch and I managed to pass him!"

The Ngong house was full of people as old friends welcomed us back and others visiting Nairobi came to stay. There was a local tragedy when a white youth whose family was well known murdered two girls. He was hung, and Olga knew the cleric, Canon Wright, who had to be in attendance at the execution; at dawn she waited outside the prison until it was over, and brought the Canon home. He said he was too sick to eat any breakfast, and Olga with many apologies said: *"Have a quiet morning, I have to go into Nairobi. The two girls are around – don't let them worry you."*

We girls were playing in the garden and saw him looking out of the window of the downstairs spare room. It was a barred window and one of us said to the other:

"*I know, let's play prisons with Canon Wright!*" We went round to his door and knocked, and told him of our idea.

"*Why not*", he said, *"why not?"* When Olga returned she found the Canon locked in his room, and we girls handing food and tins of water to him through the window. He was pretending to try to bend the bars, and shouting *"Let me out! Let me out!"*

A furious Olga sent us to our room in disgrace and turned to the Canon full of apologies. "*How awful of them! How could they do such a thing!*"

"*They cannot know what happened this morning, and you know, it was therapeutic. I feel much better*!"

At Ngong, Olga was in her element, for she could combine being a senior administrator's wife with running her own farm. The family was flourishing, the marriage had settled down into enjoyment of each other's company. If the cloud of retirement hung heavy on the horizon, it served to make the farm all the more important. The future started to map itself out. On retirement they would go 'home' and educate the girls, letting the farm while they did so. When the girls finished school they would return to the farm and live out their lives there. The recent slump, the cut in salaries, the low price of coffee and the appearance of new coffee bugs, meant that even Olga had to accept that the farm was not profitable, but it was near Nairobi and was a beautiful place to live.

Yet her life still seemed to move from one chaotic situation to another. When she had her appendix out while Phoebe was away, she appointed twelve year old Ronny as farm manager and as soon as she could, hired a rickshaw so that she could be pushed round the farm. The pushers loved it, taking it in turn to give each other rides whenever Olga got out to look at something. Wispers was now nearly ten years old, and must have been the most carefully planned farm in Kenya. The work force was divided into teams; the pruners and the carters were the most skilled and highest paid, and after them came the sprayers, and then the diggers and weeders. The least skilled of all was the picking, but everyone was expected to help with that. The 120 acres under coffee was divided into twenty areas, each with its own compost pit, and each area in turn was composted, pruned, weeded, and sprayed, the work being marked off on a map as the teams completed it. Each area had a number, each team a colour, so she could see at once from the chart in the office which corners the sprayers or pruners had not yet visited.

Olga's habit of talking to the farm hands enabled her to use each man in the position best suited to him. The men heading the different teams were those who had been with her for years. Okinde, the head man, had followed her from Koru. Ansa's son, Onyango, had come as a gardener but his fingers were not green, however his mechanical skills were excellent, so he had been sent to Jeaens School to learn about mechanics and had become Mr

Fixit. Since each man liked to spend a few months every year at home, there was always a junior work force, a group of young men who came and went, changing from season to season.

The one man who remained, regardless what happened, was old Omayo, and she devoted a whole letter to Oscar to write about him. He had a good stone hut not far from the main house, where he kept chickens. The time came when this house had to be re-thatched, but Omayo refused to move out even temporarily. When they got the thatch off, hoping to get it back on the same day, they found the rafters were rotten.

The team of carpenters were diverted from another job to the task of replacing them. The ox-cart which brought the timber had all Omayo's possessions piled in it, and they included a great many of Olga's things, including 14 pairs of corsets, some of them thrown away, some taken from the washing line, a huge pile of English magazines, (he could not read) and ten broody hens, each sitting in a Kerai, a sort of metal basin used for moving earth and stones, many of Olga's tools, and two good buckets used to take the cocoa out to the workers. When night fell, the new rafters were up, but not the thatch. Omayo insisted on staying in the hut, he would not even sleep in the cart with his possessions, now covered with corrugated iron. It rained. She had burnt all the magazines and corsets, but later that evening discussed him with the head man.

"He is very old, let him be!" said the headman.

Then she wrote to Oscar: "I feel such a swine, he has so little and we have so much, and it is so unfair. Why should he not keep his rubbish if he wants to? And he stumped off to buy a new bucket so I shall have to pay for that!"

She told the story about the corsets as a funny story, until a doctor took her on one side to tell her it was a well-known symptom of certain psychological problems connected with his inability to have sex. In Europe he would be the sort of man who cut off little girls pigtails in buses or trains. Omayo was not in the slightest disconcerted by this upset. He was always the first on the farm to greet Olga when she came back.

And now it was time to leave all this and to go back to England, this time for retirement. Oscar had never lived in England except for school and university, Olga had spent even less time there. *Home* had changed, what with the first world war and the slump.

We children had spent just one year in England. For all of us, *going home* was going into the unknown.

* * *

Chapter Ten

THE WRITING YEARS

The platform on Nairobi station was more than usually crowded for the departure of the boat train. The Governor, his wife, and his aide-de-camp stood on one side of the group, a crowd of friends on the other side of Oscar and Olga. Many of the people had been at the dinners and the receptions given for Oscar during the previous week. Others were old friends. Ronny & I climbed in and out of the carriage taking the sweets, books, and games we were given, thinking it was another Christmas. Olga had her arms full of roses and lilies friends had brought in. Someone had even provided a four-gallon tin of water to keep them fresh. The last good-byes were said, the last handkerchiefs waved, the little wood-burning engine chuffed away from Nairobi across the Great Plains and through the herds of zebras, wildebeest, and gazelle which gathered in the dry weather. It had been a wonderful send-off, and Olga was looking at one of the new books given us children when she suddenly burst into tears, very unusual for her.

"I can't bear it," she said, "what they have done to you, letting you retire like this!" Oscar moved to sit beside her, and once she was reading again he opened his old leather suitcase and took out his chessboard. It was a folding wooden box of clever design which his parents had used in India. It folded in two, and had standard designed pieces yet allowed them to remain in place when being transported. He and I continued where we had left off the previous day. As long as he gave me the queen and several other pieces, I could give him quite a good game. He never played down to me.

On board ship we were travelling second class. The scent of flowers filled the hot little box of a cabin. The porthole was open with a scoop to pull in any breeze there happened to be. Olga let us stay on deck until the pilot had been dropped on the far side of the reef and then took us down to the dining room for our evening meal. She left us with the presiding stewardess and went to find Oscar, knowing that he hurt all over to be leaving Kenya, retired at the first possible moment. The kindness and consideration of the new Governor, Byrne, the wonderful send-off, had come too late for justice to be done, and he smarted under the injustice he had suffered for championing the African cause. He felt his life's work had been wasted, and knew irremediable harm had been done to the relationship between black and white.

She paused on deck and stood to watch the sun set behind Mombasa. When would they next see a sight as beautiful as that? How were they going to manage on a small pension in England? As she leant against the rail, a young man came up and started talking to her. He too was full of sorrows and poured out tales of life on his uncle's farm, of the pests and droughts and locusts and collapse in the world markets which had caused the older man to go bankrupt and to return his nephew, penniless, to England. He was almost crying as his hand crept over hers. "I don't know what I'm going to do," he said.

"Nor do I," said Olga "except at this moment I must find my husband."

She found him in their cabin unpacking, placing the beloved chess board carefully in a cubby-hole above the upper bunk. "So here you are, I was looking for you on deck, and a young man came and held my hand!" Olga was in her mid forties and had never paid any attention to her looks. It was great to be an object of masculine admiration once again.

"Thank God," said Oscar, "then you won't object to me playing chess! There's quite a good player on board, a Frenchman." How brave he was, to be able to walk away from the job he had wanted so much without a grumble. And yet for all his courage, for the first time the journey seemed purposeless to them both.

Olga found she could not write and Oscar had only one report to complete. Both concentrated on us children. From Egypt onwards the journey was one long lesson in the evolution of Empires. As a frieze of camels moved alongside us in the Suez Canal we were made to see Joseph without his coat of many colours arriving as a slave, Moses leading his people across the Red Sea to spend forty years in the wilderness, another Joseph and Mary bringing the infant Jesus to Egypt for safety. And there were the Phoenicians and Greeks coming to meet us across the Mediterranean and before we knew it Olga had moved us from Anthony and Cleopatra, to the Merchant of Venice, although we went nowhere near that city. However, the Venetians had left their mark in Malta and we must be aware of what we would see. After all that, we could not go ashore at all: a storm was blowing and we could not get into the harbour. This method of teaching led us to wonder at the greatness and excitement of the world, so that we found many of our teachers at school dull and uninspired. But although the farm was planned our teaching was not; we had no consistent syllabus, only fascinating fragments in a mosaic of history. It took a great deal of hard work to put it together into an overall understanding.

The family disembarked at Southampton and made straight for Salisbury to visit Pella, by now a gawky, awkward and very shy adolescent. Then up to London and a desperate search for somewhere to live during the Easter holidays. They had already decided that they would spend three months at a French sea-side resort, followed by a long stay at Matzen.

It was hoped Oscar could recover his health, the girls learn French, and Olga settle down to serious writing. Only the third of these ambitions was achieved, but the holiday did serve to bring us together and weld us into a family. We had rooms in a French convent guest-house in the tiny village of L'Abbaye St Jacut which had an untidy garden running down to the beach. Here Oscar made us build relief maps for our geography lessons, with the countries and their capitals spelt out in shells and pebbles. Both parents found the holiday unfulfilling, almost frightening. The only other guests were English pensioners twenty years older than themselves, living impoverished lives far from the centre of things, ignored by the world, unable to afford such small luxuries as English newspapers or a radio. Olga had them all telling their life stories and among her manuscripts are fascinating glimpses of neglected old people in 1933. They were living in France because it was cheaper than in England, in a convent because it was cheaper than a boarding house. Retired admirals, colonels, civil servants could not afford a cottage or flat of their own. Would old age treat them the same way?

Olga had stronger reasons for empathy. Flo, of comparable age, was living in privileged circumstances, but for how long would the old lady's private income last? It had been halved by the war, and halved again by the slump. She occupied a castle which belonged to her son and which she could hardly afford to run. When in July Olga and her family went to Matzen it was invaded by visitors, Olga's as well as Flo's. There was a strange variety of guests, the Austrian and English cousins mingling with Provincial

Commissioners and typists from Kenya, school girls from England, and Flo's old Quaker friends. There was even a Chinese admiral among them, befriended by Tom when he was naval attaché in Shanghai. Willie's old shooting companions, drawn from a wide sweep of the community, the aristocracy down to the smallest farmer, dropped in from time to time, while his shooting club up in Brandenburg were in urgent need of even more of the support *their* castle had always given them since feudal times. How many of these people would befriend Flo if she became bereft of her romantic old castle? Olga could look after her in Kenya but would she agree to join her?

Olga had enrolled in a course of journalism, spent as much time as she could pounding away at her typewriter, and started writing about her mother. Soon Blackwood's Magazine paid handsomely for *Gracious Lady* stories set in the Tyrol and wanted more. By 1934 she had sufficient stories to form a book, *Tales from Tyrol*. Today they are dated, but yet retain a certain charm. They reflect well her sympathy for the impasse her beloved Tyrol had reached in the aftermath of the First World War. Although written in the third person as if by a visiting tourist, the stories show both the problems of rural communities in the Tyrol and also the extraordinary way Flo had gained the confidence and love of all around her.

In 1926 – five years after Willie's death – she had been the first woman and the first foreigner to be awarded the highest civil honour by the new Austrian republic. This was in recognition of her work in setting-up – at the time of the great hunger after the First World War – Child Welfare Centres all over Tyrol. They developed into Infant Welfare Clinics, kept going by a formidable army of middle-aged and elderly middle class ladies who put on their mountain boots and solemnly climbed to the distant villages and checked that each clinic was running smoothly, that supplies were arriving, and that someone – often the mayor's or the doctor's wife – was supervising the distribution. Someone had also to check on the children, many of whom were hungry, ragged, and in winter could not go to school because they had no boots. By the time the next disaster hit Austria, the world slump of 1932, the clinics had become self-supporting by the local community.

There was one story that Blackwood's would not publish, nor would any other magazine she approached. It concerned Olga's only recorded psychic experience, or was it just an odd dream? In feudal times, the main law court for a large section of the Inn Valley had been in Matzen; there were dungeons, a place of execution, and tucked away in the lower corner of the castle a condemned cell. Recently Flo had panelled this little room, moved two ancient spinning wheels into it, and renamed it the spinning room. Olga took over this room, in which to shut herself up to write. It already had a good work table, to which she added an arm-chair, a rug, a table lamp, and would disappear there as soon as she could escape after dinner. One night she worked so late that when she wanted to go to bed she found the door at the top of the staircase had been locked against her and she could not make anyone hear. She went back to her dungeon, wrapped herself in the rug and settled into the wicker chair, where she fell asleep.

She had a very vivid dream. She was in that same room, looking down into it from above. It was without its panelling; in one corner a pile of straw mattresses lay on the stone flagged floor. There were three prisoners sitting round a table playing cards. Each man had a number on the flaxen tunic he wore over rough leather breeches, and she noted that the numbers seemed to go in order of age, so that number one was a rangy old grey-beard, number two a short, sturdily built young man in his mid twenties, and number three a youth still in his teens. There were a number of pigeons in the room, some perched on the window bars, others on the floor. A white pigeon perched on number one's shoulder, and as he bent with the others over the card table it was almost indistinguishable from the old man's hair. Suddenly there was a great clanking of keys. The door was pushed open and a warder came in. He announced that prisoner number one had been pardoned and would be set free the next day, number two was to go back to the main dungeon and would not suffer the death penalty. The guard did not look at number three, and so they all knew he would be hung the following morning. It was a fate all three had anticipated. When the warder had gone, number one took off his tunic and handed it to the youth.

"Give me your tunic, son, and put this one on!"

"But you can't do that – it means that they will hang you instead of me!" the young man protested.

"And I have but a few years to go, and you have your whole life! Go on, do as I ask you. Let me do one fine deed before I die.

And in return, look after your mother. She has had a hard life, a washerwoman with no husband to help support you, and you spending her money drinking and fighting!"

The young man did not need much persuading, although he wondered how the old man knew he was the washerwoman's illegitimate son – he was always careful to hide the shame, in his eyes it was greater shame than that of hitting a bellicose drunk who had attacked him. He had not meant to kill him, just to deflect his blows. That night no one slept much. The old man took down a file from a hidden ledge and scraped away at the picture of a pigeon he was making in the left hand corner of the room. "That will have to do!" he said as the last candle flickered out. Soon after, dawn filtered in through the tiny slit windows, making patterns on the floor. The pattern was still changing with the sunrise when the door was flung open, and number three was called. As the old man went out he took the pigeon from his own shoulder and placed it on the youngster's.

"Look after him too!" he said and was gone. Through the slit window of the room, the boy wept as he watched the scene at the gallows. He could not see the foot of the gallows nor the noose being placed round the old man's neck, but when the rope was pulled and the figure was hoisted high, he watched the frail old man kicking and struggling. When at last he was still, the boy wiped away his tears, took the chisel from its hiding place and continued to work on the picture of the pigeon. He was still working when the door was again flung open. This time it was the lord of the castle who marched in, followed by two warders.

"Number one!" barked the warder, and the lad stood up.

"Your servant, Herr Baron", he bowed low thinking 'So I am for it after all!'

"First you kill a man carelessly, because you were drunk, then you let an old man die for you! Are you proud of yourself?" The Baron's voice was full of scorn. The youth stood there in silence. Prisoner number two intervened.

"Herr Baron, the old man was very insistent. Young Hans did try to dissuade him!"

"Has the young man no tongue to speak for himself?" The scorn and anger were still there.

"Indeed, Herr Baron," said young Hans, "I am so overcome with shame, I can hardly speak. I loved him, old Hans, that I did, and he said he wished me to live on so that I could look after my mother!"

"Your mother? He knew your mother?" A questioning tone had replaced the anger in the Baron's voice.

"I don't know my lord, but he knew of her!" The Baron took a scroll from the warder, and Hans knew it was the sentence of death.

"She is the washerwoman for the castle, is she not?"

"Yes, Herr Baron!"

"And you her only son?"

"Her only child, Herr Baron."

"And you have no father?" Young Hans hung his head, and the Baron continued: "Well, since old Hans gave his life for you, I shall set you free, but one more disturbance of any kind from you and you know what will happen." He put his hand to his throat, but all he said was: "Yes, you look exactly like him."

Young Hans was gazing out of the window where old Hans's body still hung, and missed the import of the remark.

"Free him. Free them both|" the Baron snapped at the warders and added: "I'll deal with you imbeciles later! Mistaking an old man for a youth!"

In her dream Olga watched the two men led out by the jailer, the white pigeon tucked into Hans's tunic. With the clang of the door she woke up, the dream clear in her mind. It was dawn, there were the strange shadows made by the dawn light coming through the narrow windows which she had seen in dream but never before had she been in this room at dawn. She opened her door, and heard the gentle sound of Franz, the caretaker's husband, raking the gravel in the courtyard below. He was among the unemployed and Flo paid him as a gardener in summer although he was sadly ignorant of flowers. She emerged from her cell, lent over the wall of the cloistered passageway and asked him to fetch his tools and remove the panel in the corner where she had seen the carving. It took Franz only a few minutes and there it was, the life-sized drawing of a pigeon, not quite completed. She was determined to find out if the rest of the story was true. A kindly cousin went to the archives of Innsbruck and found that a young man had indeed been condemned to death and then pardoned, that records had been kept on him, that he had obtained a small holding high on the hillside in full sight of the gallows. There he had kept pigeons and bees. His mother came to live with him; she was washer-woman to the castle, doing her washing in the pure water in the spring at the bottom of the hill. Olga wrote up the experience. She never placed the story. She did not talk about it, and the manuscript was found after her death. As we shall see, it made sense of two later appearances of white pigeons.

* * * * * * *

Among Flo's guests was a rich lady who arrived in her own chauffeur driven car. It took up all the room in the old coach house down in the lowest court-yard and Oscar's Baby Ford had to live in the top court yard outside the woodshed, exposed to summer storms. Mrs Gardner soon had all the family fetching and carrying for her. She was not used, she said, to managing without a lady's maid to look after her clothes and help her to dress and could not think how my grandmother and mother managed without them. When it was wet she would ask Oscar to take her down to the village to do her shopping. Oscar had already to spend much time meeting guests, and returning them to the station, and doing 101 other chores. Olga asked Mrs Gardner whether her chauffeur could not take her.

"Certainly not," she replied, "When it's wet, the car gets muddy and he has to clean it! He does not like to have to do that!" The good lady had perhaps more reason for complaint about the noise we girls made and the frequent dancing to the gramophone we enjoyed in the great hall. Then she announced that she wanted to come the following year and asked for a definite date when the girls would not be there. My grandmother expressed her horror to Olga about receiving her again, but did not see how to avoid it. Olga had an idea, and spoke to the lady herself.

"Why don't you get a house of your own, then you could come and go when you wanted and have your own servants, and be as quiet as you liked. It could be done for a few hundred pounds!" It is not easy to buy houses in rural Tyrol, almost impossible to find one to suit this guest. They soon decided to build one. Olga managed to find a man willing to sell a tiny corner of a field with a wonderful outlook. Building houses was undoubtedly one of Olga's favourite occupations. This time she wanted to use it as relief work for the men of the valley of Brandenburg. The men were delighted to have the work, which was carefully planned to take place between the end of the harvest and the beginning of winter. Soon a little three-bedroomed chalet was standing in the field, and the following year Mrs Gardner had her own house. It was well planned, a summer holiday cottage for one old lady on her own. I was lucky enough to inherit it and it took quite an adjustment to turn it into a winter hostelry for six of Olga's grandsons.

In the autumn of 1933 all three girls were packed off to school, Ronny joined Pella at the Godolphin and I, who had insisted on being called June, was dropped off in a school in Versailles. Oscar and Olga returned to England at a loose end, nowhere to live, nothing to do, and very little money to do it on. They took a one bed-roomed flat in Lancaster Gate in London while they looked around. Even though housing prices had continued to drop it was difficult to find anything they liked for the £700 they could afford. All the capital with which they had started out had been sunk into the farm. London was expensive and although Oscar was near all the things he enjoyed, they cost money and he did not have any. His pension was about £700 a year and his daughters' expenses came to £500.

At Easter, I brought back whooping cough from my French school. The experience of four girls having whooping cough (once again an extra girl had been wished on us) in a one bedroom flat convinced them that a move was essential. When Olga had sold Four Throws house, she had kept two fields, and had built a garage on one of them in which she had stored her furniture. She now decided to build a cottage in one of the fields. Oscar longed to go to Oxford, where he would have access to good libraries and lectures, but after Olga's experiences on their first holiday there she would not hear of it. As we girls recovered one by one, we were sent back to the Godolphin, myself included, and Olga went down to Four Throws to start building a cottage on the highest point of the field, with entrancing views over the weald of Kent. She burrowed out enough space among the furniture in the garage in which to set up camp for herself and her typewriter. By day she harried the builders to move faster and by night she warmed some food on a Primus stove and wrote by the light of a hurricane lamp. At Christmas they moved in. At last, after nearly two years of retirement, they had their own home in England. It was a comfortable, well planned, icy-cold cottage, with cherished pieces of furniture from her grandmother fitting neatly into niches planned for them. Today it has been insulated, wind-proofed and double glazed, but at the time it was cheaply finished, a north sea wind whistled through the badly fitting window frames, snow piled up in drifts against the thin walls, and the only way Oscar could shelve books he considered essential was by building book shelves up the stair case. Olga went on writing, and Oscar gave talks to many local groups, played chess at Hastings, and acted as chauffeur to all members of the family.

Olga was not happy with the Godolphin school. She considered both her elder daughters were made to feel failures because they were not apt at academic work. This was not surprising considering the lack of any consistent schooling they had received early on. I, who had the advantage of proper schooling from the age of nine, got by academically but developed a heart problem. Olga blamed the school for my affliction, which were undoubtedly exacerbated by the housemistress's belief that you could strengthen children by not mollycoddling them. She took away our Chilprufe underwear. It did nothing for girls brought up in the tropics who had suffered severe whooping cough a few months previously. Olga removed all three of us in the summer of 1935.

Benenden, very near Four Throws, was chosen as an alternative. It was more expensive and would present financial problems but at least Pella had finished school and was ready to go to Vienna to learn German, while I had to spend three months on my back, during which time my father would coach me for a scholarship. It was decided that the parents would stay in Matzen while I was laid up. An Austrian girl, Maria, an orphan a little older than me who lived with her Jewish grandfather, was invited to come regularly to talk German to me. Maria proved more linguistically gifted than myself and it was she who learnt English rather than me German, but we became firm friends. I was fascinated by the very serious life Maria had to live, learning to cook and clean for her grandfather as well as studying much harder than I did. And now her life was getting worse by the day. An anti-Semitic school master picked on her and encouraged her class-mates to ostracize and bully her, so she needed a friend as much as I did, isolated in my luxurious prison. Olga gave me great speeches of Shakespeare to learn and told me to write three different endings for the Merchant of Venice. My father made history and the bible come alive for me, drawing comparisons between the Roman Empire and the British ones. He would become so frustrated at my inability at Latin, that the Latin grammar book often sailed across the room, once to my delight out of the window overlooking the pond – all that was left of the old moat. Unfortunately it became wedged in a tree and was in due course retrieved and deemed fit for use. Between them, they must have taught me something as I did well in the scholarship examination and joined Ronny at Benenden.

With daughters sorted out, the next problem was the farm. Olga began to hear distressing reports about what was happening at Wispers. The new tenants were not fulfilling their undertakings and were running the place into the ground. Phoebe who was living on the farm could not cope. Olga decided she must go to the rescue. Could Oscar cope with three daughters, two of whom had to be bridesmaids at two family weddings during the six months she would be away? Oscar could, but did not want to, take us girls to Matzen for the summer holidays without Olga. So far he had driven all the family, sardine-packed into the tiny Ford, across Germany and back every summer. Oscar was so distressed by the obvious signs of German re-armament that each year he wrote to the Foreign Office to report what was happening. Olga was writing articles which were published in many papers, about how bad conditions were in Austria and also how Jews were being mistreated. Oscar's German was insufficient to pick up what was going on and he might misunderstand warnings of the frightening events taking place. Instead we spent the summer visiting different places in England and catching up on his side of the family.

The third problem had to do with Flo, determined to stay on in Austria under the darkening clouds of Hitler's Germany. Even before the Anschlüss, the German occupation of Austria, sudden disappearances had started, grey lorries drawing up in the middle of the night, knocks at the door and the offending member of the family removed by force. By dawn the captive was in Germany, and the Austrian government proved helpless to retrieve him. Olga realized she must be careful what she wrote, because of similar danger for her mother. Flo was not co-operative. It was at this time that a letter came from a Munich museum, requesting that Flo lend them the beautiful crucifix, reputedly the work of one of

Durer's students, Veit Stoss, for a special exhibition. Flo wrote back saying that when the family bought the castle from its Austrian owners some sixty years before, the purchaser had sworn – in the chapel and on the crucifix itself – that it would never leave Matzen, for if it did a terrible curse would come upon the place. The chapel was open to the public three days a week, and she was happy to receive specialists at other times by appointment. The museum replied: Had the Gracious lady not understood, that it was Herr Hitler himself who wanted the crucifix to be exhibited, and they were making arrangements to collect it immediately. They would take great care of it, and return it within the year. Flo was not so easily persuaded. She wrote back:

"As I cannot be certain of the pure Aryan blood of the original, I feel it unwise to let the crucifix travel to Germany at the moment!" She never heard another word from the museum, but from that moment the crucifix went into hiding, a cheap one hung in its place, the real one was produced only when some art specialist or historian wrote requesting permission to view it. Flo was standing up to the German Reich, but one old lady was not going to win the battle.

* * * * * * *

Wispers had been rented out for five years, but Olga found it in a sad state. The tenants had taken a huge crop from the coffee trees but put no compost or manure back into it. They had not weeded and so let the dreaded couch grass return. They had not sprayed nor banded against the afflictions of coffee trees – mealie-bug, thrips, antestia. Nor had they undertaken annual repairs to roads and buildings. She took the farm back from them after only three years on the grounds that they had not kept their side of the agreement, put Phoebe Meeres in undisputed control, paid the bills, filled the compost pits, started the harvesting to help Phoebe with the complicated routine she wanted followed, and went down with amoebic dysentery. Once again she was carried round the farm when she was too weak to walk, four men trotting along singing as they carried her stretcher up and down the muddy hillsides. Amoebic is a very depressing illness, it affects the liver, and Olga wrote detailed instructions to Oscar on how to look after the girls if she did not recover. It was a thankful family who welcomed her home in time for Christmas 1936.

In the summer of 1937 the family once again congregated at Matzen, weighed down by visitors. Now it was Danes Beacon which was let, Oscar and Olga were on their way back to Kenya after only four years, and taking with them – in their cabin – a Tyrolean queen bee and her hive. Olga wanted to see if an Austrian hive would improve the strain of bees in Kenya, and produce better honey. Oscar said it was the only time that he shared a bedroom with two queen bees. Neither of them liked the heat, but the one with the hive had to be put in the refrigerated larder while the boat was passing through the Red Sea. The bees arrived safely at Wispers but did not long survive the savage attacks of African bees.

At Mombasa old friends were waiting on the quayside to welcome them. Lunch was laid on at the Provincial Commissioner's house, where they had once lived, and the Indian stationmaster greeted them warmly. He replied to Olga's 'How are you' – "Oh, I have lost my daughter but I have gained the O.B.E." At the time he was once more piling Olga's always excessive luggage into the old fashioned no-corridor coach they had requested, saying as he did so, "Oh much contraband, much contraband!" Next morning, dawn found them staring out at the herds of game which stretched across the Athi plains.

A dozen old friends were lined up at Nairobi railway station. And standing behind them, reserved and silent as always, was Phoebe in clean khaki slacks and bush shirt and, Olga noted with delight, mud on her walking shoes. It must be raining on the farm. As the car turned the last corner into the Wispers drive, Phoebe's dog, Brennan, was howling and Omayo was perched on a ladder behind the hedge grinning widely. He wore on his head a red woollen ski hat and looked like a giant garden gnome. They might never have been away.

They were both glad to be back, glad that the English experience was behind them, and they settled to enjoy the golden years of retirement. At least, that was what Oscar hoped. He should have known better. The very sight of Olga going round the farm with Phoebe saying repeatedly "Well done, well done!" should have warned him. She was recognizing the hard work Phoebe must have put in to reclaim it from the run down state it had been in a year earlier. In October 1937 the harvesting season had started, the pickers were at work, the coffee pulper was running smoothly, every thing looked trim and neat as it should at the start of the season. As soon as the picking was over Phoebe would want to return to her own little farm at Machakos where she was building herself a house of sun-dried brick. When she went, Olga would have attained the paradise she had so long looked forward to, a long time on her own farm with her family around her, as they returned from England one by one. And she still had more ambitions to achieve. Whatever retirement might bring, it would not be peaceful.

*   *   *

Chapter Eleven

WISPERS RECLAIMED

"Do you wake on Monday mornings with joy in your heart at the excitement of the week ahead? No, this is not an advertisement for Eno's (fruit salts – *Ed*) but how I feel, at nearly fifty, on my coffee farm! Women can farm coffee in Kenya!" So wrote Olga for the opening lines of an article which was never published. The next few years were probably the happiest in her life.

On the journey out, there had been an architect on board, and between bouts of writing and looking after the Austrian queen bee she had found time to plan extensions to Wispers. She wanted to build on a big new room where the girls could entertain their friends. Pella would be joining them next year, her education complete. Ronny was already starting at Eastbourne domestic college and would then have a year on the continent, while I had set my sights on Oxford. I would however be brought out to Kenya at intervals, so as not to lose touch with the family; in Olga's view long separations led to disrupted families. One of these visits had to occur sooner than expected. I had a bad go of measles at school and had to take another term off, so was to return for the Summer.

Both parents wrote long letters of advice as to how I, aged fourteen, was to behave during the four week journey without a chaperone on board ship. Oscar was concerned with my behaviour. Olga's advice was more down to earth. "Remember to wear a bra, try to have a bath every day even if you have to queue, and take plenty of Eno's (fruit salts)." No one warned me that the Captain in whose care I was, had long groping fingers and at Marseilles tried to make me accompany him alone to a hotel on the Riviera. Pella, no doubt weighed down with similar advice, followed four months later, just as I was returning to England. To Olga's disappointment neither of us showed much interest in the running of the farm. I spent my time reading or riding and Pella was a party girl.

Each Sunday Olga typed out a News sheet two or three pages long for us girls and her mother, and added a personal note to each. She had altered the interior of the house, moving the bathroom from one side of the house to the other, and decided now that I was coming she must make bathroom curtains. They had managed without them, Olga would bathe at dusk with no light in the bathroom, and she thought curtains superfluous for Oscar. Now with a daughter arriving she must make some curtains. Her Wispers News sheet starts: *"What I feel about bathroom curtains is that they are always with you, a sort of back ground to other activities. They have been on my mind for some three months, and last week thought they must be pre-June! Like the boy on the lawn mower, I get round the many windowed cottages of ours just in time to start again. Metaphorically, they flap at me all the time. They won't take a minute to run up, yet look at this last week. Realignment of the factory, Phoebe moving house, two days off farm work, all quite peaceful and nice, until the phone man, an Indian, whose scarlet post office bike was stolen from here last week, and who now has to foot it out looking like a mournful sphinx, has a few words with Phoebe's bees. I was moving the 150 gallon tank at the factory that morning, heavi-hoing it off its stand beautifully up the hill to a better spot for the refilling of the cherry tank, to a tune that the boys always chant when they take a hand and each leans towards the job hopefully thinking someone else is going to do the work. With a hop, skip, and jump the tank took off down the hill, catching on to the barbecue (coffee drying) hedge which it crushed to smithereens, The jabbering and now tuneless mob caught up with it there and we had to trundle it up the hill again, moving in the oddest circles owing to its cement bottom. We stood it upright again until the green corrugations towered above us giving us no grip at all, but with thirty pairs of hands gathered closely round its lower edge we moved up hill slowly, with me as band master walking backwards until it developed into musical chairs, when I sat down with a bump and so did the tank, only I sat down first. At that precise moment news was brought to me that the headman's wife was having her baby. We jabbed the tank into position and stretchered the woman into our hospital, only to find that it was a miscarriage and all over except for high fever. I bethought me of the phone, as I thought we might need an ambulance and on asking the sphinx-like Indian I noticed that his cone-like face had two distinct hemispheres now, in diagonally opposites corners of his face, an odder looking man I never saw – poor man, it must have been painful. I found the way he had fixed the phone, was that I could not ring out, and when anyone rang in I could not be heard, but only listen as the caller with growing desperation talked to me...."*

The letter continues:- while she was trying to get through to the post-master, she was called to another baby, which arrived easily but was very small. Meanwhile she had used a hospital ward to store the goods of men on leave, and now had to clear one room in a hurry for the second mother who must be isolated from the first in case she has puerperal fever. She is busy at the hospital when one Mrs Freeston arrives and asks Olga to speak to the Mothers' Union. "On What ?" said Olga. "On anything you like!" Olga thought she would be funny. "On overcrowded lives making slums of our minds!" said Olga. "That is pure genius!" said Mrs Freeston, "Please speak for forty minutes on that!" Olga continued her letter, to write that as the Mothers' Union was dying anyway, she did not mind giving it the final thrust. And the bathroom still had no curtains.

* * * * * * *

Prime Minister Chamberlain returned from Munich to London with his infamous: "Peace in our Time" announcement.

"What nonsense!" said Olga, "We can't sit back and watch the Jews slaughtered for ever!" and she sent for Ronny to come out as soon as she had finished at Eastbourne. War now seemed inevitable and Olga considered it too dangerous to send a daughter to the continent in case she became stranded there.

The refugee problem soon took over much of Oscar's and Olga's time and abilities. They had both been overwhelmed when the Anschlüss, the German invasion of Austria, took place in 1938, Jews were now leaving Austria in their thousands; they could bring less and less with them and there was nowhere for them to go. Oscar tried to get entry permits into Kenya for men with selected skills but it was hard work. The Oxford Group movement was strong in Kenya and very anti-Semitic. Both Oscar and Olga became members of the Plough Committee, a branch of the British society formed to settle Jews on the land. Throughout the British Empire there were derelict farms as a result of the 1930s slump. The idea was to settle refugees on these farms and provide enough help to get them started. Let friends and families be grouped together so that they could support each other, set up their own skills, and they would be sure to start little industries and make a contribution to the country, while being self sufficient from the land. Olga wrote:

"This refugee business; there is a lot of propaganda going against them and O is doing it for them. That dirty dog of a man

Cavendish Bentinck is against them but was appointed by a dear old duffer on a visit as Chairman of the Plough Committee out here. He is trying to stop the whole thing. Hearing on a broadcast by some keen farmer that O was speaking at Naivasha on Friday, he ordered a committee meeting in Nairobi and all members to attend, thinking that would close down O's meeting, and that men driving in fifteen or thirty miles would go away disgruntled about the whole thing. 'All right, hold your old committee meeting, I'm damned if I let the farmers down!' 'But we want you to report!' said Cavendish Bentinck. 'Then I'll do both.' 'No you don't,' I said, 'seeing the state of the roads and your age!' So we have reached stalemate." She wrote this, but she knew, we all knew as we read the Wispers News sheet, that there was no stalemate, Oscar would do both.

Cavendish Bentinck was an extremely influential man in Kenya, and a crafty one. He realized that by accepting this position he would be well placed to slow the influx of refugees, and yet at the same time receive praise for helping those sorrowful people. It must have been infuriating having people like Oscar and Olga on his committee with a genuine interest in helping them. In Kenya widespread support was necessary, because each refugee family would need to be placed with a settler family for at least six months, to learn Swahili, English, and the ways of the country. The next move would be paid employment for a year, probably on a low wage as a manager's assistant, and then they would be on their own. Wispers took its share of refugees. It was not always easy. Olga wrote:

"Monday morning, our chief motif being refugees. They are of course a terrific nuisance wanting something or other all the time. The young woman (she was one of a trio, two young men and the girl who had arrived together) *quite confident that she is quite capable of housekeeping in the cottage, but has no notion of making bread, scones, jams, or pastry. Says she might be able to with gas. I wonder. Bread making is one of those things that came in before gas. Then I look back 25 years and I see a young ignoramus, cocksure and energetic, and devastatingly innocent, that was me. How much more one expects of the young than one ever was, or thought it necessary to be oneself! I try to think this, and then she comes up with the mincing machine in pieces, put together upside down, and says it won't mince, and one prays for patience, not with the machine or her ignorance, but the idle*

attitude with which it is thrown back at me without any attempt to see how it works, has worked, and will again work!"

One of the young men claimed to be an engineer, but came back repeatedly asking for a different tool each time – no idea of collecting all he needed to begin with. Olga continued: *"It will be so much easier when they stop working and go on picnics, and that will have to happen next week if they stay on."*

In 1939 two families arrived, one a medical consultant from the main children's hospital in Munich with his wife and daughter, the other a Viennese banker with wife and three teenage sons, plus a weakly young man who had already been rejected by two farms because he would not get out of bed before 9.a.m. When asked why, he said that Mutti (Mummy) had told him to remember that he needed his sleep. The medical family were never any problem, the doctor had one look at the little hospital and took it over from Olga, adapting wonderfully to the primitive conditions and improving the facilities in all kinds of ways. Olga need no longer be on call for medical emergencies. It was he who turned out at 3 a.m. to do a difficult delivery, and at 7 a.m. when the first minor accident needed immediate attention. He also looked after Ronny who had mumps, and sent off to Switzerland for a new drug for Oscar's pernicious anaemia, which proved more effective than the old one. His hands were remarkably deft although they looked like the claws of a bird of prey and he always hid them when he could. In Dachau, the SS had laid doctors and musicians on the floor and systematically trampled their hands with their hob nail boots. Long after the war was over, when we all knew the horrors of the camps, I took my two children to see him on the tea estate where he was medical officer. His damaged hands had gone arthritic and he did not know how much longer he would be able to work. He told me how lucky he had been to get out with only his hands damaged and added: "And I was even luckier to end up at Wispers!" He never complained about a disrupted life, a brilliant career cut short, a demotion from senior consultant in a big hospital to medical officer on a remote tea estate in Africa, or of the constant pain in the ruined hands. I remarked that he did not seem bitter, and he said no, but now when he saved a baby's life he wondered whether he would grow up to be a killer (we were in the midst of Mau Mau); and added that when Hitler's SS were jumping on his hands, he wondered how many of them he had saved when they were babies. I told him I had just driven through Munich, and he stopped me.

He had been driven through Munich naked in an open truck with a wire cage built on it, chained so he could neither stand nor sit, and as he was displayed through his own suburb he recognized some of his patients pelting him with bad fruit and tomatoes. He did not want to hear about Munich.

Back at Wispers in 1939, Olga was convinced that she could make any one into a farmer, and that her daughters would come round to it eventually. She would walk the banker round the farm every morning at six, explaining carefully in German what she was doing and why. At the same time she would be giving out the work in Luo and discussing problems with the team headmen in Swahili. The overweight banker would wear an immaculate city suit cleaned and pressed daily by his wife who had hitherto regarded a charcoal iron as something to put in a museum showcase. He trundled up and down the hills after Olga, puffing like the wood-fired railway engine tackling the escarpment from the Rift Valley. It was the rainy season, the ground was muddy, and the water ram was clogged. Olga took them down to show how Onyango, our Mr Fixit, cleaned and reassembled it. They passed the donkey and his keeper who between them carried water to the house when the ram failed. The donkey gave Olga his usual exuberant greeting and made for her pockets, which he nosed to find the carrots or sugar. The banker stared at the animal with peculiar interest. "Do tell me," he asked Olga, "What kind of horse is that? He does not look like our Viennese horses!" Olga remembered the wonderful Lipizzaner horses performing their graceful paces and steps, their riders showing their horsemanship by swooshing down from their saddles to retrieve handkerchiefs thrown by pretty girls. She saw in front of her a scruffy muddy old donkey so near the end of his working life that he carried but two four-gallon kerosene tins of water. It was for Olga the moment of truth, there were some men who would never become farmers; the smartly dressed middle-aged man in front of her was among them, as was the young man who still lay abed yearning for Mutti (Mummy) to look after him. When Olga reached the end of her bright ideas, it was Oscar who came to the rescue.

"The manager of that transport company needs an accountant – let's see if we can fit him in there!" he suggested. Fortunately that proved a success, such a success that after the war that family built up their own transport company and later transported themselves to Australia. But of course there were failures. The young lie-a-bed passed from hand to hand unwanted, even an office job was not acceptable – it started too early. Sadness carved deep lines in his dark, heavy-features, hypochondria making him ever more unemployable, always writing to Olga as if she was the Mutti who had stayed behind in Germany because she had money for only one passage. Later on, we all hoped that the real Mutti, who had given her all to send her son away from Germany, did not hear of his death from poliomyelitis before she was swept into the ovens. His hypochondria had killed him, for when he really was ill, no one – not even the doctors among his fellow refugees – took him seriously.

* * * * * * *

Apart from refugees, poultry became a major interest. Incubators heated by kerosene lined the wide hallway in the main house, and a slight smell of addled eggs permeated everywhere. There was a duck pond near the house, and although the gaggles of ducklings following a Muscovy or Aylesbury duck across the lawn looked very decorative the survival rate was not high. Wispers possessed numberless chattering cats and was visited by hawks and vultures.

It was fortunate that Ronny had arrived back in 1938, for she was the one daughter interested in the farm and capable enough to run it. After her training at Eastbourne domestic college she was an excellent housekeeper. She had always adored animals and took endless trouble inspecting the ponies and cattle. Soon she had a fat black Alsatian puppy travelling round the farm in Bully's old rucksack on her back. She called him Solomon because he was so wise. For Olga, Ronny was the embodiment of the ideal daughter. It was not long before her services were needed.

On Olga's fiftieth birthday, in 1939, Flo was staying with her sister Maud in England and preparing to go back to Austria for the Summer when she had a massive stroke, paralysing her down one side of her whole body, depriving her of speech. She was not expected to live more than a week or two, and Olga was cabled to come to England at once. Ronny could take care of the farm. Olga would travel by air.

Ten years earlier, when the Prince of Wales had visited Kenya in 1929 and King George V was taken ill, it had taken the Prince 17 days to reach England, that was with a man-of-war diverted to transport him, the Suez Canal kept clear of other shipping, and an express train waiting to take him from Marseilles to Calais. When Olga found it would take five days to do the same journey by flying boat, we all thought it was a miracle.

The Imperial Airways flying boats started in South Africa and worked their way north along the East Coast, landing at Port Reitz in Mombasa before flying six hundred miles across land to Kisumu, crossing the lake to Entebbe and following the Nile to Cairo. This route was not the shortest but gave the flying boats the shortest possible distance over land, where they could not ditch in emergency. Nairobi passengers embarking for the flight were flown in small land planes to Kisumu. Oscar took her to Nairobi's Airfield (now Wilson airport) where they had to wait interminably, because a herd of giraffe had taken up residence on the airfield and were proving difficult to chase away. At Kisumu she was driven to the hotel where she had nursed Major Gray twenty five years before and joined the passengers of the Golden Hind, the Imperial Airways flying boat, for a cup of tea before taking off to Entebbe where they spent the night in a brand new hotel. Each flying boat carried only about twenty passengers, it took off at dawn, came down on the Nile two or three times a day to fuel the boat and feed the passengers, stopped overnight at Khartoum, Alexandria, and Marseilles – calling at Athens en route, and the next morning they were in Southampton. They flew low over land or sea for the whole of the journey, and when rays from the rising and setting sun angled into the ground, Olga claimed she could see skeletons of old mountain ranges under the flat sand and scrub of the Sudan and Egypt, and see old wrecks in the clear sea around Athens. She was fascinated by the whole journey, and longed to explore each place where they put down.

Tom, now captain of the naval training establishment H.M.S. St Vincent in Gosport, met her in Southampton. In those days there was no question of a stroke patient going to hospital or intensive care, the patient remained at home, and if the family could afford it a nurse was engaged. The only high-tech service offered was a whiff of oxygen. The nurse slept in, and when she went off duty the family shared out the hours to sit with the patient.

Flo's extended family had congregated at Brownes, Maud's new home in Robertsbridge. Flo still had three sisters and two brothers alive who, with their families and those of the six dead siblings, collected round her bed. Fortunately Brownes was a roomy old farm house, with five large bedrooms, and three living rooms. It now had to develop rubber walls. Flo's nephews and nieces, many of them not much older than her grandchildren, camped in the Rookery. Camp beds appeared in the upstairs passages. Breakfast was chaotic. While the two old servants from Boxley Abbey struggled to produce elaborate breakfast dishes for large numbers, those sitting round the table played a never ending game of: "Pass my spectacles please". No one could remember where his or her spectacles had been left the previous night, and those found downstairs would be passed from hand to hand, or rather eye to eye. "These are not mine, I expect I left mine upstairs, June dear." I was spending my Easter holidays at Brownes quietly revising for my School Certificate exams, and went upstairs to search yet another room. Every time I found a pair they became an extra card in the lottery – the more spectacles passed around the less likely you were to find your own. On one particular morning, all seven elderly adults had mislaid their glasses, all so similar to look at that no one could tell the difference. It was eventually revealed that no fewer than four of the dozen pairs in circulation belonged to the stricken woman upstairs, while two belonged to our hostess, my great aunt Maud. With these six pairs removed, life became easier; I marked them with coloured cotton around the arms. Only I could remember which colour belonged to which great aunt. They thought I was a genius.

When Tom and Olga arrived, most of the others departed. It soon became clear that, although the stroke had been a massive one, Flo would drag out her life for some time. Although she could not talk, her eyes were still beautiful in the wrinkled old face and communicated a great deal. She could make sufficient noises to mimic the doctor, the nurse, or whoever it was she thought was too bossy. After each performance she would roar with laughter. She also tut-tutted when Olga dared to wear slacks and almost whenever she saw her she waved a comb in her good hand to beckon her to have her hair combed.

Olga deplored even the oxygen. "If she cannot walk or talk, why not let her die?" she kept asking. She did not know what to do. It was heart-breaking to see her active, intelligent and much loved mother confined to such a restricted life. Olga had arrived at the end of April expecting to stay one month. Soon it was June and she had to be back on the farm in October at the latest for the coffee-picking season. The journey back would have to be by sea. She wanted to take Flo with her; Tom wanted her to stay in England where he could see her from time to time. Olga yielded, a decision they were both to regret when the bombing started.

Tom begged Olga to go out to Matzen to close it down. He was the owner, his mother had only a life interest in the place, but he could not go because as a senior Naval Officer he was forbidden to travel to Germany at that moment. Olga remembered all the articles she had written. How even before the Anschluss, the Nazis had once come in the middle of the night, parking their little grey vans in Matzen park, to retrieve a refugee from a neighbouring house, and how Oscar had managed to foil their plans. She decided she must go but invited Virginia, an artist friend, to go with her. It would be more difficult to kidnap two women than one, and if Virginia were let go free, everyone would know what had happened to Olga. The two women set out by train in the middle of June.

Matzen was in wonderful order with its trusted caretaker and her husband, Franz. Franz now had a good job in the railway repair yards at Jenbach. With his wife's wages as caretaker, a free flat and fuel in Matzen, and the use of a productive vegetable garden, he was better off than at any time since his family had lost everything they had at the great inflation seventeen years before. In order to obtain his job, Franz had had to join the Nazi party. Olga was not sure whether he was a Nazi at heart or whether it was a matter of convenience. Certainly he had needed the job to restore his sense of self-respect. He was a proud man, reluctant even to accept the wages that Flo offered him as a gardener during the summer months.

If war came, the Grohman family's absence would be a long one. Would this couple be able to cope? One of the young Austrian cousins, Maria, came over to help Olga and was able to tell her how utterly Flo had relied on them, insisting that the old lady knew she would never come back, but instead of bemoaning the fact she had entertained Maria by acting out various scenes from Shakespeare – she was splendid as Lady Macbeth, stalking along the cloisters clutching silver candlesticks, and even better as the nurse in Romeo and Juliet, pausing to look up to the balcony of the North wing. Flo had been the chatelaine of Matzen for thirty years and it had become a museum of her many abilities, full of her paintings and sketches, and beautiful petit-point needle-work. In her room was a large pile of typescript notes, a biography of her own life. Locally she was remembered for starting the baby clinics and helping at the time of famine. Now the villagers called endlessly to enquire after her, flowers were brought to Olga, and even plates of precious butter, for Germany had already rationed butter to make more guns. Tyrolean butter had to go to Germany.

Despite these kind interruptions Olga worked at her usual lightning speed and did the most essential tasks first. She saw the bank, made out a power of attorney, made funds available to pay the bills, put the rooms in order for the Austrian cousins to use, put the crucifix in an even safer place, packed as many valuables as she dared to take out with her, and placed the whole building under the protection of the organization that looked after historic buildings to make sure the castle was not commandeered for military use. She still had three days to go when she woke early one morning and there was Franz raking the gravel under her bathroom window.

"Morning, Franz, beautiful day, isn't it?"

"Gracious Lady, is your luggage ready to take to the station?"

"No!" said Olga firmly. "I am not going today, not until Monday, don't you remember?"

Franz looked up at her as if he had not heard. "I'd like to take it down now, and then you could catch the night train." He looked very tense and was shaking slightly, but Olga was sleepy and her mind not as acute as usual.

"No Franz, we have not finished yet, I have a lot to do." She only realized how upset he was when he forgot to bid her good morning and disappeared to catch his train to work without saying a word. She worked over the problem and concluded that he knew of some danger to her, and she decided they would leave the next day. The two women packed their bags, told the villagers Olga had been called back to see Flo, and reserved seats on the following night's train to Zurich. They would not go out through Germany. After a long sad day Olga visited Flo's room and looked around it for the last time. It had the best view in the castle, looking west up the Inn valley to the Stubai Alps, and now she turned out the lights and went to the windows and threw them open. There was a full moon, the night seemed wonderfully peaceful, disturbed only occasionally by the low rumble of a train the other side of the River Inn. The main road beneath was silent. It was early for tourists and there would be few of them this year. Suddenly a bird brushed passed her as it flew into the room. She turned to the writing desk just behind her and switched on the light, a long low lamp with a green glass shade. She looked round the room, there perched on the gothic door of a built-in cupboard sat a white pigeon. She walked towards it, it did not move, and to her surprise it allowed her to take it in her hands, carry it to the window, and let it fly. She closed the window and walked back to the door, recalling her dream of the pigeons she had discovered six years before while working in the old death cell, just two floors below this room. Anyone less drawn to things supernatural would be hard to find, but alone in that large room in the middle of the night she wondered whether this visit signified her mother's death, or some misadventure to herself.

Inside the cupboard door where it had perched was pencilled the message that her father had written when he left Matzen in 1915. *Wednesday 28th April 1915 Goodbye to dear old Matzen one hour before leaving. Will it be for ever?*

She took a pencil from the desk and added her own message: *24 years later 1939 2nd July. Good-bye to dear old Matzen once again. Will it be for ever? Olga Watkins.*

On that same night Olga was woken from deep sleep to the sound of heavy footsteps tramping through Matzen. "The Nazis, they've come for me!" A terrible cold fear seized her. She crept to the window overlooking the park and there under the trees, stood two grey vans like those she had seen years before. Olga went into Virginia's room. She was sound asleep. Back in her own room, she tried the lights and they did not come on. Fumbling in the dark, she dressed hurriedly and packed a change of clothes, money, and her passport, scribbled a note to Oscar and hid it in the cleaning cupboard where the caretaker would find it, and policemen would not. Then she carried a chair to Virginia's doorway and settled herself astride it. It would be a pity to wake her up too soon.

Matzen is a very complicated building with two sets of spiral staircases dating back to mediaeval days and one straight one put in by Olga's grandmother. As well as a cloistered passage on each floor around the main courtyard, there is a wooden passage connecting diagonally the two corners. On the mountain side Matzen is only three floors high including the loft, but on the valley side it is five floors high. It is very easy to get lost in the building, particularly in the dark. The footsteps went on and on, round and round, in the attic above her rooms, through the entrance hall below them, but they never came to the door of her flat. Olga put her head on her arms and fell asleep on the chair. The dawn was well advanced when she woke. She looked out of her window on the valley side, the grey vans had disappeared and three floors down she could see the caretaker's lights burning. She crossed to another room and looked into the courtyard. Franz looked exhausted. He was raking the gravel.

"Morning Franz," she said. "You look tired. Now my mother is not here, you do not have to do the gravel every morning, not when you are working. Tell me, Franz what happened last night?"

"A shutter was banging in the north wing. I went to fix it!"

"Oh come, Franz, there was more action than that. I heard the tramp of boots, and the lights went out."

Franz stopped raking and looked up at her. "I tell you, Gracious Lady, a shutter was banging in the north wing and I went to fix it. And then the lights fused! I fixed them too. Now, Gracious lady, is your luggage ready for me to take down?" There was an urgency in his voice.

"No Franz, I don't want you to be seen with it. We will leave today. My friend, who is not known here, will take the train to Worgl and come back with a taxi to fetch me and the luggage. We will then be driven back to Worgl where we shall catch the fast train. No one from this village or from Jenbach (where Franz worked) will see us leave. And if anyone asks, we spent last night at Brandenburg." She noticed the look of relief that came over Franz's face.

"Thank you Gracious Lady, now I must take my leave. Be assured we shall look after the castle to the best of our ability. Farewell, and my greetings to the old Gracious lady."

"Thank you, Franz, for your courage! You have risked much for us. I shall not forget."

In June 1939 every traveller leaving Austria, tourist or emigrant, was searched assiduously. Not only was the foreign currency allowance only 10 marks, hardly enough for twenty four hours food and lodging, but it was forbidden to take valuables out of the country. Olga was fearful how she would fare at the frontier, every case stuffed with antiques she loved. To reach Switzerland she had to go through Innsbruck, and it was there that the luggage was searched and sealed rather than at the final frontier. Waiting her turn in the customs queue she noticed a Tyrolean hat hanging on the peg. It carried a magnificent Gemsbart, that decoration which looks like a shaving brush and is sometimes fixed to the back of Austrian hats. It is a hunting trophy, made from the back hairs of a chamois, and the older the chamois the longer the hairs and the more difficult it was to bring down such a canny old buck. Olga was also wearing a very fine one, from one of her father's champion animals. Now she matched the hat to its owner by the clothes he was wearing and stood in his queue although it was the longer than the others. Virginia went to the shorter queue and straight to the train. Olga did not want her embroiled in her troubles. When her own turn came she said to the customs officer: "Is that your hat, with the magnificent gemsbart on it?"

"Yes," he said, "and I shot it myself. It's not a tourist one like yours!"

"Mine's not a tourist one," said Olga indignantly, "My father shot it, and it's longer than yours!" She took her hat off and threw it on the counter in front of him. In Tyrol that constitutes a challenge – the two gemsbarts have to be measured by a third party and the owner of the shorter one has to buy the other a drink. The official fetched his hat and placed it carefully beside Olga's, gemsbart to gemsbart, and tapped his colleague on the shoulder to act as referee. The man immediately abandoned the travellers he was searching, measured the gemsbarts carefully and declared that Olga's hat won by a centimetre. The defeated man held out his hand: "Congratulations," he said, "you must be the daughter of Herr Grohman of Schloss Matzen, I went shooting with him once, when I was a boy. Now it is my pleasure to buy you a drink. Can you wait until I've finished?" He glance at his watch. "In twenty minutes?"

"I would love to drink with you," Olga said, genuinely regretful, for although she rarely touched alcohol, she would like to hear the wonderful stories he would be sure to tell. "Particularly because you are quite right, Grohman was my father. Now be a kind man and let me catch my train – my companion is already on it and it is due to leave in five minutes. My mother you know is very ill."

"I am sorry to hear that, and give her my best greetings!" He was sealing her cases with twisted wire seals as he spoke. He had not opened them. Olga looked round for her porter – he had not waited. So the official vaulted lightly over the bench, held her rucksack for her to put on, and picked up her two cases.

"You carry a heavy rucksack for a woman," he said looking at her and weighing the cases in his hands. Then he broke into a smile, guessing exactly what she was doing and lacking the heart to stop her. "Come on, or we shall miss that train!" and he led her across the tracks and loaded the bags for her, shaking off her thanks with the words: "It is a pleasure to serve Herr Grohman's daughter. He was a fine shot, a very fine shot."

* * * * * * *

Olga was surprised to be met by Tom at Dover, he must have been waiting there for hours. She had cabled her arrival from Zurich. "Thank God you are back, girl," he said, "I should never have asked you to go. I have been wondering all week how I would get you out if anything went wrong."

"It very nearly did go wrong!" Olga started to tell him.

"Wait a minute", he said, "tell me later. That youngest of yours has got her school certificate results. She has done very well indeed. I thought we might go over there this afternoon and take her out to tea. I have to go back to Gosport tomorrow, and the school is a devil of a place to get to without a car. Yes of course we'll go to Browne's first, we are lunching there."

As the two of them called in at Flo's room they looked an impressively handsome pair. He was wearing his Captain's uniform and Olga had changed into her blue linen coat and skirt. Tom was 51, Olga just fifty. He was 6ft 2ins tall, she 6ft in her shoes. They were absurdly alike, each with Flo's soft features and Willie's long lean body and dark curly hair. The old lady chortled with delight to see them, clapped her left hand repeatedly on her paralysed right arm when she heard where they were going, and beckoned Olga to come and have her hair combed.

They took me out to tea. On the way to Cranbrook they were all laughter, outdoing each other in funny stories, but in the tea-shop the laughter stopped. Olga spoke:

"The situation is very serious. The war will begin quite soon. You will have to leave school and come back to Kenya with me. I shall arrange for us to travel by Cape Town and visit the cousins in Harrismith."

"Can't I study for Higher Certificate?" I asked.

"There is not a school which offers it, or at least not a girls' school, in Kenya. We all have to make sacrifices in war time."

"Tell me, did you see Maria?" Maria was my Austrian friend. She was a Jewess, grand-daughter of a local pharmacist.

"This really is bad news!" said Olga. "You know where she lived with her grandfather above his pharmacy? Last Summer after the Anschluss German soldiers worked their way down the valley destroying all Jewish property. They marched the young soldiers all day with no food, and then filled them up with beer and turned them loose to do what they liked. Her grandfather saw the mob coming from the attic window while they were still some way off, and thought to shoot Maria so she would not have to suffer multiple rape. He took up his old rifle, his only weapon, and then could not pull the trigger, he loved her so much, but started to cry. Maria took the rifle, shot her grandfather, reloaded, then turned it on herself. It is difficult to kill yourself with a rifle, but she succeeded first shot. She was only just in time, as they were breaking down the door. The villagers who told me the story said *Wasn't she brave.* You are going to have to be brave too. We will do our best to see you get to Oxford, if that is what you have set your heart on, but we cannot leave you in England now."

"It no longer seems too important." I said. "When can I join up? I'm sixteen now you know!" I had had my sixteenth birthday the previous week.

"That's the stuff', said Tom, "Another two years and make sure you join the WRNS, quite the best service."

"Ronny is going to join the FANY's in Kenya," said Olga hopefully. "She has already attended a training camp!"

"No, I'm going to join the Air Force," I said. "They've already tried to recruit me!"

Tom raised his eyebrows at Olga. She said: "Very romantic. Last year when she travelled back home alone, a group of young Air Force officers joined the boat at Port Said. No doubt they had a wonderful time on board."

"How do you know?" I asked. I had been careful to hide my first flirtation from my parents.

"He wrote to you several times, and even came down with a large bunch of flowers, but the school intercepted the letters and sent the young man away. We have the letters at home, unopened!" I was furious and it made me quite eager to leave a school that treated me like that. Tom interrupted my outburst:

"It's time we got you back to school. The butler said you had to be back before seven!"

"He's my friend!" I said.

"So I gathered. He expressed pride in your achievements I hope that you will not let this success go to your head!"

"And I'm taking you shopping next week," announced Olga, eyeing my crumpled cotton uniform dress distastefully, "grown up clothes now you are sixteen, for board ship. You cannot go around in those awful cotton dresses much longer!"

* * * * * * *

Two weeks later we were on the *Dunnottar Castle* for Cape Town, second class in an inside cabin. I wondered how two large adults were going to survive in such limited space. I climbed up to the top bunk. Olga pushed her typewriter and box of files under her bunk. "Here, you'd better have your book box up there." I had spent five pounds on books to read on the way out, all cheap editions of history books. £5 went a long way on books in 1939.

"I suggest you stow it on top of the wardrobe." said Olga.

"But it will fall off the first time the ship rolls!" I said. And it did, that night, blocking the door and preventing Olga's hasty exit to be sick.

It was the first time in my memory that I had had the undiluted company of my mother for several weeks at a time. I did not however have her attention because Olga plunged herself into her writing, often missed meals, and did not like to be interrupted, even to go ashore at the ports of call. Whereas on my trip alone the previous year, I had always been invited to join one shore-going party or another, when my mother was there no one invited us both.

The voyage seemed endless. There was the usual ship-board routine, round and round the deck at least twenty times before breakfast, a huge meal served in the hot dining room. Then I helped Olga set up her writing things in some quiet corner. As the ship changed direction and the sun moved across the sky her position had to be moved several times a day. I retreated to the smoking room, always the quietest room on board, and read until morning break time, then took part in the games competitions. Lunch, more reading, tea, more games, dinner and some kind of entertainment often requiring money to participate. Olga thought such money wasted and went on writing.

"Do you play bridge?" asked a new acquaintance at the beginning of the voyage.

"No" said Olga firmly.

"Well then, what do you do?"

"Good question!" I replied.

Someone on board must have known because Olga it was who was asked to judge the First class children's Fancy Dress. It was forbidden for the Second class to cross into the First class without an escort, and Olga waited patiently at the appointed place for the head steward and a member of the committee who ran the children's party to meet her. She was treated as if it was a great honour to watch six kids parade around the deck – there was a prize for each so choice was not too important – and afterwards sticky sponge cake and pink ice-cream was offered. The committee members called for tea, three cups were brought for the committee members, none for Olga.

"We need another cup," said the chairman to the steward. The steward looked firmly at Olga:

"Not for the likes of 'er 'ere" he replied.

We stayed on the boat all the way round South Africa to Durban and took the train up to Harrismith. Of Olga's many first cousins, five of the women made a life for themselves in horticulture or farming, an unusual choice in those days. The two sisters we were visiting had set up their own farm high on the African veldt and managed to survive the depression, although many farms all round had gone bankrupt. They lived in a little wood-and-iron bungalow overlooking vast distances of African veldt, the Drakensbergs blue in the distance. When things got bad, Joan – who had an Oxford degree – went off to Johannesburg and took some office job for six months and Vera managed the farm alone. Discrimination was even stronger against women than it was against blacks. Neither of those women, aged then 39 and 35, could operate a bank account of her own, and had to appoint a solicitor with a power of attorney who then allowed them to draw out their own money. On the farm they were more into self-sufficiency than was Olga and she took the visit as a lesson in how to achieve subsistence agriculture to a high standard.

* * * * * * *

We left Harrismith at midday by train to join our ship at Durban; the journey should have taken twenty-four hours, but it was dusk when we eventually reached the docks, the time the ship was supposed to sail. A short squat man wearing a huge felt hat which made him look like a mushroom stood in the door of the ticket office as Olga and I walked up followed by a procession of porters with our seventeen pieces of luggage. Olga dug in her bag for her tickets.

"There is no ship sailing. The *Edinburgh Castle* has become a troop carrier."

"So we are at war", said Olga.

"You are, we are not!" he stressed. South Africa did not come into the war until fighting came to Africa the following year, when Mussolini joined Hitler and Italian troops occupying Ethiopia attacked Kenya.

"We were on the train so we did not hear. Is not South Africa coming into the war?" she asked.

"Not bloody likely," and he spat towards my feet, making me jump.

"What are we expected to do?" asked Olga, thinking that there would be some kind of accommodation arranged for delayed passengers.

"That's not my business." He spat again. This time it was Olga who jumped. The conversation was over. We stood there, surrounded by our mountain of luggage, including a splendid rooster sticking his head through a crate, a gift from the Harrismith cousins intended to improve Olga's poultry in Kenya. With the help of another disappointed passenger, and the porters, Olga managed to put the luggage into storage. With the rooster, her writing case, typewriter, picnic basket, and endless other packages as well as myself and our 'Wanted on Voyage' luggage we found a taxi. The white driver was no more pleased to hear our English voices than the shipping man had been.

"Please take us to a cheap hotel," Olga instructed him, adding hopefully, "Not too far away!" It was about 7 p.m., already dark, hardly light enough to see that the hotel was a quadrangle of two-storey blocks, each room with direct access to the street-level by wooden verandas running around each floor, like a modern motel but an unusual layout for those days. There was an overdressed middle-aged peroxide blonde leaning against the lamp-post outside the hotel who watched us curiously as we unloaded the taxi. Another figure could be seen in the shadows. We were both tired and travel worn, and were dressed for an up-country farm rather than a smart sea-side resort. Inside the office, the manager looked us up and down, taking in every detail of our appearance. It was only later that I learned that this particular expression means a man is mentally undressing the woman concerned.

"You will want two rooms, of course?" he said, leering at me without bothering to take the cigarette from his mouth. I turned my back on him and walked over to the window which overlooked the courtyard.

"No! Why should we?" asked Olga.

"Well, it's more usual!" he replied.

"Why?" asked Olga. I was watching the woman we had seen outside the hotel cross the courtyard with a man half her age.

"As you like", said the man, "It takes all kinds." He spoke in the clipped manner that South Africans use but there was no trace of a South African accent. He called a ragged black boy to carry our luggage up. As we crossed the courtyard we were conscious of faces at windows watching our arrival.

"The trouble is," Olga confided to me as soon as we were safely in our room, "I haven't got enough money to stay even here for long – and although I can cable Nairobi for more, who knows if the cable will arrive, or how long it will take, or whether we will still be here when the money arrives!"

"I suppose," I spoke while I was looking out from the first floor window, fascinated by another overdressed woman bringing back another young man, "that is why the driver brought us somewhere where we could earn money, if only we exerted ourselves!"

"What do you mean?"

"Oh, for goodness sake, Mop, just take a look. Both the tarts we saw standing outside have brought in men, and here comes a third. They've put us in a brothel!"

"Don't be stupid," said Olga, "how would you know? At your age I did not even know the meaning of the word."

"Dad told me about them before I travelled out alone last year. He said that if I went ashore alone at Port Said or Marseilles, that is where I might end up. People on board ship were more polite – they said I was pretty enough to end up in a Sheikh's harem. Why else do you think the manager expected us to have separate rooms?"

Olga joined me at the window, "My God, you're right! What would your father say?"

"Or my grandfather," I said, although I scarcely remembered the pompous elderly vicar of Holy Cross Parish, Oxford. We laughed so much that we both had to sit down on the nearest bed. What a story to tell my school friends – my mother had taken me to stay in a brothel. I recovered first.

"I'm hungry. What are we going to do for supper?"

"We are not going out tonight", said Olga firmly, as she barricaded the door with our luggage. "I have the remains of our picnic lunch in that basket. And there is drinking water here I see. No careering round during the night, do you hear? If you want to go to the lav, we go together. And tomorrow we move."

Next morning it was the cockerel who awoke us with his raucous dawn crowing and brought angry women in all stages of bedragglement to our door. "Poor old chap, you must be the only unsatisfied male in the building!" I said, filling the cockerel's water tin and crumbing some remains of our picnic for him. The cockerel went on crowing. I went to the window, pulled the curtain open, shut it again quickly, and stood peering through a crack. Outside two women were peering in at us, and a group had collected in the courtyard below. The hotel manager, in Noel Coward type dressing gown and smart blue pyjamas emerged at a leisurely pace as if to show all these women who was in charge.

"Now then," he clipped, "So you are all after the poor old cock, are you?" He turned to Olga, who had emerged fully dressed, and stood on the balcony looking down at him. He switched into broad cockney: "I didn't know you were bringing your own cock with you!" There were roars of laughter, and he turned back to the crowd: "Now then ladies, back to your rooms. You need your beauty sleep. And this won't happen tomorrow!"

"It certainly won't," said Olga, then in a more affable tone: "Do you come from Kent?"

"Yes, I was born in Tunbridge Wells."

"I was born at Dimchurch," said Olga, "and my daughter in Hawkhurst." The manager raced up the wooden steps.

"And you've just bin back on a visit?" he asked. "Tell me, 'ow are things. What is going to 'appen? Will Kent be bombed? What's this 'Itler going to do to us?" They stood there talking on the hotel verandah, Olga smart in her blue linen and the manager equally smart in his bright blue dressing gown and pyjamas, while inside the room I dressed and packed. I heard Olga explain that the cock was a present to improve her farm stock; then she was telling him about the plight they were in.

"What about breakfast?" I asked.

"Breakfast is served in the dining room," he replied, then he looked at me. I was wearing my prettiest new frock for a day in Durban and no doubt had the bloom of youth about me. "You know, I don't think you fit in 'ere. I'll send a tray over." Before we had finished with the tray he was back, this time smartly dressed in a dark suit.

"I've telephoned around and found where the other passengers are, nice little residential plice not 'alf a mile from 'ere. I'll drive you there now if you like."

"You are kind," said Olga,

"And we are not taking the cock with us!" I said, keeping my eyes away from the man, knowing if he laughed so would I, and Olga would not even see the double entendres. The manager accepted it readily as a gift, and refused to let us pay for moving us. The boarding house to which he drove us was layered with middle class respectability, white lace curtains, antimacassars, and doilies scattered everywhere. The servants were sullen young black men, forever nagged by the proprietress who had a voice like a buzz saw. It was only 8 a.m. when we arrived but African cities start early and with other would-be passengers from the *Edinburgh Castle*, we walked from travel agent to travel agent all day. Not one was polite. One travel agent asked for our passports, piled them up, then picked them up one by one and aimed them at our faces. Another tore up our tickets, and a third used four letter words. All insisted that there was no way we could get back to East Africa, and repeated that the road journey was entirely unsuited for ladies.

"But we can't stay here until the end of the war!" Olga remonstrated.

"It won't be long," each in turn insisted, "You English have got it coming to you. That Hitler knows what he is doing! Good luck to him, I say." Hitler, like them, believed in a master race.

On the second day Olga took command of the stranded passengers. One young man, son of Nairobi's leading tailor, undertook to look into the possibility of buying second-hand cars and driving up in convoy. A retired Air Force officer tried to persuade Imperial Airways to put on an extra flight to Mombasa. A bank manager called on a branch of the Standard Bank and arranged for credit for the entire group; one cable to Nairobi settled us all. A divorcée travelling with her daughter called up acquaintances and arranged for hospitality among English South

Africans, a day on the beach, an evening at a barbecue. Olga moved us from our improvised bedroom in the guest house to a nearby seaside hotel which was empty in the chilly Southern Spring. We had a big quiet room on the top floor. She retired to this room to write, and I did our laundry and then prowled around buying food for picnic lunches and suppers.

Shipping news had now become secret and it proved impossible to get any sense about shipping movements, or indeed any information at all from hostile officials. It looked like being a long wait. Every morning and evening Olga and I tramped a mile down to the docks to see if we could find out anything. On the morning of the sixth day an old British India coaster, the SS *Basra*, was nosing her way into the harbour. Olga waited patiently and despite the supposed security checks, we found our way to the gangway, just as the captain was coming down it. He eyed Olga curiously, and listened to her story.

"Have you seen the shipping agent? It is his job!"

"He's pro-German and totally unhelpful to us English." As she spoke he looked at her even more closely.

"We've met before?" he asked.

"No, I don't think so," said Olga, "but I came aboard the *Basra* in the last war!"

"I was in the Navy then!"

"Perhaps it was my brother you knew." She mentioned the name, and had an immediate response. We found ourselves being entertained to cold drinks in the captain's cabin while he assured us that certainly he would take all ten stranded passengers, even if it meant over crowding.

Crowded we certainly were. We shared a four bunk inside cabin with the divorcée and her daughter, both of them such incessant smokers that the cabin proved uninhabitable. We slept on deck, under the stars, even on the first few nights when the southern spring was chilly. Our nights were only occasionally disturbed by tipsy passengers seeking home comforts but constantly by fleas seeking a good meal. We were always woken at 5 a.m. by sailors hosing down the decks. We did not sleep well, but lying on the hard wood we talked, of life and death and war and sex and what it all meant, and how that when things looked as dark as tropical night, it was then that the stars were at their brightest, it was just that sometimes we could not see them. Even that did not explain Maria's fate. And nothing has done so since.

Olga had heard that the article she had posted to Blackwood's Magazine from Port Elizabeth had been accepted and hoped to have a second ready to post at Mombasa.

"I must finish it before we arrive in Mombasa so we are not going ashore anywhere!" she announced firmly in Mozambique. Mozambique was of course a neutral port, being under Portuguese jurisdiction. Other passengers went ashore and came back with news of a German man-of-war waiting there to get back to Germany, anticipating the peace. They had already run out of drinking water but had a good supply of beer, and extraordinary faith in the success of Hitler's much vaunted blitzkrieg, the blitz part had not yet started. Lindi, in Southern Tanganyika, was not recommended as a place to go ashore; there were no docks even for the little SS *Basra*, and the launch had broken down.

Olga could not ignore other ports so readily. Shipping lists announced arrivals days before a mail boat arrived. At both Zanzibar and Dar-es-Salaam Oscar's old friends came to meet us and would not take a refusal. The Arabs in Zanzibar and the Government officials in Dar-es-Salaam entertained us like royalty, an indirect tribute to Oscar twenty years after he had closed down his last Carriers' Depot. Even Government House included us in a dinner party, with leading Arabs and heads of departments invited to meet us.

In contrast, at Mombasa there was no one to meet us, only a telegram from Oscar to say he could not leave the farm; Ronny had mumps, the doctor was in a detention camp as an enemy alien, and Phoebe had not responded to his telegram. We discovered she, too, had joined up. At the station the Indian station master had noticed our names, had attached an old fashioned coach to the train – one without a corridor – and obligingly piled in our luggage into our roomy compartment, repeating as he always did: "Oh, Mrs Watkins, much contraband, much contraband!" Olga always seemed to break the rules with smiling support from those who should have enforced them.

Next she took a rickshaw from the station and returned twenty minutes later with two huge baskets of fruit. "Here you are, all you can eat for supper and breakfast, and I must write." She pulled up the flap-table under the window, put her typewriter on it, and started typing steadily, uttering the occasional damn as she hit a wrong key. When it got dark she found the light by the window too dim, and improvised a table under the central light, using the "much contraband" luggage.

I took up Carlisle's History of England, but was distracted by the hinterland scenery passing the window, and kept wondering what it had been like to walk all that way as the first settlers had done only fifty years before. When I woke up next morning in a top bunk, Olga was already up and typing. She was still at it when the train drew into Nairobi station and I jumped out to greet my father. That second article was also accepted. On the journey Olga had earned £100, more than most women earned in six months, enough to pay all our travelling expenses, enough to buy a new car. Even a hungry sixteen-year old has to admire her mother sometimes.

Olga's Notepaper.

*   *   *

Chapter Twelve

BELTED EARL BUMPED OFF BY BRITISH BART

These words were the headlines of American papers reaching Muthaiga club, where the run-up to Lord Erroll's murder had been enacted. People in Britain were too occupied with the London Blitz to pay much attention to the untimely death of an aristocrat in a distant colony, but the United States had not yet joined the war and made much of this real-life 'who dunnit'. Since then books and television programmes have proliferated, and it is mentioned here only because the victim, Lord Erroll, was the member of Legislative Council for Kiambu, and Kiambu was the district in which Olga lived.

Only after the fall of France on 10th June 1940 had Mussolini decided he would become an ally of Germany. A few years previously he had invaded Ethiopia and taken that poverty stricken country as the first (and as it turned out the last) colony he, Mussolini would add to the Second Roman Empire he was so keen to establish. To hold Ethiopia he had a large army, massively equipped and armed with the gadgets of modern warfare. The Italians could easily have marched as far south as they wished, for the British had few troops available, not one tank, a handful of planes, and limited motor transport.

In East Africa the altitude at which most white settlers lived was said to make them highly volatile. Certainly there was little trace of British calm, as everyone contemplated the possibility of the occupation of Kenya by Ethiopian troops under Italian command. Many families planned to send their daughters to South Africa. Every European was called up, men and women, aged from 18 to 60. Thousands of Africans volunteered. Olga reviewed what the Watkins family could contribute. She would grow more food, and out came ten acres of much treasured coffee to make way for cattle and pigs. Oscar, aged 62, had tried to enlist but had been rejected as two stone under weight. He had taken on two other jobs, broadcasting the news in Swahili and setting up the first newspaper, Baraza, in that language, under the auspices of the East African Standard. A newspaper for Africans still had to be subsidized, the literacy rate was then only about twenty percent, but it was soon found that about ten people heard the news from each copy as it was read aloud round the evening cooking pot.

My two elder sisters, Pella and Ronny, had both joined the FANYs, (First Aid Nursing Yeomanry) started in Kenya by the Lady Sydney Farrar, the first woman elected member of Kenya's Legislative Council. I had already found a niche in the Meteorological Office, working as one of a team of weather clerks. As soon as Italy came into the war the Air Force demanded weather reports at night, which meant shift work. This was awkward for us weather clerks as we could no longer share transport to and from work with other members of our families, and petrol had already been rationed. In order to minimize these problems, the office turned one room into a rest room for us girls, where we could sleep, eat, or just take a break from work.

Olga was sure that there were going to be air raids and wanted to ensure her daughters had reasonable means of protection. Once she had fixed Lady Sydney about her two older daughters she charged into the Met Office. When the very shy young meteorologist on duty that evening was challenged by an excited Olga demanding to know what provision had been made in case of an air raid, he showed her into this room, barely furnished with two beds, two chairs, and a table. No curtains had been provided, so we girls had hung up a blanket instead.

"You see, Mrs Watkins," he said, "the young ladies can take refuge here, we have even hung a blanket over the window for them!" The young man had huge moustaches reminiscent of Pilot Officer Prune, and when he was nervous stroked them hard with the stem of his pipe. I wondered if they were going to fall off under the stroking they were receiving that evening.

"I'm not talking about canaries," said Olga indignantly. "I'm talking about daughters." I was still only sixteen, an age when mothers are acutely embarrassing, and bent my head over the great chart I was working on to hide my blushes, and even more my giggles. Giggles, as the young man hid his shyness by making himself into a stern task-master and none of us clerks had seen him so discomforted before. Like so many people whom Olga challenged, he became a firm family friend and visited us at frequent intervals. In fact he seemed determined to become Olga's son-in-law, proposing first to me over the shiny bonnet of his large car, and then to my eldest sister. He told me he loved Olga's fighting spirit.

The outbreak of fighting in Africa had at once brought South Africa into the war on our side. That country, unlike the Dominions, had stated that it would not declare war on Germany unless Germany attacked African countries. In 1939 that had seemed unlikely. Now Italy had come in on the side of Germany Kenya was – with the exception of the Channel Islands – the first country within the Empire to be invaded by the enemy in the form of Mussolini's troops from Ethiopia. South Africa was in no way prepared for war and many South Africans were still unwilling to fight. However the authorities cleared out the jails, rounded up a number of other undesirables, put them all into uniform, drilled them for a week or so, and rushed them up to Nairobi. They were tough men spoiling for action, but unfortunately used up much of their aggression on arrival in Nairobi, where they considered the Africans much too uppity and proceeded to show them who they thought was boss, or should it be *baas*. Black had to be separated from white as never before, and harsh colour discrimination, which had not previously existed, was introduced.

Nairobi was flourishing in the boom of war-time demand, every hotel bed taken, every dance floor crowded, every tailor too busy making uniforms to take on other work, every hall bustling with volunteer ladies running canteens for this and that group of soldiers, every garage full of ancient de-registered cars being made road-worthy for re-registration – clearly there would be no new vehicles until the end of the war.

The infamous Happy Valley crowd emerged from their up-country mansions, put on smart uniforms and went to Muthaiga club to live it up. My parents also belonged to Muthaiga club which was conveniently situated half way between Wispers and Nairobi, and only three miles walking distance from the farm. We girls used it for games, dances and as a useful meeting place. It had a good library and took a wide range of illustrated magazines, an important feature in pre-television days. Parties seemed to go on day and night while the rest of us laboured away at our wartime jobs. Lord Erroll, elected member of Legislative Council for Kiambu, was among the party-goers.

To serve this influx of activity, up-country Africans poured into Nairobi seeking work – for the first time in most of their lives it was a seller's market – too few people for too many jobs. And where were all these people going to live? Appalling slums were thrown up; the Municipal Council started once again to build 'bed spaces', as large dormitories for the workers were called. Olga could hardly believe they could be so stupid. She thought she had stopped this practice twenty years earlier when she had been on the Municipal Council. So it was that on the morning of January 24 1941 she visited once again the Municipal Native Affairs Officer, Tom Colchester, begging him to do something about it, insisting that she could provide garden city housing for the same price as a bed space in the dormitories the council were building. He told her wearily the Municipal Council could do nothing for her, she must approach members of Legislative Council if she wanted to improve African housing in Nairobi. Olga complained that she had approached every member of Legislative Council and not one member had shown any interest.

"I would stand myself, but there is unlikely to be an election until the end of the war, and by then all the dormitories will be built and it will be too late!" she said.

"Why not stand in the Kiambu by-election?"

"By-election?" she asked. And he told her about the murder of Lord Erroll. It had been on the morning news but had been too late for the papers. Olga did not listen to the early morning news as she was always out on the farm. In case a reader has not heard of this *cause célebre*, Erroll's preference for other men's wives had caught up with him. He had delivered another blonde bombshell home in the early hours of the morning and four hours later Erroll had been found shot dead in his car a few yards down the road from the British Baronet's home. The cuckolded husband, forty years older than his wife, was tried for murder and acquitted. Many of us who knew him believe it was not he who was guilty of the murder but his errant wife, and that he was drawing the blame on himself to protect her. She had told him that she wanted a divorce, to which he had agreed. When she told the Belted Earl she would soon be free to marry him, he rejected her. The last thing he wanted was to be landed with a penniless divorcée with expensive tastes. Infuriated, she took his gun from under the seat of the car where he kept it and shot him while he was driving. The gun was never found, but the bullet inside the belted earl's head could not have been fired from the Baronet's guns. While I was working on this book, Errol Trzebinski has published a new book on Lord Erroll's murder, attributing it not to the inglorious ending of a sordid love affair, but to SOE, a British secret service organization. Her book is very carefully researched, and she gives chapter and verse for her assertions. Lord Erroll had been among the numerous British aristocratic families who had given great support to the Nazis, and to whom Rudolf Hess had been sent to negotiate a peace in 1940. Had Lord Erroll spoken of his knowledge, he might well have brought down the Churchill government with drastic repercussions on the outcome of the war. However, it is not my intention here to discuss a sixty-year old unsolved crime, political or *passionel.* Erroll was dead and his seat in Legislative Council would have to be filled.

* * * * * * *

Kiambu was a large rural constituency bordering on Nairobi and peopled mainly by coffee farmers. It was the constituency where Olga had stood unsuccessfully for election in 1926, where she had wanted to stand in 1938 only to find she had been taken off the register during her years in England, and where she had determined to stand against Lord Erroll at the next election. It was the area where she was most likely to succeed. Although she could hardly stand in a settler farming constituency on the platform of better African housing, she had many other ideas on how to put the world, and more particularly Kenya, to rights. She declared that she stood as a woman determined to improve conditions for all women, black and white; that she was a farmer determined to improve the lot of small farmers, and rescue coffee farmers from the wicked rings of wholesalers who pocketed their profits. She wanted to protect small farmers from being taken over by big-estate owning companies. This tendency had been growing since the slump ten years earlier, fortified by the opportunity to buy farms cheaply as many small settler farms went bankrupt. She also spoke as a patriot determined to contribute to the war. She was widely known as a kind-hearted person who would go to endless trouble to help anyone in distress, a doer of good works who could get things done. Back in the thirties a friend on leave in England had sent her a letter addressed: *Olga, Kenya* to see if it arrived. It did, quicker than another test letter fully addressed and posted the same day.

Her main platform was provided by her opponent, Geoffrey Hunter. He was not only the employee of a large Nairobi company which dealt with coffee wholesaling, he was also on the board of two of the big estates his company had accumulated. So he had two major disadvantages: he was working for a company which was a member of the coffee ring, and was also buying up and consolidating small farms into big estates. He had the minor disadvantages – which Olga was quick to point out – that he had not been in the colony long, did not speak Swahili or have any interchange with Africans, and from his comfortable suburban life had learnt little about the country. Olga was convinced that a board of directors made bad farmers, understanding neither the needs of the land nor of the people who worked on it, and so were out of touch with the day to day problems. The platform on which Olga stood, the platform on which she was returned, was to encourage the small individual farmer and do away with the coffee retailing rings. In her manifesto she claimed a real knowledge of local interests, and that she would make the time to get to know her constituents as individuals. She had no axes to grind, no board of directors to please, no other irons in the fire.

Olga hurled out ideas for manifestos, speeches and articles. Oscar fielded them, put them into more politic words and into a comprehensible order, adding quotes and references. It was an unbeatable partnership. Poor Hunter did not have a chance, gaining only 92 votes to Olga's 220. Even this small total meant that 60% of the electorate had voted, considered a high turn out with so many men and women away at the war.

Olga put enormous energy into the election, visiting every constituent, meeting old friends and making new ones. She had a great way of drawing people out and was a sympathetic listener. When she asked constituents if they were going to support her, a number said: "I am, but my husband won't vote for a woman!" Settler women voted for her not only because they were tired of discrimination shown against them, but also because they felt frustrated that African women were so badly treated. It was usual, right up to the 1960's, to see crocodiles of African women walking into Nairobi each heavily laden with an enormous load on her back, often topped by a toddler, with a man walking behind, carrying nothing but a stick. Anyone who had helped these women in childbirth, as so many settler women had, knew how the deformities caused by carrying great weights on the lower back made the event even more painful. So did the extensive genital mutilation which was widely practised by the Kikuyu people around Nairobi. If anyone could help change these age-old customs, it was Olga.

When Olga won, the press were exceptionally generous in their congratulations. The East African Standard headed their main leader *The Lessons of Kiambu*, described in some detail Olga's support of the smaller farmer and coffee marketing problems, and then continued that there was a more important issue. *"We believe that the Kiambu result is strong evidence of a revolt against complacency and apathy in high places and that in this sense it reflects the opinion of the majority of European electors throughout the country. For a long time now, even before the outbreak of the war, there has been a feeling which has grown steadily into a firmly held conviction that the electors are not being adequately represented by the Elected Members. The result has been an increasing public irritation and a tendency to regard sittings of the Legislature as largely a waste of time since for all practical purposes the Colony is subject to what is almost a totalitarian form of government by decrees.*

"Mrs Watkins represents people who see an urgent need for change, for independence of outlook and a determination to challenge official proposals whenever it seems that they run counter to the views of the majority of the electorate or that they are capable of amendment in the public interest. Even if in all the circumstances her voice is the only one raised as an opposition, the unofficial community will feel that it is no longer without effective representation and will hope also that her example may stimulate some of the Elected Members to a sense of their responsibilities and opportunities."

Even the East African Traders Magazine, which kicked off each month with a *"What we Think"* column, wrote: *"In the first instance we wish sincerely to congratulate the new Member for Kiambu – Mrs Olga Watkins – on her victory at the polls of the Kiambu election. The only reason that we are invading the territory of politics on this occasion is that it seems to us that there is a political awakening in the minds of the Kiambu electors which we sincerely trust will percolate throughout the electorate in Kenya. …… We do not wish to criticize unduly but unfortunately the apathy which consumed the Members of Legislative Council in pre-war days has followed us into the war period. ………*

"In reading the manifesto of Mrs Watkins we heartily welcome her high resolve to attempt to alter the conditions of political representation in Kenya. … It seems to us that the electors of Kiambu have lighted a torch which should ignite the feelings of all electors, which should enable them to stress strongly their opinions as to what they require from their representatives."

When Olga was asked how she had achieved such a high turn out, she said she herself had worked like a beaver, and she had a most able and energetic agent in her husband! She was quite overwhelmed by the congratulations she received, and surprised by the excitement that her election had achieved. She soon came across an example of the apathy of other members. Her predecessor, Lord Erroll had not one file, not one letter written, not one record, among his papers. There was nothing to take over, to help her to come to grips with constituency work.

*   *   *   *   *   *   *

When looking back to the newspapers of the time, most of them read as if only the white races existed in Kenya, and Olga is mentioned every time she takes up a niggle – and she received hundreds of minor niggles from all over the country, most of them entirely superficial. There was, for example, the shortage of bedding for travellers on the trains. Now that the majority of European children were educated locally instead of being sent to Britain, it meant that six times a year there were migrations of children across the country. There were also many soldiers travelling. The Railways could not supply enough bedding, and could not buy any more during the war, so school children were told they must bring their own rugs and some mothers were objecting – all this is reported in detail.

Much nearer Olga's heart were the hard luck stories, often the result of over-zealous bureaucracy. One classic example was the treatment of a woman whose school-master husband joined the Navy and was taken prisoner of war. She had at once to leave her house at the school to make way for another master. She received only the family allowance part of his pay and no help with a housing allowance because her husband had been *provided with accommodation in his POW camp!* Olga's success in bringing relief to this woman and her three young children was highlighted by the press, but her success in getting an estate of bungalows, each set in its own garden, in the Eastleigh Road of Nairobi for the use of Africans, was hardly mentioned. These houses were nicknamed, as her electricity huts along the Muthaiga road had been twenty years before, *Little Olgas*, and the joke was that they stood on either side of Watkins Road, the road which led to what was then the military airport, Eastleigh. The road had been named for Oscar, whose main Carrier Corps camp in the previous war had been situated on the old race course near Muthaiga. Today the only name which commemorates the British past is *Kariokor* (Carrier Corps), the adjacent area to Eastleigh where the Carrier Corps main depot camp once stood, where Olga had nursed the soldiers in the First World War.

Nor were reporters interested in her comments on how bad were travelling conditions for Africans in the trains, nor in her seconding S.V.Cooke, a retired District Commissioner, when he put the motion *"that this council urges government to pursue a far-seeing Native production and welfare policy, that non-official Europeans be associated more closely with the formulation of that policy. ... and increased African representation on council, better native elementary education, and improved health and welfare measures in their areas."* Some twenty years earlier Oscar had been Cooke's immediate superior and had drawn down gubernatorial fury on his own head when he had tried to protect Cooke who had refused to let a settler occupy African lands. He was delighted that Olga could now support Cooke's liberal views in council.

It was fitting that her first session should have been much occupied by the problems of the Coffee Industry in war time, and the endless discussions on how it should be controlled at the end of the war. She took every opportunity to point out that it was not the size of Colonial Office grants which had held back economic development in Kenya, but the way in which the coffee wholesalers' ring kept prices of coffee down to less than a quarter of the retail price. If this extra money could flow into Kenya, an enormous amount of development would be achieved, including better labour conditions.

There was much more behind Olga's drive to meet the need for African housing than meets the eye. Olga had long been in touch with those trying to ameliorate conditions for Africans in South Africa. The provision of good town housing for African families was an attempt to avoid the mistakes which that country had made, with its reliance on migrant labour. Migrant labour resulted in large numbers of young males forming gangs in the towns and impoverished families growing up without their father in the homelands, a situation which had not been planned, but had grown out of historical circumstance.

At the end of the XIX century, most of Africa was organized on a tribal basis, usually with young men aged from about 14 to 26 passing through two warrior stages, the senior group training each new intake of adolescents in such things as how to bear pain, how to kill a lion, and how to go raiding for cattle, women, and land. The next door tribe would be training their men folk in the same way, and ensuing battles would provide a life time of excitement. Arab invaders encouraged such pastimes, as the conquering tribe provided a steady stream of captives to the slave traders.

When white invaders stopped both tribal wars and the slave trade, what happened to the groups of young men deprived of their twelve years of warriorship by Pax Britannica? They usually sought adventure going out to work in groups on any undertaking available, building towns, constructing roads and railways, working for individual employers, in South Africa working for the mines, work which did not raise adrenalin levels as satisfactorily as warfare had. As time went by, each man returned to his home land, purchased a wife or two, started a family, but life was dull in the villages and off he went again back to his employer. The woman was left to manage the land and the family. This system of migrant workers could not have succeeded had it not suited the men. It did nothing for the woman or family life.

Another way of organizing labour was the squatter system, which allowed whole families to migrate into land taken over by the settlers, in return for an agreed amount of work, usually for one adult male in each family to work for six months of the year. This suited the immediate needs of the pioneering farmer, who had too much land allocated to him. It was extremely popular among certain tribes, particularly those accustomed to cultivation rather than herding, because they could obtain access to more land than they had at home, land previously denied them by warlike neighbours. Olga had foreseen the problems it would cause when she was in Koru; it would develop a peasantry tied to the landlord's land. The worker would be unable to leave, however unpleasant the landlord, and the landlord would not be able to sack a worker, however inefficient or troublesome, because with his wives, his children, his extended family, his herds, he had nowhere to go. And in the event the squatter system was proving even worse than foreseen. The African population was increasing faster than had been considered possible for any population to do, so pressure on settler land was great; and farmers needed less labour as mechanization took over. Tractors and motor transport were reducing the demand for labour while the supply was increasing.

The settlers were aware of the Malthusian problem of a population increasing faster than the means of food production, but they had no idea of how fast the problem was growing. Registration and counting are extremely unpopular in Africa and any suggestion of recording vital statistics was strenuously opposed by the Africans. Oscar had endeavoured, in the 1920s, to introduce the registration of all births, but in a country where a polygamist may be unaware how many children he has, the thought of government recording such facts was totally unacceptable. In one district, Machakos, in the dry years of the early 1930s the growing population had put such pressure on land desiccated by a long drought that famine struck. In pre-British days the tribe would have marched to war to grab the land of a neighbouring tribe. Under British rule food was imported from other areas and the tribe concerned (Wakamba) marched to Government House to demand that more land be allocated to them. Much negotiation took place on the amount of agricultural improvement that must be undertaken on this new land. The problem was put succinctly by an unpopular governor: *You cannot build a modern state on the back of a woman with a digging stick.* In this particular case it was a succession of wet years which revived the land and the bonus of plenty of employment for adult males outside the reserve, plus the hard work of teams of government agriculture and veterinary officers working with the African farmers. This was the more successful because the officers could work with the women. As we have seen, young African men went out to work on settler farms and learned new ways of farming, how to make land more fertile, how to prevent soil erosion, how to keep trees as windbreaks and shade, how to make dams, and how to protect livestock from disease. But it was the women who grew the food, struggling to feed themselves and their families while the men were away working. It was difficult to get any training, any learning over to them. Very few spoke ki-Swahili, even fewer were literate. Olga picked up one of her favourite slogans: *Educate a boy and you educate an individual; Educate a girl and you educate a family.*

In 1905 it had been estimated there were 2.5 million people living in both East African protectorates of Kenya and Uganda. Settler farms had been allocated mainly in no-man's land between warring tribes. Now many settlers said that they were sure there were twice as many people living round them as there used to be. The Colonial Government sent out a man called Kuczynski, the Colonial Office Consultant on vital statistics, who reported in 1947, that such an increase as the settler's claimed was impossible, no population could increase so fast. He recommended that a census should be undertaken as soon as possible to prove it. This was done, and the settlers as well as the Colonial Government and their expert, Kuczinski, were all proved wrong – the population had not doubled, it had nearly trebled. When Kenya gained Independence after sixty years of British administration, the population had more than quadrupled to 11 million, despite all the vicissitudes experienced in that period – locusts, plague, drought, famine, economic slump, and two world wars.

If then the African subsistence farmers were not to become tied serfs on large European estates, if they were not to be migrant labourers away from their wives and families and social responsibilities, how were they to be moved from the land as they outgrew it? Olga expected it to happen as it had happened in the countries she knew. In Britain it was still continuing when her English grandfather returned from America as a boy. She had been brought up on stories of how the enclosure movements and industrialization had driven workers gradually, reluctantly, from the land. In Austria on the other hand it had not started until 1848, at the time her Irish grandmother had arrived in that country. In that year the Austrian peasant had been given his land tithe free, but legislation had been introduced to prevent him fragmenting the land between his children. Surplus sons were apprenticed to artisans, the more intelligent were selected to become priests or school masters. The more successful artisans trained their sons, and then set up small industries, leather- work, furniture making, glass works, gun-smiths and silver smiths, all based on local materials. In this twentieth century there were ways of mitigating the pain of resettlement. Improved transport meant that industrial centres could be distributed near the different centres of population; all kinds of food processing could be started right away, and various cottage industries could start in a number of different areas. This was Olga's hidden agenda behind her political thinking, and accounts for some of her apparent contradictions.

Africans did not accept any of the solutions offered, either then or now, they developed in their own way. Jomo Kenyatta had lived in Europe, mostly England, from the early 1930s until 1946, when unemployment and homelessness was at its worst. He was quick to spot one advantage African social organization had over British. In Kenya there was no such thing as homelessness. Even now every man, woman and child in Kenya has somewhere a fragment of land which he calls home and to which he may return. It may be desiccated or flooded or beyond producing food, but it is his. He may find begging in the streets of Nairobi a more productive way of living, but he knows where home is. It is his castle, and he does not want any one to tell him how he should handle it.

Olga was in a unique position. Most of the other elected members knew their own workers but had little idea of the realities of tribal life. They had been elected by settlers to represent settlers, as she herself had been, a permanent opposition to the officials who governed the country. Official members were still in a majority and African affairs were their business. Olga had lived and observed and breathed African administration since she first met Oscar some twenty- five years earlier. Africans had at first been represented by specially appointed members, usually missionaries or schoolmasters, now they were being represented by appointed African members. Olga considered she must also interpret African interests, particularly those of the women. Appointments of special members were made by the Governor, who was appointed by the Colonial Office and whose policy changed every time the British Government changed. This made it difficult to maintain a steady policy of improving education and development for the African.

Meanwhile the pursuit of war overlaid everything else. The Ethiopian episode had soon been solved, an occupation government of experienced administrators set up, and the Emperor restored to his empire. The troops moved on to Egypt, where 1941 was a year of defeat and retreat for Britain. In Kenya the war was almost forgotten until at the end of that year Japan's unexpected entry gave Kenya a whole new series of problems to solve. The battle for control of the Middle East was at its height, the Mediterranean closed to British shipping, thus lengthening the distance that troops had to travel to the Far East. Kenya, lying just across the Indian Ocean, provided not only a haven for people evacuated from Burma and Singapore, but also a bread-basket and a supplier of experienced troops and willing recruits to both theatres of war. With the Mediterranean closed to shipping, all supplies to the Eastern theatre of war had to take the long route round the Cape. Hardly had the convoys steered their way through the German submarines of the Atlantic than they hit the threat of Japanese submarines off the coast of Portuguese East Africa. Kenya had to become not only self-sufficient but also an exporter of food to both the Middle and Far East.

Nor was Olga's home life without its distractions. Her second daughter, Veronica, was married at the end of 1941 to an Army Captain who was soon posted to Burma, where he rapidly became a brigadier. Veronica went back to her FANY posting to Mombasa but a few months later she was home again waiting to make Olga a grandmother, and it was she, smitten by morning sickness, who noticed that Oscar was also being sick. In his case it turned out to be cancer of the stomach. On Sept 8, 1942, their Silver Wedding day, he was operated on, just at the beginning to the coffee picking season. There followed a dramatic fortnight with Veronica at one end of the Maia Carberry Nursing home holding court with a fine son and poor Oscar at the other end bravely trying to learn to live on a limited diet with a very small stomach, while the farm house was surrounded by trays of wet coffee, Phoebe struggled with the picking season, and Olga with speech-making in Leg.Co.

Early in 1942 I had managed to transfer myself into the WAAFs and went up to Cairo to be trained as a cipher officer. It was an exciting time, with the Germans only a short distance from

Cairo, Malta in a desperate state, and Egyptian business men busy translating their shop signs into German. RAF Advanced HQ retreated East of Cairo, leap-frogging over Rear HQ to which the cipher unit was attached. It was an important unit in that we deciphered messages not only for the RAF but also for Combined Services Headquarters. We were on alert to leap-frog over Advanced HQ, and as we could not stop work even for a few hours, part of the unit would join Advanced HQ and work under their protection while the remainder travelled with Rear HQ. Some of our machines were to be moved in special trucks so they could be plugged in to any electricity supply and we could work on board. My part in all this was tiny, and I was given a compassionate posting to Nairobi to be near my father. He recovered for a year, but then the cancer returned, and proved inoperable. He died two days after Christmas 1943. There was to be an election in May 1944 and all the time he was ill Olga was electioneering and trying to attend to constituency business as well as doing the coffee harvest and nursing Oscar.

Dr Anderson, the surgeon who had operated on Oscar, was a devout member of the Oxford Group, a Christian revivalist group. Every day each family of groupers gathered their entire households together for prayers and readings from the Bible, followed by a quiet time during which God spoke to them of what they must do that day. The good doctor decided God had told him he must stand for Council against Olga. Only he never told her. Immediately after the funeral Olga did not attend the constituency meeting to start the election campaign – she had taken a few days leave to recuperate some strength to see her through it. Dr Anderson attended this meeting, was welcomed in Olga's name and announced he was standing against her. Olga read about it in the press and was bitterly hurt that he had not told her beforehand, and that her committee had accepted him in her name. To be fair, he had written to her just before the meeting, so the letter did not reach her until afterwards. She found it hard to stand against this kind and gentle man, who had been a firm friend for countless years, a sympathetic surgeon, and a support to us all in the last difficult months.

She was not alone in thinking he was not the right man to stand. Owing to the war, there was a great shortage of doctors in Nairobi, and Anderson worked very long days and frequent nights with his patients. He was also totally unsuited to represent this productive constituency, knowing little about agriculture or trade and even less about the intricacies of coffee farming. When Olga was returned with an even larger majority than before, he retired for a long holiday in South Africa. When he came back, he never again wrote or spoke to Olga although they both attended the same church. Olga retired from the Parish Council so as not to embarrass him. Then four years later, in 1947, when she was on holiday in Austria, he invited her to attend an Oxford Group meeting in Switzerland. She replied courteously that she had insufficient currency left (foreign currency was as strictly rationed as butter at that time) and she was quite taken aback when he promptly offered to pay her expenses. She still declined. Sitting meekly together, as the Oxford Groupers did, enjoying a *Quiet Time* and waiting for God to speak to them was not part of her character; she once said to me that she found herself praying: "my will be done, not thine!" Given her propensity to spoonerisms, I was not surprised.

It was at this election that Wilfred Havelock first came forward and took over much of the organization of the Kiambu electors union for her. He had come out to Kenya in the twenties to work on a coffee farm, had subsequently invested a small legacy in a farm near Limuru, and had been released from the war as many farmers in Kenya were when the fighting in Africa was over. He devoted himself to this work and was greatly appreciated by Olga. She needed a reliable hard worker to help her and now she had one. He would eventually replace Olga as member for Kiambu.

Olga's slogan for this campaign was: *Win this War*. We had just passed the fourth war-time Christmas and the end still seemed a long time away. True, Germany's main ally had succumbed and our forces were landing in Italy, and we all knew that preparations were building up for the invasion of Europe, but in Burma the fighting was bitter and the outcome by no means determined. And when it did end, the world would need even more food. Olga took out another ten acres of coffee and increased her livestock. Her poultry was flourishing and she sold most of her produce direct to people in Nairobi. When Council was sitting, she would drive in with her baby Ford loaded with farm produce, sometimes live hens loose inside the car, and a farm lad would make the deliveries on foot while she, also on foot, made her speeches in Council. One day she was in such a hurry that she arrived in her best linen coat and skirt and with one foot in a tidy town shoe, the other still encased in a muddy walking shoe she used on the farm.

Even before Italy surrendered in 1943, the many prisoners of war taken in the Ethiopian campaign were allowed out to work on farms. Olga at once took on a horde of them. There was the mason who was asked if he could build a pigsty, and replied "Not a pigsty, but a Palazzo Porco!" The palazzo still stands to this day though the pigs disappeared two generations ago. Olga had all kinds of buildings going up all over the farm, limited only by the shortage of materials, cement and other imported goods. The Italian prisoners were hardworking, easy-going people who wanted only to get out of the camps.

It was quite a sight to see Olga doing the farm round to give out work to her workers, talking to them as required in French (Seychellois), German, when some refugee had nowhere else to go, Italian, Kiswahili, and Luo, the last three languages spoken fluently with no grammar, a small vocabulary, many gestures, and even more errors. If Oscar was around when she was speaking Swahili he would wait in silent laughter until the family were alone, and then say "Do you know what you just said?"

"I told him I wasn't born yesterday – so I did not believe his story!"

"No," said Oscar, "You said *I did not have a baby yesterday!*"

On another occasion she tried to say to some malingerer one of her favourite admonishments, "My God, you get my goat." While we were having lunch the man turned up with a goat. A little book was published on up-country Swahili, someone said it should have been called Olgarisms.

She grew to depend on her Italian prisoners who were yeoman farmers from Northern Italy and craftsmen to their finger tips. There was nothing they could not make, an old tin became a cigarette lighter, firewood proliferated into colourful wooden toys for the grandson, the coffee pulper worked more vibrantly than ever before, the car engine purred, and the farm roads improved beyond recognition. One of the men was intent to come back as her farm manager as she had no son and two others wanted to migrate to Kenya. She missed them dreadfully when they departed and while in Austria in 1947 she went down to Italy to see them.

They gave her a tremendous welcome and arrangements were made, but it was not to be.

Sometimes the POWs' improvisations were too inventive. One day she commented on the splendour of the dahlias in the garden. "Oh yes", said the gardener happily, "They came from Closeburn", the Graham-Bell's market garden two miles away where also were employed Italian POWs. Olga was horrified and phoned at once: "Harry, I am afraid my Italian gardener has some dahlias from you, I must pay for them." Harry's kindly drawl cut her off. "That's all right, Olga, we had two delicious ducklings for dinner last night!"

The only man with whom Olga had any difficulty was the Italian cook. He had come to us when Oscar first came out of hospital, needing frequent meals of well cooked easily digestible food, using limited ingredients available in war. The man was excellent at his job, and after Oscar died he stayed on, but he could not understand how Olga hardly noticed what she ate. He sent worse and worse food to the table each day, with no comment from her. Then one day when we were all at home with visitors, he sent in one uncooked potato on a large serving plate. At last Olga commented long and loud, none of it repeatable. He said he wanted to leave, the personnel officer was sent for, and Olga asked him to question the man as to what was wrong. Was his accommodation inadequate? No, it was much the same as he had at home. Was he getting enough food? The food was excellent, thank you. Then what was wrong? "It is just the signora, it makes me tired to watch her work!"

Olga had of course her share of rude and derogatory letters. There was one who wrote deploring that Olga had supported the call-up of all women between 18 and 60. "Some ladies of gentle birth are of delicate disposition and unsuited to the rigours of war work." She, and it obviously was a she, had put on a post office box number but the letter was unsigned. "Wait until you experience the whip of the Nazis or the Japanese!" Olga wrote back. Another woman wrote asking Olga to find her some soldiers: "suitable as paying guests in a lady's home." Then, in almost illegible handwriting scribbled on the page of a school exercise book, came a real gem. At the time the Young Men's Christian Association was looking for a building which could be adapted as a hostel for women war workers. The request came before Leg.Co. and Olga spoke in praise of the organization, but was doubtful that accommodation could be found. "The only building I know which is not already crammed to the brim with war workers is the Coryndon Museum." It was said and accepted as a joke, the idea of the three tiny galleries and one large hall then possessed by the museum being suitable for war workers was considered amusing. The letter read: *"Instead of touring the country around to explain the meaning of total defence in beautiful phrases which deceive no one, may I suggest that you come down to everyday matters in which you could and should help. As you yourself have explained, a hostel for women war workers is most urgently needed, but instead of taking the one and only museum for this use why not take Muthaiga Club, the most ideal place because it would mean real sacrifice for its members, of which I believe you are one, and a certain group of people all over the world believe that real unpleasant sacrifices are for other people to make, not they, oh no, but they are living in a fool's paradise and will certainly be shaken to the core one day when the truth for the first time dawns on them that this is a total war and everybody, even the Muthaiga clique who still have time to play bridge and drink their time away must make every contribution to the war effort they can. I thought you were different, Mrs Watkins, but the Museum plan disgusted the woman in the street."* signed Woman worker.

We had to laugh at this, for Olga hated alcohol, had never played bridge, and used the club as a useful meeting place and a good library. There were a number of small hotels which would have made far better hostels, but the whole point was that there was such a shortage of accommodation in Nairobi that there was no point in taking it away from one group and giving it to another. Muthaiga club offered superior accommodation, which was in very short supply, and was a convenient place to dump transient senior officers and V.I.P.s who streamed through the capital.

* * * * * * *

Olga spoke strongly on the land-drafts bill which came up early in the new session in 1944. The purpose of this bill was two-fold; one was to restore some land put aside for settlers for African use, and the other was to make large areas of undeveloped land held by some settlers available for new settler-farmers at the end of the war. Much of this land was occupied by squatters, mainly Kikuyu squatters. The Kikuyu reservation was suffering from overgrazing and erosion was threatening crop failure, as it had in Machakos some ten years earlier. She stressed that many Africans had large farms, but never large enough for the number of cattle they wanted. At the same time Africans were refusing to terrace their land and plant trees to prevent erosion, to dip their cattle against disease, or to cull their herds since in tribal life, a man's status was judged by the number of cattle he kept.

She came back continually to the need to reorganize African agriculture, and to set up industries near or within the reserves as well as outside them to enable Africans to become wage earners without having to leave their plot of land. She wanted each unit set up to make a profit, but profit would not be the main aim. Here the contradiction in her thought became clear, she was wanting to set up capitalist organizations without the profit motive, yet it is the profit motive which drives capitalism. She was aware of the mess Communism had made in abandoning the profits motive, yet she somehow wanted industry in Kenya to rise above it. And she thought communal farms would work. She was undoubtedly driven by her Quaker antecedents, and indeed was fond of quoting Cadbury and Fry in the same breath as she quoted Henry Ford. She wanted to mitigate the harshness of capitalism, just as she tried to mitigate it for her own workers.

"The paramount need of this country is to a rising scale or standard of African life, based on the improved achievements of the Africans themselves. You cannot do that without secondary industries. There are two questions to consider: Do you foresee an entire reorganization of African agriculture in the immediate future? And are you preparing during this coming year to start those secondary industries within and outside the reserves which are at present within our knowledge and our grasp." Only this would give men the opportunity to have one foot in country and one foot in industry. In the American depression Henry Ford had revived depressed towns by introducing just one factory to each town, and employing men for only six months of the year. Here in Kenya it was becoming essential to move people off the land. "Houses for Africans should be built by Africans, by small contractors, not by large firms importing materials at huge cost. Family housing was important since families were the future. At the moment government money spent on housing pours out of the country to buy the materials. Yet Kenya had all the materials needed, clay for bricks, timber, stone. Prices should be stabilized over years, but there must be no monopoly, The Livestock Marketing Board should continue after war…."

Eager as she was to introduce new means to forward the African's economic development, to improve his education and well being, she was harsh on idleness. She considered that everyone should work hard for his living, and deplored the idleness of African youth now their traditional occupation of becoming warriors had disappeared. Tradition prevented him taking part in agriculture, which was women's work, and there was little incentive to work for a low wage on European farms.

* * * * * * *

Peace came at last, in May 1945. Olga longed to visit her mother, now aged 83. By June she was in England. She had been careful to pack copies of her major speeches. We met unexpectedly at her mother's beside. The old lady lay, nearly totally paralysed, in a London nursing home run by nuns. I had been invalided back to London from Italy in April, and when I arrived, my relations all told me my grandmother's brain had gone, and she would not recognize me. No blame to her if she does not, I thought, as I walked into her room soon after my arrival. I had not seen her since I had been a hulking sixteen year old dressed in school uniform, now at twenty-one I was taller, much thinner, and looked grey and gaunt in my air force blue. How would I greet her? *Hallo Granny*? might be too sudden.

I need not have worried. She recognized me as I came into the room, clapping her good hand on her useless one to welcome me. Then she pointed to a picture of Oscar, shaking her head sadly; she pointed to one of Veronica and her baby and did her clapping gesture; and then picked up that of Olga and looked at me imploringly, her large grey eyes fixed on my face. I was holding back tears, thinking of her lying there, knowing everything, her daughter in Africa, her son and grandsons in the Navy, and herself being treated like a cabbage. I walked over to the window, and said: "Granny, you see that cherry tree just coming into flower?" she nodded. "By the time it fruits Mum will be here, I am sure she will!"

As I left, the Sister Superior called me in to her room, and welcomed me with tea and biscuits, thanking me for my part in the war. Everyone treated us as heroes. She asked when my mother would return?

"As soon as the war is over and she can get a passage," I said.

"Good," she said, "She's just holding on to see her, you know. We read all her letters out to her as she cannot read, and she always cries." From then on I visited the old lady at least twice a week, cycling fifteen miles each way between my mess and the nursing home. I knew Olga was trying to get a passage, and I was watching the cherry tree anxiously. They were growing fast but not yet ripening when one day she burst into the room, her hair all windblown in her hurry. The old lady picked up the comb which lay on her bedside table with her left hand and waved it at her. Olga came and knelt down to have her hair combed. Only then did they hug each other. I realized that this gesture which I had seen a hundred times before was their symbolic ritual, of daughter submitting to mother love.

Sister Superior proved right. Once Flo had seen Olga several times and heard her news she died peacefully in her sleep. She was buried in the churchyard at Nutfield in Surrey where both her parents and several of her siblings lay. Two old schoolroom friends of hers still lived in the area and entertained us afterwards. No fewer than fifty of the huge Nickalls clan managed to be present, nearly half of us in uniform. For the immediate family it was not a harmonious occasion. One of the great aunts handed a cruel letter to Tom berating him for his neglect of his mother – hardly fair on a man who had taken such responsibility during the war. And sadly, it became obvious that Tom and Olga were going to quarrel over Matzen. The will bequeathing it to them, one third to her, two thirds to him, was customary in Austrian division of property, but Tom felt that the property should have been left by English custom entirely to him, with no need for him to buy his sister out. Moreover their father's will had been written before the first World War, and now conditions were very different. The worst constraint from the point of view of Britishers who had property abroad was the fact that it was very difficult to transfer currency from one country to another.

Whoever owned it, it was going to be difficult to keep Matzen, and in the aftermath of war, impossible to sell it. There would be six years arrears of taxes and repairs to catch up on. No one knew what condition it was in, knowing only that the valley had been heavily bombed by allied planes because it lay on the main route of supplies from Germany to Italy. I knew it was in good condition, because I had seen and interpreted aerial photographs of the area, some of them taken after the bombing was over by a friendly pilot. Such was wartime security that I dared not mention this fact.

Olga went down to our cottage, Danes Beacon, and I joined her there for a few days. We were both exhausted, and in the afternoons would take a bus to the bluebell fields and lie on the damp grass in woods smelling deliciously of bluebells, both of us thinking of the man we had both loved so much. She spoke of the little things she missed, the lamp which he brought out to meet her when she came home late from electioneering, the pencils he sharpened, the typewriter ribbons he put in the right way round, the letters he stamped, the car that was always serviced. We did not talk of the deeper things, the wonderful letters he wrote, the gentle spiritual advice he gave, the tactful way he would help each of the family to face her choices in life. Yet even without her mainstay and prop, she never found life purposeless or sad. With the farm, the daughters, and her work on council she filled every minute with an hour's work. She had very occasionally, during her married life, taken a relaxing holiday with him. I was glad that she took a long weekend relaxing with me. She never knew how to relax when she was on her own.

I was posted to Slough, and one day we met in London to go to the theatre. I had been given two excellent seats in the stalls as a birthday present. As the lights went down, we were surprised to see three empty seats immediately in front of us. There were thousands of men in uniform in London and empty theatre seats were rare, particularly good seats in the middle of the stalls. It was a few days after the election which had thrown Churchill out of office. Then three figures slid into the seats in front of us. They had hoped not to be recognized, but everyone knew the stout old man and his tall elegant wife and cried out: "It's Churchill! It's Churchill!" and started cheering and clapping. The entire cast came on stage clapping, and someone started singing: "For he's a jolly good fellow!" Churchill stood up, turned back to the stage so he was facing the theatre (and us), tried to say something, and choked. Tears started down his cheeks. Clementine and Mary each grasped an arm firmly, turned him round and sat him down. The play started. In the interval Olga leant forward and introduced herself – she had written to him several times and received brief handwritten notes in reply. She started questioning him about Colonial policy. He gave her a list of names to see, including that of Creech-Jones, who was likely to be the new Colonial Secretary of State. I was told to write these down. "Don't let them spend money without sense!" he said, and Olga wondered what he meant. Never one to miss her opportunities, she followed up all the contacts.

On August 16 we were again in London, walking down Oxford Street when suddenly we caught sight of a news seller's poster, "Bomb ends Japanese War." We looked at each other, but for once we did not say a word. She was thinking thankfully of all the men who were saved. I was remembering the many brave men I had met and worked with who would not be coming home. Yet it was impossible to be sad for long. There was almost no traffic in London, so Oxford Street was joyous with pedestrians walking down the middle of the road. A line of six American sailors with linked arms swept down kissing every woman they passed. Olga looked slightly surprised when her turn came; I was expecting it, I had been there on VE night. Our progress to Oxford Circus was slow.

She wanted to get back to the farm. I hated to see her go, as I felt so ill. She departed leaving behind her as always endless chores to be cleared up, visits to be made, bills to be paid, shopping to be bought, parcels to post and research to follow up on. These were made easier to accomplish because she had made me promise to consult the heart specialist I had seen as a child. When I eventually did he wanted to put me into hospital at once, and when the RAF hospital said there was a waiting list, he insisted I be given sick leave. It transpired that I had had amoebic dysentery since 1942, and I was still in and out of hospital in March when exams for St Anne's entrance came up.

Meanwhile it had taken me two weeks of hard work to finish Olga's jobs – I had plenty to do but nowhere to do it, now that my uncle's London flat had closed down because he was in Kiel taking over the German Navy. In Kenya, Olga found as always that it was time that was short. The coffee- picking season, the main session of Legislative Council, and a second grandchild were all happening at the same time.

*   *   *

Chapter Thirteen

A VOICE IN THE WILDERNESS

"Sir a woman's preaching is like a dog walking on its hind legs. It is not done well but you are surprised to find it does it at all." Dr Johnson.

This quotation was actually made by a member from the official side of the house after Olga had delivered a long and carefully considered speech on the short-comings of the budget. She interrupted immediately, addressing her remarks to the Governor who acted as speaker in the colonial legislature: "On a point of order, Your Excellency, do I understand that the honourable gentleman is referring to me as …er…a female dog!" The house roared with laughter, and a friend told her afterwards that the man concerned had been heard to mumble: "Olga's stupid school-girl jokes." Such was chauvinism in those days that men were unaware when they were guilty of it.

Twenty years earlier Governor Grigg had suggested that introducing guilds would be the best way of introducing democracy to Kenya. This was the way British democracy had developed and he had proposed it as a better way of introducing equal rights than one man, one vote, when there was such a gap between the illiterate masses and the educated few. Up until 1946 the Electors' Union were still discussing this possibility, which would give each man, black, brown or white, a chance of representation according to his trade and skills. All this now changed. The British government, with pressure from the Americans, were being pressed for political equality for all citizens.

In January 1946 Creech-Jones made his first speech in the House of Commons as Secretary of State for the Colonies.

"Strong far-sighted government is needed in Kenya in the interests of all races and will not be found without considerable change in the system of Crown Colony Administration ... Autocracy in the modern world depends not merely on the possession of force but on the suppression of opinion. We have not attempted it with Indian opinion in India and we are hardly likely to attempt it with British opinion in Kenya. We have

therefore to find some means of making a strong and independent executive acceptable to our own people in Kenya, and to find a way of evolving such a government." He also spoke of the need for a commodity marketing scheme to help producers.

Olga had done her work in London well, for Kenya was the first colony he visited. Although he stayed at Government House rather than Wispers, he did come to dinner with her, where she had laid on a suitable guest list of settler farmers. She dined and wined them well – telling them with pride that everything she served, except alcohol and sugar, had been produced on the farm. Then she withdrew from the room, leaving an all-male dinner party to discuss the issues affecting agriculture in tropical Africa. I do not think she believed, as most women of her generation did, that men were more intelligent than women; but she certainly knew that if women were present at a meeting it would detract from the level of discussion, for the men would automatically dumb down the conversation into something light and amusing until the pretty little creatures left the dinner table for the drawing room and the men passed the port around. There were of course no bottles of port available in Kenya, but Olga had laid in whisky which proved a very acceptable substitute and they got down to serious discussion immediately she left.

Sir Alfred Vincent who was leader of the elected members told Creech-Jones that equal representation was entirely unacceptable not only to the settlers but also to the Africans out in the reserves, it would be a betrayal of our trusteeship. It would satisfy a few urban academics but no one else. (This was partly born out by time, for Gerald Hanley reported that when he returned to Kenya in the 1970s, ten years after Independence, the Masai Laibon with whom he had become friendly years earlier said to him: *"Look what you Europeans have done, we gave you the country and you have now left us and given it to those Kikuyu!"*). Sir Alfred also took up the extreme argument, that if Kenya offered equal representation, what would happen in Rhodesia, South Africa, and other countries. From the distance of the 21st century we can look back and ask one of the 'ifs' of history. If we had given instant equality at that moment would we have avoided Mau Mau and all that bloodshed? Or would we have involved Kenya and indeed all East Africa in a long drawn out civil war and chaos, creating an ungovernable state, as in the Congo?

Today (2005) both democracy and the economy are much stronger in Kenya than in most other ex-colonies in Africa. Settlers would claim it was because the infrastructure in Kenya was so much stronger, while officials would refer to the strong Local Native Councils set up in each area in the early 1920s, giving men a taste of running their districts without spears in their hands. Yet in 1947 it still had not penetrated the minds of many white settlers that Kenya would one day be governed by the African majority. A decade later, Prime Minister Macmillan with his *Winds of Change* finally convinced them.

During Creech-Jones' visit there was also much discussion about agriculture. One by one, the land of the different tribes was becoming exhausted and needed restoring. Before the British came even the agrarian tribes had practised shifting cultivation, moving from one area to the next every five years or so. The Nandi tribe from West Kenya had expanded their herds of cattle enormously during the war, supplying much meat to the meat factory. Now they were running out of grazing. The government had cleared many square miles of forest for them, but they did not like this new land, and instead smuggled their stock into squatter settlements on settler farms. This settler land they now favoured was the very land where they had found farming too difficult before the settlers came, because it was at high altitude and therefore too cold. Now for the price of an ox, a man could buy warm blankets and sweaters for all the family, and he wanted the highlands because European farming had shown him how cattle thrived in the cool uplands. The Wakikuyu also were outgrowing their land and the squatter families outgrowing the settler farms. As they were so near to Nairobi it was more difficult to find them room for expansion. When a survey was eventually undertaken it was discovered that this particular tribe were reproducing faster than any population ever recorded. When over half the population is under the age of sixteen the adults will always find it a struggle to provide for the young.

The discussion about suitable development projects for East Africa did not deter Creech-Jones from insisting on investing millions of British tax payers' money in totally unsuitable countryside in Tanganyika (Tanzania) in order to grow ground nuts. It was hoped the nuts would provide the British with much needed edible oil and the Tanzanians with much needed jobs and money, but like so many large scale experiments it proved a total failure, just as the Kenya settlers had said it would. Tanzania had few white settlers and they were mostly producing coffee in the highlands and had little experience of other crops and little clout with the inexperienced government officials. More than six million pounds in 1940s money were wasted and almost no groundnuts were produced. However, Creech-Jones did not insist on any such schemes for Kenya. Instead, teams of agricultural and livestock officers were recruited and allocated plots of land in different districts to demonstrate improved agriculture, and to encourage keen young African farmers to use new methods, and plant a wider variety of crops. Cattle dips were built, steep slopes were terraced, wind breaks were planted, water conserved in dams. Only the Kikuyu resisted such developments. They looked enviously at the settler farms, newly wealthy because of war-time demand for food, and soon became easy prey for agitators and the beginning of the Mau Mau movement.

During the immediate post war period, for the first time in the history of the colony, there was a sellers market for agricultural produce. Kenya had become a land of milk and honey and the honey was not trickling down fast enough. Tremendous improvements were made in local production, and in raising the quality of African produce so it met the quality required by the canning and preserving industries. Meat and butter, fruit and jam were canned, milk was powdered, leather made into shoes, sisal into ropes and matting. The canned and dried foods were particularly important in those pre-freezer days – food could be exported through a large area of the tropics, and indeed further afield.

Olga's greatest contribution was probably to change attitudes to education, particularly the education of women of all races. In her speech moving the government to declare its development policy for women, she had said:

"Your Excellency, I shudder when I think what remains to be done on the subject of African women's education, but we have got to make a start some time. We need a director of Women's Education on this council." And she quoted her much loved formula, *"educate a man and you educate an individual, educate a woman and you educate a family."* As the years proceeded she was pushing for new buildings for the Kenya High School and the

new Nyeri school, both for European children, to go ahead. Miss Janisch, the new Director of Women's education for whose appointment Olga had worked so hard, was a brave woman and had to fight a tough battle. She was working under the same Director of Education who had assured Olga in 1939 that it was not necessary for girls to go further than *a mild school certificate with plenty of domestic science*, and that it was absurd of her to think of sending a daughter to university. He changed his tune fairly fast when the new governor arrived with two daughters bent on university education, and a sixth form appeared in the Kenya High School, but he showed in a hundred niggling ways that his heart was not in such foolish projects.

Nearly all white children were now being educated in Kenya because it was too difficult to send them back to England. Of the £300,000 allocated for education of white children, there were to be three academic streams for boys and only one for girls, enough to prepare them for the three openings available for them, secretaries, nurses, or practitioners of domestic science. Miss Janisch had other ideas and found an outstanding head mistress for the Girls' High School, Miss Stott. Soon every girl in the top two forms was working towards a career plan, an unheard of idea for girls in those days. Soon this school was gaining more university entrances in England than any girls' school outside England. Fifteen years later this same girls' high school was one of the first to go multi-racial under the guidance of the same headmistress, and for years continued to gain the same excellent results.

In 1946 African girls were offered serious schooling for the first time, and although many fathers were reluctant to send their girls to school, a firm foundation was laid. Miss Janisch talked repeatedly of the steadying influence women had on society, and goes on to define education: *"The term is used to cover all organised efforts to influence the lives of women and girls, of which scholastic institutions are only one kind …… Women's and girls' work must be planned on a community basis. It is vital that education should be sufficiently inspiring to give an impetus not only to the individual and personal ambition, but to the development of public service."*

One of the problems was that most official members of the government still remained unconvinced that a population explosion among the Africans had taken place, and therefore far too few schools had been provided, and much too little money invested, only £600,000 when there were probably nearly three million under the age of sixteen. Even those children who did attend school were inclined to attend irregularly, and often for as little as two or three years. When children come from illiterate homes, four years of regular schooling are the minimum required to attain basic literacy, and six years are needed for that literacy to be lasting. To educate a child for two years only is a waste of money. 76,000 boys entered the first stage of primary school, five years later only 10,000 remained. The idea was to limit the number entering school but to make sure that they stayed there. Wadley, the male director of education, assured the settlers who were showing such concern about African education that there was no need to worry, he had a wonderful scheme which would enable all African children to enter school so the whole country would be literate in twenty years time. Needless to say no such scheme materialized and it was not until after the census had been taken that a real drive was made to educate children. During the 1960s 80% literacy was achieved, a figure which has sadly fallen since independence.

Olga saw the main aim of education as enabling Africans to leave their land and live by their work. In particular, she wanted to introduce an apprenticeship system for artisans. *"We also need to introduce apprenticeship schemes. It is essential so that the young adolescent male learns to stop at one job for two to three years and to do a reasonable amount of work. He should be able to choose his job but not be able to choose not to be trained and to live on the community."*

Pat Williams, the Director of Training, had another idea. He was suggesting compulsory literacy camps, where boys of 16 who were illiterate would live for six months and be taught concentratedly the whole time. This might also short-circuit Kikuyu refusal to cooperate with government in improving their agricultural methods. Pat Williams thought that during this six months compulsory camp each boy could be brainwashed into better agricultural practices as well as into literacy. Terracing, dam building, cattle dipping, crop rotation, creating and using compost, could all be demonstrated. Olga was interested in this idea, and consulted Carey Francis, Headmaster of the Alliance

High School, the first fully academic secondary school for African boys. The camps would not of course effect his pupils who would become the future professional elite, but his views on African boys would be pertinent. He commented:

"African boys are good stuff, their brains are as good as ours and they are really good fellows who have ideals by which they mean to stand. They could develop into fine men if only they grew quietly under the right guidance. I find African leaders are quite dreadful people. African men go out into a world in which almost every big man of their race is bad, in which the crowd is now moving after their leaders, shouting their slogans."

Shortages of all sorts of commodities continued long after the war, and with the shortages crime boomed. During the war Olga had suggested a penal battalion be set up in the KAR, but this idea was not popular. It was not the paltry efforts of petty thieves which worried her but the growth of organized crime. She spoke in Council:

"The employers' section in the crime world is made up of modest persons who shrink from public advertisement but who pay well for successful work. There is careful planning beforehand, speed and ruthlessness in execution and rapid distribution of stolen goods to pre-arranged destinations. Owing apparently to a weakness in the law the root of the trouble is not being got at, the principals in the background are still safe and no doubt prosperous. The Committee proposes that criminal law should be made more stringent in regard to receivers of stolen property and that any vehicle used with the knowledge of the owner in the furtherance of a crime should be confiscated, etc."

It was these receivers who troubled Olga. Veritable schools of them were growing up in Nairobi, training young Africans in the art of theft, and paying them generous wages. If one of them was caught, he went to prison but when he came out his wages were waiting for him, and he returned to work, probably for the same receiver. The receiver was never touched and was nearly always non-African, and in Olga's view these men should be sought out and deported. As a result of Olga's second speech on this subject two years after her first, letters of congratulation poured in. Every elected member supported her and many of the officials. Of course there was the usual lunatic fringe, the man who wrote in that corporal punishment should be restored because a tingling bottom did a man good; and another who commented what a pity it was that Leonard Beecher (later the first Archbishop of East Africa) who represented African interests had not been born a negro (the lunatic's word, not Olga's!).

On January 11 1946 another of her speeches was reported at length in the East African Standard. This time she was moving a motion that the government should formulate a comprehensive native policy in the immediate future. She was seconded by ex-DC, S.V.Cooke. She wanted to consider the attitudes of the African himself, his attitudes towards the world into which he was now moving, and then to consider the attitude of the government to the African, and that of the man in the street or on the farm (meaning her fellow settlers) to him too.

"The man in the street regards him with benevolent irritation. We feel we are bringing him so much, and he does not want it, that we could improve his agriculture and he merely maintains that we are cheating him of his cattle. We know of no country on earth where every individual can claim to be a landowner, yet the African wishes to follow this idea to the bitter end, which would be that within an appreciable time there would be no land fit for anyone. We know that the women of any race should be prevented from doing heavy tasks during the years of child-bearing and rearing, yet the heaviest burdens and the most grinding drudgery are left to the African women year in year out lest we interfere with the man's freedom to impose these burdens on her.

"What does the African think as he proceeds into this new world where everybody has more than one set of clothes, where most people eat three meals a day, where we move on wheels in preference to our own feet, and where we do away with much of life's drudgery by the water tap and electric switch. What is he thinking? I think that like most of us he would like to find his own niche in the world provided he can do it without too much physical work, or perhaps without any effort at all. Otherwise he prefers to sit under a banana tree watching his perambulating currency which in due time by its progeny will have produced the purchase price of yet another wife who is by African custom the slave of the land. What he does not realize is that he has not this choice. The world which is so familiar to him and which he still regards as a happier alternative to working out a new salvation for

himself and his tribe is fast disappearing. The impact of civilization is here.

"What does he want? I believe it is safe to assume he desires very much what we all desire, freedom from fear and want, a modicum of security and a little something extra that makes life worth living for each one of us; but he has less experience of setting about getting it. We cannot expect him to know what it has taken us so many centuries to learn, and he shows a marked apathy towards the necessary efforts and self-discipline required to improve his own well-being. He prefers to look to a paternal government which seems to provide everything from its capacious pockets.... It is not now a question of whether the claim of civilization in Africa is a good thing or bad, but that it is inevitable and the question is how soon can he absorb it?"

In 1947 Creech-Jones in London sent a paper to each of the governors of the three East African territories: *"It is now fourteen months since the proposals for inter-territorial organizations in East Africa were published in Paper Colonial No.191, in Decmber 1945. These proposals have since been the subject of wide discussions in the East African territories, and during my visit to East Africa last year I was able to discuss them with members of all communities in each of the territories. More recently the Governors of the three Territories have held consultations with the unofficial members of Legislative Councils. I am now arranging for modified proposals to be published as a basis for further discussion.*

These proposals were for an East African High Commission to be set up, with a Central Assembly and an Executive Organization. The Central Assembly would be set for four years, and within this period its continued existence would be reviewed. The purpose of the High Commission would be to administer certain scheduled services, exercising the usual powers of a Colonial Company. Olga insisted that both the debates, and particularly the accounts, should be on record. Unofficial members must be chosen from Legislative Council and proposals must not go through if violently opposed by this council. She considered that the proposals for the Conference supported the African, and gave him a fair deal. She dismissed Indian criticism with *"And Mr Indian, the British do intend to keep control of their own Empire and to protect the African from the likes of you!"* (this was in a letter to me and was put more diplomatically for Leg.Co.)

The Conference (of East African Governors) had developed considerably during the war when co-operation was clearly necessary, and even Olga and other settlers who had been against it now saw the need if more research organizations and better services were to be provided. The idea was that economies of scale could be achieved by uniting for certain services, one railway organization, one post office, one set of research institutes, one meteorological and statistical department, one customs department, and one taxation policy. It was not going to be easy to introduce because, although all three countries were administered by Britain, they all had different legal status. Kenya was mostly a colony with a small protectorate at the coast, Uganda was a protectorate and Tanganyika a mandated territory for which Britain was responsible to the United Nations. Neither Uganda nor Tanzania wanted to be joined closely to Kenya because they did not want her problem with settlers. Yet because of those settlers, Kenya had much the strongest economy, provided much better services for all her inhabitants, more doctors, more roads, more buses, more schools, more research centres, more agricultural and livestock officers, and she did not want to take on board her poorer neighbours. Geographically, she was the middle country and the other two could hardly share services if she did not participate.

While this was being discussed in constituency meetings up and down Kenya, many comparisons were drawn between the plans for a High Commission, and those drawn up some twenty years earlier, in 1927, when Governor Grigg was working for Closer Union. In that year a Commission of Enquiry had been set up and their report, known as the Hilton-Young Report, had recommended that a Governor General for all three territories be appointed in Nairobi, to whom the other governors would be responsible, and Africans would be indirectly represented by chosen whites, usually missionaries, head masters, or retired civil servants. Under the new High Commission the three governors would be equals, and Africans would represent themselves. Now settlers with long memories harked back to Closer Union, saying they preferred it to a High Commission. As far as the British Government was concerned the choice was not on offer.

Clarence Buxton, a retired Provincial Commissioner turned coffee-farmer, a great friend of Oscar and Olga's and now one of her constituents, stepped in and gave Olga the constitutional advice that Oscar would have provided. He pointed out that the Kenya Constitution would have to be amended so that Kenya could enter into closer union with the other two countries which were not colonies. The Governors' Conference was easier to arrange, and could always move into closer union if so required. Buxton said he supported direct African representation because leading settlers, including Frank Joyce, had declared for it. The High Commission was in fact a great success, and lasted some thirty years, half of them after Independence, when the three countries' eagerness for self determination pulled them apart.

The Press was also presenting problems, especially to Olga. There was then only one daily newspaper, and after the 1944 election it was continually misrepresenting discussion in the council. Angry MLCs would send in corrections but these were never acknowledged. It became so bad that the Electors' Union held a meeting to discuss the matter. They agreed to write to the directors of the East African Standard asking members of the board of directors to meet them and discuss the problem. The meeting occurred, the directors promised to look into the matter, and the misreporting continued as before. Olga thought she knew the reason. The Anderson family were a close knit one, a missionary family who had pioneered from the beginning of the century. Claude Andersen who was brought up in Kenya was editor of the newspaper, his brother Gerald was the doctor who had stood for Legislative Council in opposition to Olga and had lost to her. Both were deeply religious men who wanted to change Kenya into a country where anyone who shared their views would be treated equally. Unfortunately theirs was a minority view and an idealistic one, considered by settlers and administrators alike to be unworkable, and by Africans to be too patriarchal.

When Gerald Anderson was thwarted in his desire to get on to Legislative Council to promote his views, Olga believed that Claude hoped to achieve their ends by misreporting or ignoring those views with which he and Gerald did not agree. An example of this was when a man by the name of Davis wrote to the Standard saying the British government was interfering far too much in Kenya's affairs and quoted the recently published book of letters between Margery Perham and Elspeth Huxley to illustrate his point. Margery Perham had made herself extremely unpopular in Kenya when in 1931 she spent six weeks in the colony at a time when locusts, drought, and world slump were causing great hardship. Regardless of the problems besetting administrators trying to cope with famine and disaster, she insisted on constant attention and hospitality for herself. She refused even to meet settlers, and criticized those officials who happened to bring one near her, for example when my father had Lord Kitchener to lunch. She attributed the colony's poverty to the presence of settlers rather than the happenstance of natural disasters. Elspeth Huxley, herself the daughter of settlers and already a recognized writer, was momentarily unpopular with some settlers, but not with Olga, in that she had recommended training courses for new settlers' wives. The Standard published Davis's letter but omitted the names of the two women, which made the letter meaningless. When Davis complained, Anderson replied he did not want to draw attention to the two women who relied on publicity and controversy in the Press for their influence and if he had mentioned them by name he would have confirmed them as being influential in East African affairs. Davis at once wrote to Olga asking her to take the matter up with Claude Anderson. Olga replied:

"I have long ago given up either hoping for or counting on any accuracy in the things that do not in themselves coincide with the opinions of the editorial staff of the Standard. The only cure would be competition...... If we backed up the other newspaper and got them to use better print and so forth (there again Anderson is paper controller so it is very difficult) we might make them the organ for public comment. Competition will of course come, but until it comes we shall have to sit down under the Standard. You have no idea what it is like to be represented entirely wrongly on matters of urgency to the constituency and to have both correction and apology refused."

The other paper was the recently started Kenya Weekly News and Olga wrote frequent leaders and commentary for it. (I was horrified to discover that she had also published many of my letters written from Italy in 1944 where I was serving with the RAF cipher unit at Caserta, headquarters to the Mediterranean Allied Air Forces.)

In other cases she was more successful. Olga was known for taking up lost causes, and winning them. John Ainsworth, long considered the founder of the Kenya's administrative service, and much loved by those he administered, died and left his widow no pension, only a lump sum of £2500. This was enough to buy a very small annuity but she wanted some money to leave to their son. Olga went to the Pensions department in Nairobi and pointed out that the government was contributing to serving officers' pensions, and they should also contribute to one for Mrs Ainsworth who had supported John so courageously in the pioneering years. When she was refused she appealed to the Financial Secretary, Troughton by name, and was again refused on the grounds that since Mrs Ainsworth had such a considerable sum in savings she needed no help. Most people would have given up at this stage. Olga wrote to the Secretary of State for the Colonies, and Mrs Ainsworth got her pension.

There were many penniless old women scattered about Kenya, survivors of the pioneer days, nurses, school-mistresses, widows of farmers who had lost their farms in the slump. Each European community had built its own church and Olga decided that the ideal solution was for each little church to build a cottage near it where the very elderly could live. More cottages could be built as need demanded. Books were always in short supply in Kenya. A collection of books would be assembled and the old person in each cottage would run a library. During the week people who came into the settlement to shop or to attend to the church could easily drop in and would be able to change their books. No doubt many callers would bring a small gift, some eggs, a ready plucked chicken, a loaf of bread, (we all baked our own) and so on. It was a generous scheme but one which would require supervision and co-ordination. Olga had built one cottage at Limuru and was building another at Kiambu when she died. Soon afterwards the two cottages were sold and money put into a more central scheme, where one out of twenty bungalows was named for her. I was asked to go and speak about Olga at the opening of this house. I could not say what I felt about it, it was just what Olga was trying to avoid – as she put it:

"They take the elderly from their communities when they would much rather stay put."

She was trying to make it easy for people to continue as part of their own community, not to be shut away with their own inactive contemporaries. She did not like the idea of old people's homes.

Olga herself drew no pension, the widows' pension scheme had not been introduced when Oscar joined the service. On retirement he had a pension of £700 a year and Olga would not accept the payment offered to MLCs because she said she and Oscar were already receiving enough from the government. She did accept other privileges, free travel on the railway, and extra petrol coupons, which she needed for her work. After Oscar died, she still did not want to accept payment for her work, and my sisters and myself had to persuade her to take it, saying it was not fair to us when there might come a time when she would no longer be able to run the farm. There were few luxuries at home, we never owned a refrigerator, rarely a second car, and alcohol was only offered to guests on special occasions. When she was feeling hard up she would wash her hair with ordinary soap and clean her teeth with soda bicarbonate. We daughters had also to take a firm line with her when she needed new clothes, and insist she obtained them. We slept on African frame beds woven with strips of hide, with thin mattresses and cheap coarse cotton made into sheets. Any one of us who was working would make constant gifts, electrical gadgets, tools, whatever was needed. She so often gave these away that when her mother Flo made her a gift of good quality pillows, she wrote a little rhyme:

"Not for the governor, not for the king,
Not for the chicks, but for you, old thing."

The one thing on which she never economized was generosity to others. The house remained packed with guests, and as many as twenty-odd uninvited but never unwelcome guests would turn up for tea on Sundays, to enjoy her company and wander round the farm. Oscar found constant entertaining at the week-end exhausting when he had to work all week, and he complained he had no time for gardening. She built him a potting shed, a round African hut with no walls, and placed a large notice on it: *"I am not at home. These are not my legs."*

One day when we three girls were tidying the ruined sitting room, Ronny asked:

"Why do they come? They get no alcohol, stewed tea, an untidy house, and rock hard cakes! And yet they come week after week."

Pella did not hesitate with the answer: *"When Mum gets going, she's much more entertaining than the flics."*

Another of Olga's interests was the prevention of cruelty to animals, and in 1946 she became a member of a special committee of Legislative Council to enquire into instances of cruelty. The African often has an amazing rapport with wild life and with his cattle, but his treatment of other animals can be horrific. A witch doctor trying to heal a patient would half suffocate a goat or sheep, then while it was still living he would slit its stomach open and take out the entrails. Customs such as these the RSPCA had to recognize lay beyond its jurisdiction. They were however very concerned with the methods of slaughtering cattle. There were many Muslims in Kenya who had to have their meat ritually slaughtered, and an electrical stunner had always been used with no complaint from Muslim leaders. Then a Jewish refugee noticed that a stunner was used, pointed it out in the newspapers, and the Muslims decided that this was wrong and reverted to the crueller methods. The committee considered *"the cruelty applies not only to the actual killing when performed by untrained slaughterers with blunt or unsuitable instruments, but to the preliminaries ... the throwing of the animal into position for the throat cutting. We are satisfied that the act of throat cutting does not of itself involve cruelty. In order to avoid the cruelty which now accompanies ritual slaughter we consider that steps should be taken to procure casting pens for all abattoirs and slaughter houses as a matter as of urgency."* They made many other recommendations, including that slaughterers should be trained and registered. Dr Williamson of Williamson's diamond mines made a donation of £1,000 – a very considerable sum in those days, to alleviate the suffering of animals in the slaughter-houses. A special committee was set up – Dr Williamson's humane slaughter fund committee.

Most of the Arabs lived in the coastal strip, including of course Mombasa, which was a protectorate and not a colony and was only rented from the Sultan of Zanzibar. Arab administrative officers worked on Arab concerns while British ones administered all others, and the Union Jack was never flown from the ground in the coastal strip, only the Sultan's flag. It was a very British solution to a political problem which usually worked well but in this case did not. The Liwali of Mombasa, a Muslim, did not see any necessity for improvement in the way cattle were slaughtered. Of even greater concern was the treatment of dairy cows on the island of Mombasa. The dairies were licensed to hold 1,200 cows, and probably held many more. The cattle had to be kept permanently in stalls because there was insufficient grazing on the island. The conditions of overcrowding in the tropical heat amounted to considerable cruelty, and recommendations were made that the herds should no longer be kept on the island but moved to the mainland, for now the war was over trucks and petrol were once more available and the milk could be sent in daily. Here the Liwali refused again. It was well known that he had vested interests in the dairies. In the long run the dairies had to be moved for reasons of hygiene but he was able to delay the move for some years.

Donkeys were also being maltreated, and it was hoped to introduce legislation to prevent them carrying weights of over 120lbs, and also to insist that any carts they hauled were fitted with brakes. As Olga remarked, the poor things were underfed, overladen, and overworked, just like African women, and making the lot of donkeys better might make that of their owners' wives worse. Who else would transport the loads?

It was no doubt because she had been involved in all these discussions that just after Christmas 1946, the incident of the monkeys occurred. Olga had kept one morning free to clear her Christmas mail when the telegram arrived from someone in Mombasa that 93 monkeys were being transhipped from ship to train, in very cruel conditions, and would she inspect them at Nairobi. She wrote to me: *"Down I went, having done the milk round and rung the Railway police. There was Swaine from the police, a friendly but non-committal stationmaster and a transport officer. The monkeys were from the Rockefeller Institute in India travelling to Uganda for testing yellow fever vaccines, poor things. They were in a terrible condition, closely packed in crates, twenty-five in each, seven had died en route, others so weak from lack of food and air that they could only wave a feeble paw in the back ground. It was impossible to get food to them as the front row seized everything. I bought up all the oranges and bananas at the station, cut them up and pushed them in. Then I phoned the senior Vet at Kabete Veterinary station and said: 'Expect 93 monkeys to stay with you at your lab!' 'Not on your life!' said he. 'Then come down to the station, with your shot gun!' He came without it, saw the poor things, and took them all back to Kabete. I had meanwhile rung the PWD for crates and so had someone else, so there we were. Now we are running the culpable folk, but of course the damned old Indian at the Rockefeller Institute in India is really the one, and I expect he gets off scot free!*

"More important was of course the fact that I had already got a 'Cruelty to Animals' government committee going, for alterations in our law and in our practice, and this could not have been better evidence of what is needed before granting import licenses etc. The joke is that it is to such departments as the Rockfeller Institute, the Railways Authorities, and the Uganda Medical Research Dept that quite a lot of the blame attaches. But it is no joke at all when you see it happening. It is amusing to think that there is a large body of R.S.P.C.A here in Nairobi and in Mombasa, there are two members for LegCo. For Nairobi, there is the Veterinary Department, there is the Railway, there are the Police, all by their positions more concerned with this case than I am, yet those who saw it in Mombasa wired me."

* * * * * * *

In the Autumn of 1945, Tom had managed a visit to Matzen from Kiel and found it in wonderful condition, looked after by our caretakers and financed by our Austrian cousins who had used it as a bolt hole from the bombed cities of Austria. Tom had retired from the Navy that Christmas and in the Summer of 1946 when I was demobbed he invited me to spend my summer with him at Matzen, occupying the rooms which my family had always used and which now belonged to my mother. Travel was difficult as permits had to be obtained from the occupying power, in this case France. The French were very unpopular in Austria and it was not always easy to keep on good terms with them, but fortunately the French General was delighted to welcome a distinguished British Admiral to his province. The Admiral had two handsome sons and the General one very pretty daughter, with whom one son became very friendly, as did I. I obtained a pass not only for that summer but for Christmas also, and was on the top of the world.

I wrote fully to my mother with descriptions of life in post-war Austria, from the bombed village with its temporary bridges over the River Inn, the church wearing its onion at an angle, to the shortages of food, clothes, consumer goods, transport, and indeed most other conveniences of modern life. I also stressed the warmth of my welcome, the fond enquiries after her, and how friendly everyone was, despite the havoc the bombing had caused. In 1947 Olga decided she must come and observe the situation for herself. She could not quite believe that I was putting myself through Oxford at the cost of a grateful government, and not drawing on her exchequer; she wanted to see how I was managing. She decided that Pella needed a break to get her away from a boyfriend Olga considered undesirable. She was sure to pick up a more suitable young man in Oxford.

As so often, she was right. Olga and Pella arrived in Oxford days before they were expected, just before a week in which I was to attend both a Commem ball at Magdalen and my own more modest college dance. I had to obtain a partner for Pella for both. I had already become engaged although I could not announce my engagement or I would have been sent down. My fiancé, Oliver, obligingly produced a man who was an instant success, falling head over heels for Pella, so much so that he could no longer continue with his studies. Alas for Pella, he was still shell-shocked from terrible war experiences and proved a long-term disaster.

Olga next set out for London, where she had arranged many appointments with Members of Parliament, the Colonial Office, the Board of Trade, farmers' organizations and other institutions of interest. She already had appointments with Lord Cornwallis and with Mr Knollys who was secretary of the Farmers' Union. She was now recognized as a VIP in her own right and a young man from the Colonial Office was allocated to look after her during her stay. He was Andrew Cohen, later Sir Andrew and Governor of Uganda. His diplomatic skills were sorely tested. Olga wanted to attend a certain debate in Parliament and he promised to escort her to the gallery reserved for members of Imperial Legislatures. They arrived just before the debate was due to start, to find that Olga was refused entrance because she was a woman. Cohen had to think quickly. He went to the gallery reserved for Peers and Peeresses. Here Olga was admitted by a courteous Peer who invited her as his guest, but protocol did not allow him to invite Cohen. I was always grateful to Cohen, he obtained such a wonderful wad of petrol coupons for her which found their way directly into Oliver's car!

As soon as term was over, she and I set out for Austria, a long and complicated train journey through a war torn France, a luxuriously wealthy, well fed Switzerland, to the little border town of Buchs where the clean and comfortable trains stopped, and the Austrian carriages with their boarded-up windows and hard wooden seats took over. It was in Buchs that we spent the night in a bed and breakfast house in sight of the station. We had eighteen pieces of luggage including the kitchen stove; that was without Pella who was visiting her future in-laws. Early the next morning the station-master phoned, grumbling: *"The Austrian train is on time, the first time this year! And now we will have to wait for you."*

Two years after the end of the war the contrast between two small alpine countries could not have been greater. Everyone in Switzerland looked plump, healthy, well fed, well dressed. In Austria the guards, ticket collectors, porters, and indeed almost everyone looked gaunt and hungry, their uniforms shabby and patched. At the station buffets there was nothing to eat, no sandwiches, no biscuits, no milk, no soft drinks, only bitter black acorn coffee. The stations had mostly been bombed and were piles of rubble with some kind of Nissen hut placed in a clearing. We had to change trains twice and when at last we arrived at Brixlegg, the old porter almost embraced Olga, and started reminiscing about the day she had left Brixlegg for Kenya thirty three years earlier. He was distressed there was no car, no carriage to meet us and insisted he would walk up with us bringing our lighter luggage on his hand-cart.

Our progress through the high street of our village, where the Church tower still wore its onion at a rakish angle, was like a victory parade but slower. A party of young American volunteers were helping to rebuild the villages their countrymen had bombed so flat only three years earlier and we stopped to watch them working on the upholsterer's workshop. They were digging a particularly deep cellar. The owner recognized Olga and appeared from nowhere to deliver the warmest of greetings. He explained that his house had been bombed and now the American volunteers were making him a cellar extra deep where he could keep his leather.

"So I see," said Olga, "You did not have such a deep cellar before!"

"No," he replied "but it seemed such a good opportunity – I always wanted a bigger one!" As we walked up the street, two grocers, two butchers, the doctor's wife, two innkeepers, the ironmonger, the shoe-makers, the draper, the hatter, the watchmaker, and the post master, all came out to greet us. As we passed the market gardener, Olga arranged with him to fetch our heavy luggage with his horse dray. By the time we reached Matzen it had taken us over two hours to complete a twenty minute walk.

We had hardly reached our rooms before a stream of visitors arrived, people whom Olga had entertained at childrens' parties long ago, people whom she had helped in the slump, people to whom she had shown friendship. Food was desperately short, but each brought a gift, apologizing it was so small – farmers had sent a few ounces of butter carefully wrapped in leaves, a sliver of cheese, a wine bottle half full of milk, a cut of veal. There were bunches of roses, bundles of vegetables, honey and even a tiny pot of jam and two eggs. It was remarkable, that despite the war and the bombing, enemy aliens were given such a welcome home. Tom arrived in the middle of this, our flat still full of visitors, flowers, children, and in the courtyard stood the horse dray with our heavy luggage. There had been no such welcome for him. No one knew him, since the age of fourteen he had always been away in the Navy, with a few days of leave snatched here and there.

Olga stayed for two months. We had no car so we cycled everywhere. She was approaching sixty, and found the long pulls up hill and down steep dales exhausting. She knew she had cancer, but never told me, saying the pain in her left arm which prevented her from lifting was a touch of rheumatism. She longed to visit her favourite places and old friends farther away, at Kitzbuhel, on the Achensee, up the Zillertal. Never once in that long Summer did Tom offer her an outing, an expedition, in his car. At Matzen as at Wispers she acted like a magnet, bringing us a stream of English and Austrian guests. Olga went down to Italy to visit her

Italians, the ex-P.o.Ws who wanted to migrate to Kenya. I went to Vienna with a delegation of Oxford undergraduates to make contact with Austrian universities, visiting also Graz and of course Innsbruck. Most of the delegation ended the journey at Matzen. Tom did not approve; student guests let down the tone for his posh ones. We were all shabbily dressed, most of us had been at school when the war started. One could not build up a suitable wardrobe on 16 clothing coupons a year, and of course for the Austrians it was even more difficult. There was an Italian girl who walked around barefoot wearing on old sack with a rope round her waist. This outfit did nothing to detract either from her beauty nor her sex appeal.

Oliver arrived to stay with us and we decided to visit the Austrian Hochschulwoche, a gathering of students from all over Europe which took place in the little village of Alpbach in a branch valley only a few miles from Matzen. Its purpose was to bring together university students from all over Europe to heal the wounds left by war, and by furthering understanding and friendship among the young to make another European war impossible. Olga decided to come with us and see what was going on. On arrival, Oliver was allocated to a dormitory of men and Olga and I were allocated a double room in a hotel annex quite a walk away from the lecture venue. We went straight into a lecture, then supper, and another lecture before we went to find our room at about 10.30 p.m., Oliver carrying our cases for us. I opened the door of our room, switched on the light for him to take the cases in, and stepped to one side. He stood in the doorway stock still, moving only his jaw with no words coming out. I looked over his shoulder, to see a very surprised and irate-looking priest sitting up in bed, wearing his dog-collar under stripy pyjamas. Oliver had no German, I was laughing so much I just managed *enschuldigen* before pulling him from the room. With the door shut, we had a discussion with some other inhabitants of the house. There was an empty bed in a four-bedded room of girls. Olga said I should take that bed and that she would prefer to sleep on the balcony. We decided to move the spare bed from the priest's room. With plenty of knocking and more enschuldigens we re-entered the priest's room. Austrian beds at that time consisted of a solid head and foot board connected by a sturdy frame within which rested a sprung padded frame a foot or more high. On this rested a substantial mattress divided into three biscuits. We did not have to move the heavy bedstead, only the padded frame with mattress and bedding, It took only a few minutes to have Olga comfortably settled in a protected corner of the balcony where, at sun rise, she would have a wonderful view of her favourite mountain, the Wiedersbergerhorn. When I woke next morning her bed had been tidied, her rucksack packed; there were no signs of her, and I knew that the view must have tempted her to take a walk. I hoped it would not be a three day one. As I made for the staircase, the priest emerged from his room.

"Come, look at this!" he beckoned me. I followed him into his room. There on the floor, neatly placed within the empty bedstead, lay a man still sleeping off a heavy hangover. He had been so drunk when he came to bed that he had not noticed that the mattress and its stand were missing.

"It was you who took the bed last night", he asked, and I admitted I was the culprit, saying it was for my mother. We went over together to breakfast in the main building, shook hands all round as is the custom and sat down at a crowded table.

"Und was ist neu?" (What is the news?) I asked.

"Have you not heard, a drunken middle-aged English woman tried to get into bed with the priest!" The priest choked into his coffee. So he did have a sense of humour after all. It had been difficult to detect it the night before.

Despite the warmth of her welcome and moments of hilarity with my student crowd, it was not a happy holiday for Olga. She realized that not only would it be impossible for Tom to buy her out but that he was under great financial pressure, trying to repay the debts incurred during the war, and he knew that even on an Admiral's pension he would not be able to keep up Matzen. He realized also that immediately after a major war was not the moment to sell it. Even the organization for looking after Ancient Monuments could not afford to take it on. One of his sons, Michael, had been demobbed and thought he could make Matzen pay by taking in Summer guests willing to pay high prices to live in a castle, but it was not a good time to start such a venture. There were few people in Europe who could afford expensive holidays. In England foreign currency was strictly rationed. Americans had the money but not the wish to travel. Michael was about to marry a wealthy wife and Tom was transferring the castle to him, but they could not move her money from England. All the time they were pressing my mother for use of her rooms.

Fortunately the storms at home were offset by the warm welcome she continued to receive wherever she went. She called on all the Austrian cousins, even the Nazi ones whom Tom had conspicuously snubbed, and tried to repair the tremendous rifts made by the war, laying down a firm path of friendship. I had not been able to do this the previous Summer because Tom had forbidden me to meet up with them and I had been his guest. Quite suddenly in early September there came a telegram recalling her to Kenya. On the last night we were in the big room of our flat, going through papers. Suddenly there was a tapping on the South window, not a usual occurrence as on that particular exterior wall we were five floors above ground level. I went to open the window, and found a white pigeon was crouched there. I carried it carefully over to show her. She went almost as white as the pigeon, and her voice was quite different, almost shaky, when she said: "Do let the poor thing go, it will only make a mess on the furniture." I took it to the window and set it free.

When Olga got back to her room that night, she opened the cupboard on which she had written the message back in 1939. Underneath the two messages on the door, when Tom was an Admiral in charge of Kiel in 1945, he had visited Matzen and written: *19–24th August 1945. Am back again. All in wonderful order although war came to our very gates. Empty without Mother.* When Olga had arrived in July 1947, she had added: *"Yes, back again in Mother's room. All in order. Can we hold on?* And now, on 7th Sept, she added: *New crisis. No English money allowed. I am going back to Kenya. Beloved Matzen, au revoir. I am doing my best that Mother's ghost may rest in peace.*

Olga had never wept before when we parted, not even when I was going into war zones like Egypt and Italy – she was usually too busy to see me off, let alone cry over me, but this time she wept and wept. It was only years later that I found her unpublished manuscript about the pigeon room, how white pigeons were associated with a death in the family. Not knowing about the cancer, I tried to cheer her. "Mum, I have only two years to go and then I am going to spend a whole year at Wispers before I do anything else! And Oliver has been accepted into the Colonial Service and will be going to Kenya." She looked even more sad.

In England she went into a hurricane of activity to clean and redecorate the cottage, putting the garden in order, and finding tenants. It never entered her head to employ decorators. Instead she and two of our recent guests at Matzen, and one or two other hangers-on all descended on the cottage, which had been left very dirty, and cleaned it up and painted it room by room. Olga of course worked harder than anyone, getting up early to have breakfast ready on the table, walking a mile down to the shops to buy the lunch. After a very hard week's work she left, leaving again a trail of unfinished calls and chores for me to do when I returned from Matzen.

Olga had intended to stay in Europe until the end of September, and had taken on a manager for that period. Alas, she made the same mistake she had made on her Koru farm; she had employed a man willing to take a very low wage without checking up on him properly. She knew she was not a good judge of character, but could never turn away a man who said he really needed a job. It turned out he was almost illiterate, drank heavily, and relied entirely on his wife, who was a well-spoken, able woman. The wife walked out on him soon after Olga left, and on his own he proved a disaster, not paying or rationing the labour, neglecting the livestock, and driving Olga's new pickup truck on a 700 miles round trip on appalling roads to the coast in pursuit of his wife. He signed chits for everything, petrol, hotels, meals, and everyone gave him credit, because the truck he was driving had Wispers Farm on it, and everyone knew that Olga would pay. On return to Nairobi, he drove straight through the level crossing gates near the Nairobi post-office, missing a train by inches. He then abandoned the truck, fortunately not far from the Ford Agents who had supplied it to Olga only months before. They recognized it, took it in and repaired it. They would also need payment.

Ronny's husband was by now demobbed and was working as a district officer some 250 miles from Wispers, and Ronny herself was close to the birth of her third child. Even so, Patrick took a long week-end and drove her down to sort things out. They found chaos on the farm, cabled Phoebe to come back and also cabled Olga, the cable we had received in Austria.

Flying boats now landed at Naivasha, which was more convenient for Nairobi, but Olga disembarked at Kisumu in order to visit the new grandchild. Back on the farm it was the picking season again and also the new session of Legislative Council was about to start. Olga moved into a round of constituency meetings. She was exhausted and unhappy; things were not going well at Matzen, nor in the Kentish cottage, nor even on Wispers, and she knew she would soon have to have the dreaded cancer operation. She asked the surgeon to fix a date when the Budget debate was over. He said now. She persisted – after the budget.

Just after she returned in September, Troughton, the Financial Secretary, moved a fiscal survey which he had undertaken, but Olga complained it was blurred through lack of knowledge. Recently 20,000 Asians had been lost in the statistics. The Government were working on a population of 3.5 million. She was prepared to bet there were over 5 million. In fact as we have seen there were nearly 7 million. Higher taxation would be unnecessary if we knew how many people there were. She agreed that there should be fingerprint registration for the whole population, a measure which made tax collection easier.

The budget speech of 1947 was very unpopular. E.R. Vasey, an elected member who was later to become Financial Secretary, referred to this budget as Old Moore's Almanack, and had written *"In the absence of the statistical information required for a theoretical estimate of Kenya's taxable capacity I have attempted to gauge the volume of unavoidable expenditure."*

At her consituencey meeting at Kiambu she said that she had not heard of the suggestion that all the elected members walk out. She would certainly put it up to the other elected members if that was what her constituents wanted, but she personally thought sweet reason achieved more than a total strike. *"But sometimes if we are forced to it - we have to have a general strike."* She wrote to me the next day that this meeting had been very much more pro-Olga than it used to be, and the chairman thanked her publicly for her last speech in council. The hot headed old Colonel Grogan, later nick-named the Lion of Africa, wanted to send the budget back to the Financial Secretary to have it redrafted.

In her own comment on the budget she asked how long the country could afford the tremendous cost of the leisured classes, the men who sat about all day doing nothing. She pointed out that Pella, who had stayed in England, had tried to draw unemployment pay but had been made to lift potatoes in

Yorkshire while waiting for a boat, and if that applied to Pella in England why not apply it to Africans in Kenya – no famine relief unless you work. There should not be seven men sitting in a row along the road selling charcoal, nor markets crowded with men selling a few razor blades. The sugar factory set up as part of the processing of local food in the war had to reduce output because it could not get labour. There was now insufficient sugar to keep the fruit canning and jam-making factories supplied. If conditions in the sugar factory were bad, then why not improve them? And when they are improved why not deny sugar to the nearby reserve until labour co-operates? It was not only the Africans she belaboured. When the male members of Leg.Co. threatened opposition to more money being spent on schools and hospitals for all races, Olga threatened to mobilise women-power in their own households.

She reviewed the budget under eight heads:

1. A reliable census of the population was essential. The whole budget was blurred by lack of reliable statistics.

2. Education was not only schools or technical training, but to teach the essential values of life, of creating happier homes and better citizens; nobody wanted to create a body of discontented clerks, which she feared the schools were turning out.

3. There must be a limit to African territorial ambitions; otherwise there would be no land left fit for anyone to live in. There was need for better farming methods, proper villages, and development of village industries.

4. Labour. On the subject of labour, she said: *"Words fail me... Never in 34 years have I known such lack of discipline, such breaking of contracts, such cheating, such stealing and so many agitators. I speak not only from my own experience but from that of my neighbours. The first difficulty is that it is difficult for the honest African to remain honest when he sees the dishonest one getting away with perpetual stealing, making five times his wage in petty theft of the crop concerned... . They had got away with it because of the receivers... ."* (Naughty Mr Indian again.) Continued registration was essential, if better conditions and better training were to be achieved. At the moment men wandered in and out of work, and training schemes, taking everything he had been issued with and quite a lot he had not, making production difficult for his employer and a settled life impossible for

himself. (It was customary to issue a new employee with clothing, a bed, blanket, cooking pot, and so on – all these goods were in short supply, and many men would leave after a few weeks taking everything with them.)

5. African industries should be given more encouragement, specially in building, and small scale contracting.

6. Crime could be dealt with by a review of the judicial system and deportation of foreign receivers to their country of origin.

7. Social services should be the reward of achievement. For workers outside the African lands, she suggested a compulsory insurance contribution made by both employers and employees.

8. Political status must be the result of education and achievement. She welcomed and congratulated the two new African members to Legislative Council.

Olga's recommendations were no new fiscal policy without better statistics, a graduated poll tax for Africans, a sliding scale of school fees, a reorganization of the post-office, a cheaper inland letter rate, more rural telephones, and a T.B. sanatorium to be built at Nanyuki by the private sector.

It was her last speech in Legislative Council. Ten days later she was dead.

* * *

Chapter Fourteen

A HURRIED DEPARTURE

It should have been a solemn affair, the funeral of Olga Watkins, Member of Legislative Council, who was buried on the farm she had carved out of a wild slice of Africa, but nothing about Olga had ever been solemn and it was not solemn now. She left the world with the same speed she had entered it some 58 years earlier, while seemingly recovering well from a cancer operation. It was December 7, 1947, and in those days in the tropics funerals had to take place immediately, within twenty four hours of the death.

Ronny had driven herself down from Kakamega, 300 miles away up-country, to be with her mother, bringing her two infant daughters with her. It had been planned that her husband, his mother, and five year old Richard would come down to Wispers for Christmas. Ronny spent Saturday afternoon sitting beside Olga planning a children's party and writing out the invitations. Olga gave Ronny a long list of preparations which needed to be done. Then she told her firmly to take the children home, she was tired and needed to rest, and it was getting near the children's bed time. She was coming home the following day and would see plenty of them then. Ronny could sense that all was not well with her mother, and drove home thoughtfully, her mind not at ease as she picked her way over the rutted murram surface now slippery with rain. She was an exceptionally good driver for she had driven long distances for the forces in the war, on appalling roads and in all weathers. As she climbed the last slippery hill, a froth of blue jacaranda flowers hung over the road, the red mud blue with fallen blossoms. Her heart lifted as she rounded the last corner and saw the familiar red brick farm house covered now by golden shower and blue potato creepers.

Before she could park the car, an African dressed in the long white robe of a house servant had reached her. The hospital had phoned, she was to return at once. She turned the car round and drove as she had never driven before, breaking a spring in her hurry but driving on. A nurse met her. Olga was already dead. The last ten minutes had been bad. It was a thrombosis to the heart. Ronny went into the room. It was hard to believe that the familiar figure so still now under the covering sheet had been so happy, so lively, less than an hour before. The long body was almost too tall for the bed, and as Ronny drew the sheet back she saw that her eyes had been closed, her hands crossed over her chest, her hair lay dark and unruly on the pillow. She could never remember seeing her mother so still before, nor seen the long thin fingers without their familiar rings, her wedding ring, Oscar's signet ring, and the solid gold ring Wellington was supposed to have worn at the battle of Waterloo. The invitations to the party and the list of guests lay piled on the little table. The nurse took down the worn crocodile dressing case from the top of the wardrobe and helped Ronny collect Olga's things.

Friends who had come to visit Olga were gathered round the main door, waiting for news. Ronny kept her eyes down and walked through them. Not now, please God don't let them speak to me now. She must keep herself from breaking down, from weeping and letting go, for at least twenty four hours, until the funeral was over. Until then there was so much to do. Then she thought a moment and turned around to face them. "The funeral will be at Wispers, tomorrow afternoon, at 2.30 pm," she announced, "Please tell as many people as you can." She fled for the car. The children were still in it, the baby had gone to sleep.

She drove to the post office, long since closed for Saturday afternoon except for a night telegraph office. But there had been so much rain that the up country telegraph line was down, and there was no way she could contact her husband. "Why don't you phone the wireless station, here in Nairobi. It will go in the early news tomorrow, and he will hear that way!" suggested the clerk. It was by public announcement that Patrick heard of her death, as did the British press. Her death was announced in the British papers on Monday morning, before the telegrams sent to Pella and myself, both of us in England, had arrived.

Ronny drove her children home, bathed and fed them and put them to bed. Supper was brought to her and she was about to send it away when she remembered she must eat, she was still breast feeding the baby. Rain clattered down on the roof and she moved over to her mother's chair where the light was better as she tried to plan what had to be done. Would the rain lift sufficiently in the early afternoon to allow the service to be held out of doors? Would the vicar at Limuru be free to take the funeral? Would the farm road stand up to the traffic?

There was a knock at the door. One woman, Nora, one of the many lame ducks Olga had helped, had been at the hospital and had seen how stricken Ronny looked.

"I've come for the night!" she announced, "you cannot be alone on an occasion like this." Ronny's chance to sit and meditate quietly on what had happened, to enjoy the warmth of her children even as she mourned her mother, had gone. It was a gesture kindly meant but unwelcome. Yet Nora brought one blessing, she had infinite patience with Kenya's quirky telephone system and could usually make it work – there was much telephoning to be done in the morning.

First on the list was the municipal funeral department. Would they be sure to send a hearse with an experienced driver, seeing that when Oscar died the hearse had got stuck on the farm hill and this time there would be so many VIPs coming it was vital to keep the road open. The manager insisted all his drivers were experienced, in Kenya they had to be, and wanted to know where the cortege would start. He clucked with annoyance at Ronny's steadfast refusal to drive into town to be driven out in a huge car just behind the hearse. She insisted she must be at home to welcome those who arrived early, and also to feed the baby.

She went outside and rang the gong for the workers. It was Sunday but they had to be told of the death and she needed men to dig the grave and then in the afternoon to stand along the road in groups to help any car in trouble. While she was talking to them, Harry Graham-Bell arrived with a van full of flowers and a team of labourers. He insisted he would do the grave, he remembered Olga so well when she had stayed with them during the First World War Indeed it was he who had guided her to the raw patch of Africa that had been Wispers in 1922. He had wanted her as a neighbour. Despite the rain, he managed to make the raw earth of the new grave look beautiful under a mantle of flowers which spread over Oscar's grave and the surrounding stone walls. By the time Ronny had fed her daughters it had stopped raining and the sun came out.

Perhaps it was this which caused the driver of the hearse, driving down the hill towards the bridge, to go a shade too fast. He skidded into the hillside, leaving very little space for the cars behind him to approach the bridge. In the absence of family in the procession, hierarchy had prevailed and it was the Governor's car which followed the hearse. The driver was keen to demonstrate his driving skills and attempted to pass the hearse but skidded in the opposite direction, ending up with one wheel over the bridge. The groups of African labourers descended on the vehicles and attempted to move them, but they were too heavy. The Governor organized the unloading of the coffin, and it was shouldered by eight willing workers and started its journey up hill. The rain came again, a dismal drizzle, just as Oscar had said, all those years ago, was appropriate for the chieftainness returning to her lair.

The Governor took up his large and heavy wreath and followed after it. The groups of workers stationed up the road joined the procession as it passed, singing as they went:

"Agishu, Agishu, has gone, gone,
Agishu has gone to the hills.
We bring Agishu home,
Agishu has gone to the hills,
Where she will be heard,
We bring her home!"

Every now and then they stopped, and another team took over, each team picked by the headman. The singing got louder and louder, sung in chorus form, with the headman singing every alternate line, the chorus joining in full throat. Ronny was waiting in Wispers house as the minutes ticked by and when she heard the singing she knew that something had gone wrong.

After the Governor processed the other senior government officials, the Chief Secretary, the Chief African Commissioner, the head of the Police, and then came the members of Legislative Council, including the portly Sir Alfred Vincent who was finding the climb hard. Each carried a wreath, and the mud crept up their shoes and on to the trousers of their best suits. Ronny led them into the house to await the end of the procession, people who would have had to leave their cars further and further away and walk an extra half mile or so. Archdeacon Beecher saw the procession of stuck cars, turned round and led late-comers in by another route.

A group of eight elected members approached Ronny; they had been chosen by the others to be pall bearers and here they were reporting for duty. Ronny had already promised eight senior farm workers they could carry the coffin from the house to the grave. She thought a moment. "Thank you. We will have two teams, it is a long and slippery walk and we'll change half way." The two teams, farm workers and elected members, sized themselves off.

It proved a wise decision. One pall bearer only made it half way across the lawn. The three alsatians had all been shut up in different rooms, but with all the coming and going of waterlogged guests Olga's dog, Pauline, somehow broke out and though normally the gentlest of dogs she made straight for the pall-bearers carrying the coffin. Ronny managed to grab her, but Pauline had come away with a piece of expensive gent's suiting in her mouth. Fortunately the leg underneath was untouched. By the time Pauline had been locked up and Ronny returned to her place, Patrick had arrived and took his place beside her while his mother ushered Richard into the house. They had driven three hundred miles through rain and mud since hearing the news at 7 a.m. that morning. By chance, Patrick had chosen the shorter route, the one that was not blocked.

The sun was trying to come out again, bringing out the bright colours in the herbaceous borders, cannas and roses, dahlias and bougainvillea, plumbago and pinks, lilies and oleander, all carefully colour co-ordinated by Oscar over the years all the way down the long grass walk. Half way down the jacaranda trees had covered the grass with blue blossoms, and through these blossoms ran a thick moving stream of safari ants, carnivorous ants that can kill a puppy or a chick in minutes. Several people stepped in them, including Sir Alfred Vincent. He dashed through the flower bed on the left hand side into the lines of coffee, using the trees as a screen. A few moments later the head of the procession also turned left, then left again to face the little graveyard. Ronny had her eyes down, trying to hold back tears, but when she heard the Archdeacon stifle a laugh she looked up. The Archdeacon, laughing at a funeral? Ahead of her, facing them, was Sir Alfred, his trousers round his muddy ankles, concentrating intently as he picked the biting ants off his more delicate parts. Now she also was suppressing laughter, and she swore that at that moment she heard Olga laugh too.

It was five o'clock when the guests left, wanting to get their cars out of the muddy road before dark. Ronny went into the house, there were so many chores to be done before she could relax. Richard found her. "Mum, where is Wispers Gran? I've looked everywhere and she is not there!" She sat down and took him on her knee. "Darling, she has gone to heaven to join Granddad. She is happy there with him but we shall be very lonely without her and will have to be brave." She kissed him, put him down, and picked up the belt on which Olga wore all the farm keys and put it round her own waist. Richard watched her, then suddenly went into a rage.

"Those are Gran's keys, put them down. They are not your keys. Take them off! Take them off." It is said that a sorrow shared is a sorrow halved, but for Ronny at that moment it was a sorrow doubled, to realize how much the child would miss his grandmother.

* * * * * * *

Ronny now found herself in the same position that Olga had been in in the early 1920s. She had a husband working one side of Kenya, a farm without a manager the other side, and young children at the centre of her life. She knew she did not want to struggle as her mother had done, nor did either of her sisters. All our lives, every penny anyone had, had gone into the farm. It had taught us hard work, responsibility for others, respect for the soil and those who work on it, but it had been a hard task master. In our first jobs, both Ronny and I had been saving up to buy Wispers its first refrigerator. By the time we had enough money there were no refrigerators to be had. Yet we could not bear to be rid of the farm, not now that both parents were buried on it. We decided to take out the coffee and put the land down to grazing, far easier to look after. It is easy to be wise after the event, but we were not to know that by 1950 the price of coffee was to double and that within ten years of her death it would reach a price ten times the £40 a ton that Olga had received. And that thanks to her fight against the coffee rings, the farmer was now able to enjoy a far larger proportion of that price. She had done the work, fought the battles, and was not there to enjoy the victory.

What then had Olga achieved? She had turned two areas of wilderness into productive coffee farms and demonstrated that women could indeed farm in East Africa, and usually managed better relationships with their labour than did men. She demonstrated that better conditions for workers made them more productive. She fought the monopolistic coffee rings, and pioneered better marketing for coffee through the planters' own marketing organization.

With Oscar she rescued some two hundred refugees from Nazi Europe and led them to better lives. For some ten years after her death it was nearly impossible for her daughters to pay for anything at a Jewish shop, the owner always wanted to give us free whatever we wanted. In her writing she showed exceptional ability and I am always sorry that she only resorted to this when she found herself in frustratingly boring surroundings.

In her seven years on Legislative Council she did away with the idea that large dormitories of 'bed-spaces' provided adequate housing for Africans, and put up an exemplary little garden city of houses which she hoped would be copied but never was. She laid the foundations for better education for women of all races, and showed by example what women could do. At least three other women on Legislative Council were persuaded there by her.

She had concentrated everyone's mind on the need to work for the war effort, and persuaded the government to encourage far greater production of food. This stood the farmers in good stead, immediately after the war, when serious food shortages occurred almost throughout the world and the farmers prospered as never before. She was not so successful when she tried to make government tackle the crime problem by starting with the big men who organized it rather than the small time thieves who carried it out.

She used the power given her by being on Leg.Co. to meet such men as Creech-Jones, Secretary of State for the Colonies, and managed to fend off successfully the British Government's determination to set up in Kenya huge crop production units, like the groundnut scheme in Tanganyika which wasted £5 million of British tax-payers money. Instead, she encouraged them to send many more trained agriculturists to work with the African farmers, particularly the women who produced most of the food. Later, after her death, Kenya became the first country in the world to produce tea and coffee as peasant crops, grown by small land-owners instead of big estates.

She accepted that self-government would come, was the target everyone was working for, but did not think it would come so soon. When she died, the three great technical developments of the war were only just starting to make them selves felt. These were better transport with the introduction of universal travel by air, better communications with much improved radio and telephone transmission, and most of all, better health with the conquest of many illnesses. Tuberculosis, leprosy, and yellow fever disappeared, malaria and venereal disease were brought under control, and antibiotics made blood poisoning a minor inconvenience. Better health, better education, wider understanding of world events and faster travel greatly speeded up the whole process of education and brought the East African territories into the modern world as never before. Olga had made contributions in many ways; better health by encouraging refugee doctors into the country as well as her own contribution in nursing Africans, better education in her insistence on educating African women as well as men.

At Wispers she created a centre of hospitality, kindness and understanding. She supported her husband through his difficult career and brought him enormous happiness and pride – nearly all his letters mentions how proud he was of her. She brought up three daughters all of whom have led a more domesticated life than she had done, but her ten grandchildren have all made their ways successfully into middle age, while her 26 great grandchildren are doing well in their youthful activities. One daughter still lives in Wispers, three generations of her own descendants around her, and the rest of us visit at intervals. Olga remains the most generous and helpful person I ever met, and I still weep at the thought that she never saw my four lively sons, so much the family she herself would have liked.

Over eight hundred letters of sympathy were received. Everyone mentioned some kindness, some hospitality, some help given. The last word must go to one of her oldest friends, Clarence Buxton, a District Commissioner who, like Oscar, had taken his retirement in the colony. He was not a man known for his approval of up-and-doing women. He wrote her obituary in the East African Standard.

Kenya has lost, by the death of Olga Watkins, a remarkable personality. Olga devoted 35 years of her life to the development and service of this colony. Many will remember her with affection and gratitude. She was always ready to help a person or a cause and never spared herself, or those who opposed her, in whatever she undertook. Her vitality, courage, humour, and warm-heartedness won the admiration of a wide circle of friends who will miss her vivid interest in them and their affairs.

Energetic and dauntless were epithets which were applied to her at the last meeting she addressed in Limuru a fortnight before her death. She was not looking well. Now we know why… She spoke at Limuru with her usual eagerness and her unhesitating style, direct and persuasive.

Twenty-eight years have passed since I first met Olga and Oscar. The friendship once begun grew till each of them left the scene. Her enjoyment of life overflowed wherever she was. But perhaps she was happiest at Schloss Matzen, her lovely home in the Tyrol. A few weeks ago she sent me a picture postcard of and from it, to 'recall memories'. She had had a wonderful reception from all the inhabitants who were again able to hand back the beloved home which they had guarded through a second war.

In reading her fascinating stories, 'Tales from Tyrol', you will have a glimpse of what that life meant to her. When I was last in Matzen in November 1934 she was arranging the building contracts for winter relief in various villages. She was a striking figure in any garb, but nothing suited her better than the Tyrolese costume in which she strode forth to succour the poorer villages. The response of that alien people was a revelation of what British sincerity, kindness, and good cheer can achieve. Their devotion to that lady of the Schloss was intense. There was nothing of the fairy tale in Olga's handling of these many problems, domestic and communal, as she went from village to village, and yet there was romance and adventure in medieval mythology. Those who only knew her in Kenya missed the real clue to her character. In Matzen she was in her perfect setting; with Oscar's inspiring companionship, amidst the flowers, the mountains, and woods, and above the Valley of the Inn.

Olga has been a household name in her Kiambu constituency where she devoted her last thought and energies to it. Her interests and enthusiasms never failed. One day you would meet her absorbed in the selection of a suitable present for a grandson, the next in the subject for a meeting. Her mind and spirit never rested. She filled the unforgiving minute with sixty seconds worth of distance run in her service to God and man, with the result she got 20/- in the £ out of life for herself.

Her humorous appreciation of the incongruities of men and matters kept her outlook young and lively. It was always good fun to hear her describe some event or interview. The ability to take things seriously, and yet to enjoy a little judicious levity about them is a great asset in public life. She certainly had it as a natural gift when she was a senior official's wife, and later when she herself became a leading unofficial, Oscar stimulated this talent of hers by his quick and ready repartee. Meals at their house, whether at a government bungalow or at Wispers, were

always a treat. They did a great deal of entertaining, especially for those in need of it.

They both had facile tongues and sympathetic understanding so conversation never flagged or was dull. When Oscar and Olga had an argument, the phrases fairly flew with scintillating sallies. One learnt a lot by listening to this friendly duel about every variety of subject which concerned Kenya or their friends. The salt and erudition of Oscar's cracks were matched by the speed and spontaneity of Olga's retorts.

Those blessed with memories of Olga and Oscar in 1919 and 1920 will have a picture of such a pair as would have excited interest in ancient Athens. Pheidas would have adorned his Parthenon with a marble figure of Olga while Plato sought out Oscar for his symposium. They exemplified the great ideal of the "The good and the comely".

Wispers Farm

Flight to Palestine

By Olga Watkins

This story was written by Olga Watkins in 1933 and was published by Blackwoods first in their Magazine and subsequently, in 1934, in the book Tales from Tyrol. She published at least half a dozen articles on the same subject during the early thirties.

"Into the garden of the little inn at Ellmau in the Austrian Tyrol, where I was sitting reading a paper and sipping the local red wine, came a German boy. A fair haired youth tanned mahogany by the sun, in shorts and an open necked shirt, and a very heavy rucksack. With him was a girl, a slight young thing, with a small rucksack, obviously weary.

They ordered one coffee, and sat down at the next table to mine. When the coffee came, they shared it sip by sip. They ate nothing. When they had finished the girl moved a few paces away, stretched herself on a bench beneath a chestnut-tree, and slept almost immediately. The boy counted out a few groschen for the coffee, and sat on while the girl slept.

I spoke to him. "You are both done in!" He nodded sullenly.

"Far to go?"

"Vienna."

Vienna is about twelve hours by quick train from the little Tyrolese village in which we were sitting. I pushed the red wine over to him, with a spare glass.

"Finish it for me," I suggested.

He looked at me suddenly and sharply.

"I am a Jew," he said.

"And so you won't drink with me?"

He laughed bitterly. "Christians have not been drinking with Jews much lately, where I come from." He was silent for a moment, then added more graciously, "Yes, I thank you, I will drink with you since you offer it to me, and I need it. It is a long walk."

He drank the wine slowly, savouring it, and this is what he told me. He spoke haltingly at first, then, as the wine refreshed him and he sensed a lively interest, he spoke more freely.

"I am a Jew, and I come from Bavaria across the mountains. Eighteen months ago I married."

"You were a brave man in these bad times."

"I had a good position," he parried quickly, "for some time now I have been earning four hundred marks a month. That is good pay for a young couple to start on. I married a Jewess. We had a little flat and we were saving. Then this accused thing….this terror, came to Germany. My employer, the chief of a very big firm, was also a Jew. He was interned two months ago. The business was shut down, and I was one of fifty-seven men who lost their jobs just like that." He brought his hand down on a horsefly that had settled on his knee, squashing it flat.

"They confiscated our savings in the bank, and searched our flat for papers, and found such money as we had there. Luckily my wife had a few notes tucked away at the time of unexpected search which they did not find. Or we should have lost our last sixpence. One of my best friends who was searched at the same time received terrible maltreatment at their hands, a thrashing among other things. We had just enough cash left to start walking. We just walked out. I have one change of clothes and shoes here, she has two changes. We have a blanket each, mostly we sleep out, and a heavy coat each. That is all we have. While we have been in Tyrol we have found some barn to sleep in most nights, and a stream to bathe in daily. But it is getting very cold. We crossed the boundary by night. We are walking to Vienna where there is a Society of Jews who may help us. Perhaps they will send us to Palestine, where we can have a patch of land, and grow potatoes, and live.

"Just now we are walking on insufficient food, for we must save our few remaining coins for wet nights or towns, so we beg our way. Today one woman gave us a hunk of bread and butter, which we shared. That is all today, and it makes one very sleepy: that is why she sleeps so soundly now." He glanced at his sleeping wife. "I must wake her soon, as we must make Kitzbuhel tonight, or sleep just this side of it perhaps."

"I will order you some food."

He nodded gravely. "Thank you. I cannot say we do not need it…." He looked at me sadly, and said softly. "I hope you will never have to get up one morning and walk round your home taking only that which you can carry easily, and walk out, leaving all else behind you. Leaving first your home, then your town, then your country behind you, because there is no room for you and yours there any longer."

"You have no family?"

"Not yet," he said, his brooding eyes were on the girl beneath the chestnut tree.

"What will be the outcome of all this, do you think?"

"Do you remember what happened in the history of Spain, when they turned out the Jews?"

"I remember vaguely that they brought much trouble on themselves."

"But Spain will remember vividly, from generation to generation." He laughed and stretched himself, then added "But I wish my country no ill. They persecute us because they think the country will be better without us. We shall see. Come, Annerl," he cried; "come, there is going to be food."

But she slept on.

"Let her sleep until the food is ready ," I told him.

He nodded, I went to hurry it up.

When the food came, a mountain of roast potatoes flanked by an omelette, half a small cheese, and two double portions of coffee, his eyes brightened. He went over and woke his wife.

"Wake up, Wake up. There is food here; no beggar's dole but a guest's portion." He took her hand and led her up to me. They stood there hand in hand, a pair of children. He made a formal little bow.

"No guests of yours have ever been more grateful."

I left them eating.

*   *   *

Other Kenya biographies by Elizabeth Watkins

JOMO'S JAILOR: Grand Warrior of Kenya.
(Britwell Books IBSN 0-9528952-0-X pbk, pp.266 £9.50)

"Skilfully and most readably put together and set in context by a younger Kenya veteran, with a foreword from the queen of imperial history, Elspeth Huxley." (The Spectator)

"As fascinating a biography as could be imagined." (Africa Magazine, Eire)

"A first rate and lovingly told biography" (Journal of the Anglo-Somali Society)

"This is a first class biography of a man who deserved one." (The Overseas Pensioner)

"This is a book to be enjoyed." (The International Journal of African Historical Studies)

OSCAR FROM AFRICA

(Radcliffe Press IBSN 1-85043-948-6 hbk. pp.265 £24.50)

"This fascinating book...the story of a very remarkable man, well researched and engagingly told. (Oxford Magazine)

"Both instructive and fascinating. It is well researched and well written" (Women in Kenya)

"Essential reading for everyone interested in the colonial period in Kenya and in the operation of the colonial service." (The African Studies Association of Australasia and the Pacific Review)

"Fluently and not uncritically told." (African Affairs)

Olga Watkins MLC Summer 1947

* * *

* * *